DATING UP

THE HYPERGAMY FACTOR

Written by
Bobby Cenoura

DATING UP: *The Hypergamy Factor*

This is a work of fiction.
Names, characters, places, and incidents either are the product of
the author's imagination or are used fictitiously. Any resemblance
to actual persons, living or dead, events, or locales is entirely
coincidental.

First paperback edition April 2021

ISBN 978-1-0879-4148-6 (paperback)
ISBN 978-1-0879-4149-3 (eBook)

Cover design: Christian Mirra
Layout design: Lazar Kackarovski

www.sliceofpain.com

SLICE OF PAIN

PUBLISHING AND MEDIA

Published by Slice of Pain Publishing and Media, all rights reserved.
Other works published by Slice of Pain include, but are not limited
to: *Seoul Revelations; Male Angst Vol. I: FML: I Always Get Those Chicks,
Black Names Matter: The Black Names Book.*
All of the aforementioned titles can be found on multiple platforms
such as Amazon, Apple Books, Nook and others.

马到成功

(The Horse's Success is a Reality)

○ My Creator–Some of the roads you had me travel down took me on emotional rollercoasters, but I am faithful and thankful for the signposts You have put up for me.

○ BFR – Thank you for taking me under your wing as a young'un and being a strong foundational father figure. Thank you for the old southern proverbs and work ethic that you instilled in me.

○ RAR – Thank you for always encouraging me to read during those summers of my young life, taking me to the library and getting involved in my schooling.

○ Kylie (aka "LJ") – I would need a whole chapter to express the thanks I have for how much you contributed to my later adult life, mental, financial, and emotional health.

○ TK – Thank you for lighting a fire under my ass to get to work and complete this book.

○ MaTeese Falcon and Valerian Root– thank you for the support, especially through my later education and training for providing shelter and encouragement.

○ B. Furmong – Salamat Po! Thank you for telling me to always keep my "nose to the grindstone" and mentoring me during those rough times in my life. Your humor is #1 ("It depends" joke!).

○ Freelancers, editors, and other contributors – thank you for the work you put in, and even the work you could or would not finish, either through the increasing complexity, conflicting belief systems, or my demands—everything happens for a reason.

○ Wang2 Jie3 (王姐) – thank you for helping me to get my emotional "ducks" in a row, introducing me to the practical and somewhat stoic Chinese life view of "生老病死" (birth, old age, sickness, death). As a result, I became more comfortable with my perceived shortcomings and incorporated this with the East African "Hakuna-matata" approach. You will always have a special place with me. As you once told me: "没人知道上帝的安排"("Nobody knows God's plans.") but one thing I do know—if you are reading this—then 这匹马一定到了成功 (I must be successful).

TABLE OF **CONTENTS**

OUR CAST OF
CAVEPEOPLE

O UR CHARACTERS ARE A part of a hypothetical tribe that exists
in the Holocene period—just before the Mesolithic era. At this
point in time, there was an overall warmer climate; and various
human and prehuman tribes that were formerly isolated by glacial
topography were now more active and migrating.

The assumption here is that as human migrations occurred, so
did interactions between various groups of humans. This would have
resulted in sharing of culture, knowledge, tools and yes, mating. As a
result, the members of our tribe ("characters") are phenotypically and
genetically diverse and coexist united under prescribed customs and
norms.

As the reader goes through the book, the reader will come to realize
that the tribal innovations (i.e. like having a market for goods in the
"Occupational Benefits" section or a tavern where food/drink is served
in the "Sexual Marketplace Value" section) are moving the tribe closer
to settling in a specific area where resources are abundant and the
environment is favorable for all of the tribe's members.

With no further ado, I introduce the three main members of the
tribe who make repeat appearances throughout the book to illustrate
the points made in various chapters and to add humor to the crucial
topic of what determines whether or not we get to pass on our genes.

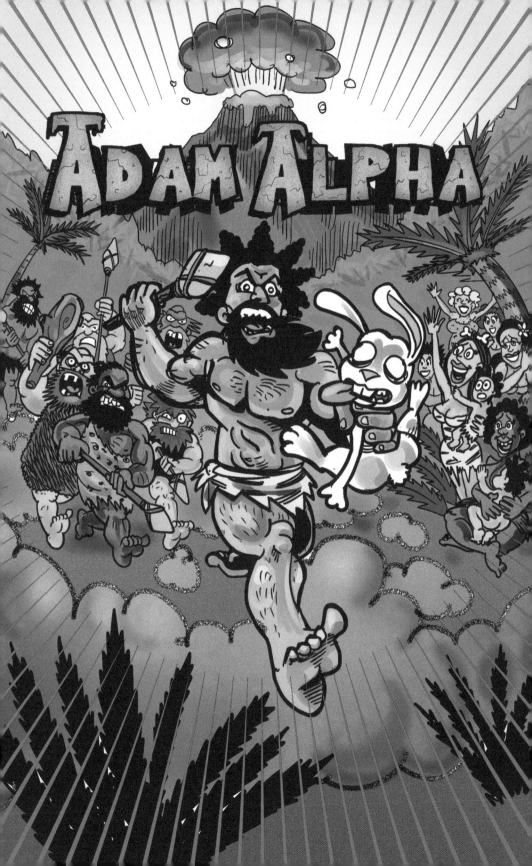

ADAM **ALPHA**

ADAM IS THE TRIBAL and hunting leader, battleground general, and the most sought-after male in the tribe. Adam's political activities are governed by a triad of tribal elders ("The Three") and his vision for the tribe (occasionally curtailed by appeals to The Three by Benny and Brianna) is tempered by their expectations. Adam is often seen with Sherman, the traitorous rabbit who works with Adam to trap other rabbits. Adam is also the head law enforcement officer enforcing tribal law handed down by The Three.

Adam's raids focus on potential targets to expand his tribe's territory and power. First, Adam sends scouts to conduct surveillance. After the leadership of the target tribe is confirmed, he will send an envoy to negotiate with the tribal leaders. If the negotiation is favorable (i.e., they will acquiesce to his demands), Adam absorbs the conquered tribe and allows the former tribal leader to govern his former tribe, but with the caveat that homage is paid to Adam's tribe.

Adam is generally a just leader, but while fulfilling his pleasures, often finds himself making new enemies, because of his selfish and somewhat narcissistic behavior. Fulfilling his pacts often include bedding someone from the outside tribe, and in the case of the Amizunians, the tribal leaders.

As Adam's tribe grows, and other tribes are assimilated, Benny advises Adam to take heed on bedding other men's women (at the same time hoping that he'll leave Brianna alone), and to start to prepare their society to stay in one area rather than expand and migrate. Though Adam often likes the thrill of the hunt, Benny, seeing the long-term strategy, says it's more predictable to stay in one spot, where the statistics of resources are known (climate, rainfall, etc.).

Adam is the distant ancestor of all ethnic "big hair" and "big beard" folks like Bob Marley, Lenny Kravitz, Jimmy Hendrix, Jaggi Vasudev, Colin Kaepernick, Osama Bin Laden and the "Yogi Tea" guy.

BENNY **BETA**

B ENNY IS ADAM'S RIGHT-HAND man and second in command, and the tribe's lead tactician, treasurer, and engineer. Before Adam conducts any offensive strategy, he consults with Benny. Benny collects data from peacetime and wartime activities, and conducts an analysis to determine the fastest and least injurious method of attacking. Benny's war tactics have a 95% success rate, and thus he invented the 95% confidence interval methodology that was later attributed to statistics. Besides the Amizunas, the only tribe that has been evasive enough to resist are the "Proto-Xulus" a tribe known for their physical endurance, weapons innovation (instead of long spears, they use short, sword-like spears for close range attacking), and ability to cover immense distance over a short period by running. As a result, Benny negotiated a territory deal between Adam and Chakara the empress of the Proto-Xulus. Everything was fine until Adam had sex with Chakara and then tried to pipe down Chakara's sister.

As a treasurer, Benny came up with the shells-and-clams economic system that the tribe uses to barter with each other and determine the values of various goods and services. The Three are in possession of the coffers of rare shiny shells that gather at the tribe's western shores. Benny often has to stop Adam from squandering the tribe's resources for his own personal pleasures, including but not limited to, excessive gifts to Brianna.

Like most men in the tribe, Benny is smitten by Brianna. Although he is fancied by other women in the tribe himself, Benny knows that Brianna, per the "Fire Woman" prophecy, will bear offspring that will usher in a new age of prosperity.

Benny has the right to lead if Adam is killed or injured, and thus he carefully tends to Adam, not liking everything that Adam does, but questions him when it threatens the existence of the tribe. Adam values Benny but gets annoyed at his contrarian opinions. The two have not come to blows yet. Benny is the ancestor of all cool bald folks like Richard Cooper, Patrick Stewart, Jason Statham, Jason Alexander, and Bryan Cranston's Walter White before cancer remission.

BRIANNA BONEZ AKA "THE FIREWOMAN"

IF BRIANNA EXISTED IN present day, the song "What you won't do for love" would be the song that best describes what many tribesmen have suffered to woo her. As the most popular female and the predecessor of all red-haired people on the planet, she mysteriously appeared on the scene. Many legends exist about the origin of Brianna Bonez. Some say she is a demigoddess or a part Amizunian, because of her flawless genetics. Some say she is a gift from the "Gods" (read: Ancient Aliens). In her future, she's destined to be the ancestor of tribes that settled in the Isles, the Proto-Celtic tribes. Brianna is a lover of life and admirer of all things colorful. She leads many foraging and gathering expeditions and is a master of horticulture (along with her cousin Mimi (½ protoxulu), who grows their cannabis). She keeps records (well her assistants at least) of the numerous amounts and types of flowering and fruit bearing plants and what they are used for (i.e., food, medicine, or poison). If it's a good weapon, it goes into testing/labs under Benny's supervision, and he'll have the spear heads coated with it. Under her oversight are the primitive infirmaries and the food culture.

Brianna has been labeled as the "fire woman" or "fire queen" by the proto Cathayan tribes—as the first red haired mutation. If you're a ginger or redhead, you're probably her descendant. She's the ancestor of Julianne Moore, Carrot Top, Bill Burr, Gillian Anderson, and Marcia Cross.

INTRODUCTION

"A woman's loyalty is tested when her man has nothing
and a man's loyalty is tested when he has everything"

~ Dread Reed, YouTuber

Preface

Let me get this out of the way right now. You will likely be offended,
amused and/or intrigued by this book. It is part research data and part
anecdote. The assumptions and anecdotes are not out of the "blue sky",
but observations based on averages. There will always be exceptions to
the rule—the Asian family whose son is a mass murderer; the white guy
who grew up in the ghetto and has several "baby mamas"; the Ivy League
black couple who were both born and raised; well-to-do black parents in
southern California who are still together and have strong family ties; the
Native American CEO of a multinational corporation whose parents are
both Native and come from the "Rez". All these occurrences are possible,
but they are more often the exception to the rule rather than the rule
itself.

In 2008, I re-entered the dating world after being a somewhat non-
participant for about seven years. In the span of the previous seven
years up to 2008, I had two long-term relationships that averaged about
3.5 years each—me rebounding as a "serial monogamist" from one
relationship to the next. I was somewhat insulated from the external
social changes because, like most people in relationships, I was in my
own world and I had a routine going.

After the second relationship ended, I found myself at sitting at the
bar in a pool hall listening to "DJ's Got Us Falling in Love" by Usher,
and across the bar table from me, looking directly at me, was a woman,
presumably single, sitting by herself. I took the eye-contact as a signal to
approach; the feeling of liquid courage and the music in the background
made me feel like I was in a movie. "*I'm ready to get back on my horse and
ride*", I said to myself. After approaching her and having a somewhat
decent conversation whereby we both laughed and joked, I thought I
was "in there like swimwear". She subsequently gave me her number
and that was that.

I was still old-school, so I waited a day and gave her a call. I was
expecting to hear her voice and for her to respond to me like I had

experienced in the early 2000s—something like "Hey! I remember you—you were at the bar, right?" and then we'd start talking and setup our next meeting schedule. Instead, I got the standard voicemail cover. I figured that she didn't recognize the number, so I just shot her a friendly text telling her who I was, where we met, and for her to contact me when available. Then I played the waiting game. After two days of not receiving contact, I sent a final message asking, "Is this [name of woman]'s phone?" and I received no response.

Then something occurred to me that rocked my belief system to the core: maybe she didn't like me, and she just gave me her number to be nice when she had no real intention of getting together. This was a culture shock to me. In my heyday, women told you to your face whether they were interested in you or not. A guy had to have thick skin. But at that time, I realized that this new landscape would be more psychologically insidious.

The event that happened in the bar sparked me to question myself—was I not attractive enough? Was I getting too old? Was she afraid to tell me she was not interested? All the questions started to bounce around inside my cranium like a schizophrenic game of bumper cars. After a few more "electronic" dating experiences, I realized that technology had totally changed the sociocultural landscape.

I perceived social media interactions between men and women had reduced to men exalting women (i.e., "you're a Princess/Queen/Goddess") and over-competing for their attention. Men had flooded the market, doing "extra", and consequently, men's values took a dive. This behavior accelerated as time went forward. These observations inspired me to draw the following diagram:

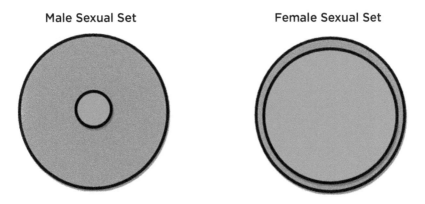

Figure 1. Male and Female Sexual Sets

The grey represents all the people of one sex that are sexually attractive ("fuckable") to the opposite sex. The green represents all the people of the opposite sex that are considered relationship worthy (i.e., you would bring home to momma). My observation of male and female behavior, regarding sexual versus relationship partners, is that there is a disproportionately larger range of women that a man would consider for sex versus worthy of "pair bonding". Based on this logic I illustrated the following:

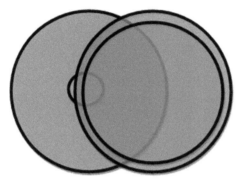

Figure 2.   "Easy Lover" Set Overlap

I named this interaction "Easy Lovers" as inspiration from Phil Collins, who sings the song about a man who laments that he can't change his girl to be exclusively with him. Like Nat King Cole's "Rambling Rose", or Mos Def's "Ms. Fat Booty", this woman who is happily free with her options and her sexuality has no intentions of settling down. Her "grey zone" of fuckable guys lands inside of this guy's green zone—he wants to settle down with her, but his love is unrequited. Then we have the widely known, yet sometimes hated "playboy":

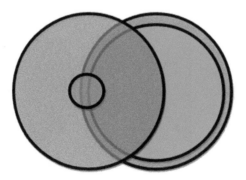

Figure 3.   "Playboy" Set Overlap

The playboy set is the opposite of the easy lover set, whereby a woman's green is heavily in his grey zone, this gives the perception that men are "dogs". Even with "perfect" overlap, the condition would be in disequilibrium:

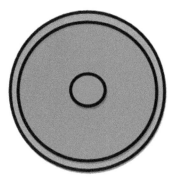

Figure 4. Perfect Sexual Set Overlap

As the conditions surrounding human mating preferences, even if a men's green zones were completely inside women's, most of the women's green zone coincides with grey. After making these observations, I went online to see if it was just batshit crazy. I discovered my observations were a symptom of a larger phenomenon called "hypergamy".

HYPERGAMY

❍ "Hypergamy" is the phenomenon by which heterosexual women tend to choose men of a relatively higher physical attractiveness, income, and/or level of societal status.

❍ The "80/20 Rule" is a post-modern theory that the top 80% of women look to engage in relationships with the top 20% of men.

❍ In 2009, women using the OK Cupid app were more likely to find men on the app unattractive 85% of the time, while men found the women unattractive less than 50% of the time.

❍ An independent analysis of dating applications shows that that the "differential" in the attraction tendencies of women and men rendered large portions of the dating population "incompatible" and gives the appearance that there is a shortage in "good men".

❍ A speed dating study showed that despite the "progressive" qualities men and women said they were looking for in a mate before the session, during the session they "regressed" to "primal" mate selection tendencies.

CHAPTER 1

HYPERGAMY

"What's yours is mines and what's mines is mines"

~ Onyx "Throw Ya Gunz"

ALL HETEROSEXUAL MEN—AND I would argue gay men, too—consciously or unconsciously understand hypergamy to some degree. Hypergamy, in a nutshell, means to date/marry "up". "Up" in this case means up the social ladder, the looks scale, economically—or a combination of all of these. Hypergamy is dynamic and, depending on where you are (your market); will determine what hypergamy means there.

Human beings, as you will see in the upcoming pages, are hardwired for this and would not have survived so long without it. Women choosing the strongest and the fastest in the stone age and the most industrious in the industrial age is what kept the human race going. This behavior can be seen in all types of animals—the strongest survive and get to mate and eat first. They have earned that right and tend to pass it on to their offspring.

The question of the current time is whether we still need to engage in this behavior. With technology, we no longer need to hit other people and animals over the head with a jawbone to get them to acquiesce to our desires. We have a court of law and law enforcement to keep us safe, we go to the grocery store to purchase food instead of killing and quartering it ourselves, and most of us have homes with A/C and heating that allow us to weather the most inhospitable climates.

Regardless of the back-and-forth between modern men and women, the fact is that those traits that have kept us alive for eons are not going to disappear in the next 50, 100 or even 1,000 years. Despite what we are told to value, biology is the driver that has shaped our behavior, causing us to, in turn, shape our environment.

The 80/20 Rule is an unwritten "rule" that asserts that the top 80% of women are attracted to/interested in dating in the top 20% of men. One way to interpret this is if one were to look at attractiveness-based interest on a decile scale ("a scale of 1 to 10", but it can be in different ranges, and in this book will be called the "Max/Min or the "Min/Max" scale) it would be like saying: "chicks who are 2s and above are interested in guys who are 8s and above". I believe what people mean to say is "if you asked a random heterosexual woman/man, she/he is likely to find the top 20% / 80% of men/women physically attractive".

Data from a 2009 Ok Cupid article written by Christian Rudder entitled "Your Looks and Your Inbox" [37] proves the existence of hypergamy. OK Cupid has since pulled the majority of this type data from their articles and blogs, possibly because issues dealing with human attractiveness and relationship prospects are controversial.

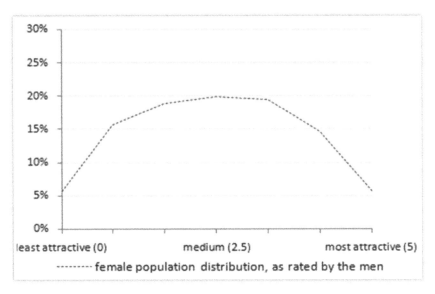

Figure 5. Male Appraisals of Female Attractiveness

The above graph reports non-normalized representation of how men rated women. Here we see that male appraisals of female attractiveness are normally distributed—meaning a woman is just as likely to be "hot" as she is to be "ugly" and most women were rated as average—or somewhere between the two extremes. Here, the OK Cupid data is rated on a 5 "Max/Min" scale. The above graph can be read as: "a little more than 5% of women with an OK Cupid profile are considered most or least attractive; and the rest are of average attractiveness". Now, let's consider the female appraisal of men on OK Cupid:

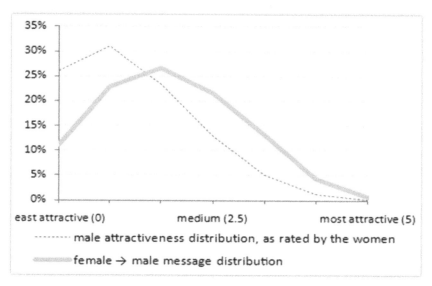

Figure 6. Female Messaging and Male Attractiveness

The grey dotted line in Figure 6, is analogous to Figure 5 above. The female appraisal of male attractiveness is skewed right—with most of the distribution to the left of the average ("medium"). Same 0 to 5 scale, but the result is about 10% to 15% of guys considered average attractiveness, with the rest considered "least attractive". This could be read as: "10 to 15 percent of the time, a guy on OK Cupid is likely to be considered of average attractiveness; less than one percent of the time "most attractive" and the rest are considered "least attractive". The line that demarcates attractiveness versus unattractiveness per the OK Cupid assessments are shown here:

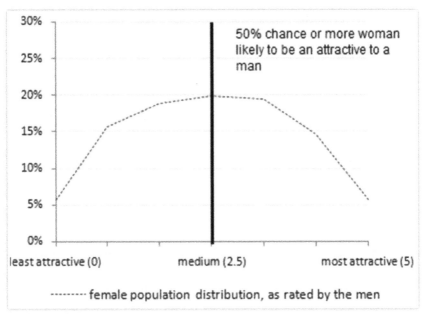

Figure 7. Male Appraisals of Female Attractiveness

Where, imagine a woman right at medium attractiveness would be deemed so 50% of the time. If we do the same for men, we get this:

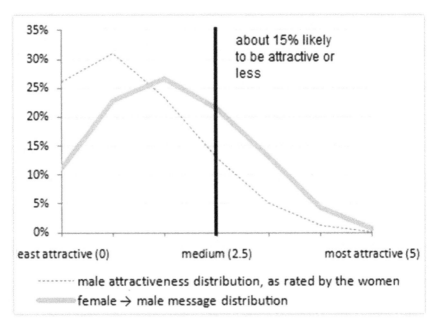

Figure 8. Female Messaging and Male Attractiveness

The blue curve represents the message responses. The OK Cupid article had this to say about the response rates and the attractiveness ratings:

> [women] rate an incredible 80% of guys as worse looking than medium. Very harsh. On the other hand, when it comes to actual messaging, women shift their expectations only just slightly ahead of the curve, which is a healthier pattern than guys' pursuing the all-but-unattainable. But with the basic ratings so out-of-whack, the two curves together suggest some strange possibilities for the female thought process, the most salient of which is that the average-looking woman has convinced herself that the vast majority of males aren't good enough for her, but she then goes right out and messages them anyway [37].

Without responding to the OK Cupid male-bashing tone of the article quote (well not in this volume anyway, but possibly in another volume), they make an important point about messaging ahead of the curve, or the "adjusting their expectations" part. While it is stated that this is a "healthier pattern" they have not considered that women tend to be less visual than guys and factor other things into the equation like income, status etc. So maybe it's possible that the "balding accountant who dates the Russian model" motif exists because that balding accountant has the means to provide resources for the Russian model—not because Russian models are running some sort of charity case for balding accountants.

While the article mentioned "the two curves together" they did not actually illustrate it, but I will do it for you here [38]:

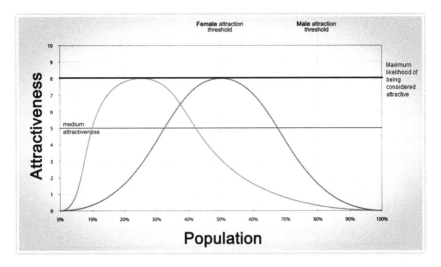

Figure 9. Gender Attraction Differential (PDF)

The unfiltered attractiveness ratings of women show the grey dotted line reaches the medium attractiveness threshold at the 15% mark (a random man on OK Cupid will be considered attractive 15% of the time). But, since the Pareto principle preaches 80/20 and the title of this section is "The 80/20 Rule", I will go ahead and be extra conservative and assume that men are considered attractive 20% of the time. I illustrate this with the horizontal line tangential to the optimum points on both curves—the maximum likelihood of men and women being considered attractive at 20% and 50% respectively.

A more helpful way of viewing it would be considering the medium attractiveness line as the "attractiveness threshold" [38] for each respective sex (considering that a person at the medium level or greater would attract a mate) by finding the absolute position that a person occupies when it comes to attractiveness (i.e., their position on a 10 scale—we'll dig into this in more detail further on).

This can be found by taking the integral of the PDF (the bell-curve shaped functions for likelihood of attractiveness for men and women above) which then becomes the CDF—which will tell you what attractiveness percentile a person with a certain level of attractiveness will occupy. For example, since women are likely to find men attractive 20% of the time or less, this means that attractive men occupy the 80th percentile of the attractiveness threshold. It would look like this:

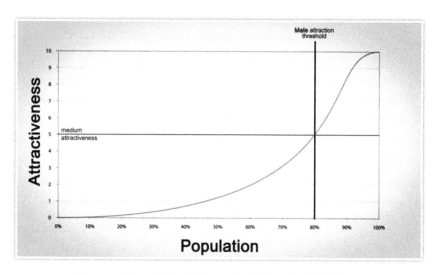

Figure 10.   Male Attraction Threshold (CDF)

Using the same logic regarding women (that they are considered attractive 50% of the time or less), attractive women would occupy the 50th percentile, and we can overlay their attractiveness position like so:

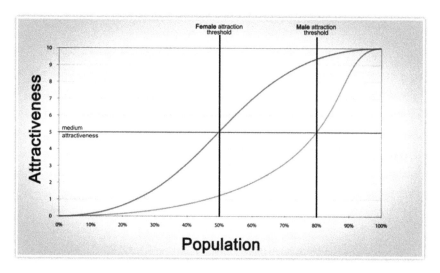

Figure 11.   Male and Female Attraction Threshold (CDF)

This difference in absolute position conveys a much more concrete interpretation than the overlay of probability functions above, because it shows the positions, or the rating on the 10 scale, relative to the probability of getting that rating. For example, the blue curve that is the analog for men's attractiveness shows that a man in the 80th percentile is considered a 5 by women, whereas a woman in the 50th percentile is considered a 5 by men.

This selectiveness is reinforced by a CBSNews.com article commenting on a dating study evidencing that women are more selective in mate choices than men. The study in question was a speed dating event conducted in Munich, Germany of 26 men and 20 women ages 26 to early 40s. Before the session, participants stated what their preferences were for a significant other from items ranging from wealth and status, family commitment, physical appearance and health. After the session, researchers compared the results (who the participants noted they wanted to see again for another date) versus the previously stated preferences regarding what they were looking for. What the researchers found, was that

> [humans] were similar to most other mammals, following Darwin's principle of choosy females and competitive males, even if humans say something different [1]. In addition, that men selected females based on looks, choosing every woman that they interacted with who was above a minimum attractiveness level [analogous to the attractiveness threshold illustrated earlier] showed men being less choosy than the women; and the women made more discriminating choices, and adjusted their expectations to select more desirable guys.

Researcher Peter M. Todd, the head of the cognitive science program at Indiana University, stated, "Women made offers to men who had overall qualities that were on a par with the women's self-rated attractiveness. They didn't greatly overshoot their attractiveness, [because] part of the goal for women is to choose men who would stay with them [but] they didn't go lower. They knew what they could get and aimed for that level" [1].

While the article commented that men chose primarily on looks, its stance on how the women were "discriminative" in their choices was vague. The article only mentions that the women adjusted their preferences to choose "more desirable" men, since they knew men went for looks. The article didn't mention exactly what women found desirable in the "more desirable" men. Among the initial preferences, the article mentioned certain attributes such as wealth and status, family commitment, physical appearance and health.

If the article says that men chose based primarily on looks, then attributes of physical appearance can be mapped directly to looks, since one's looks are derived from their physical appearance. Because speed dating is a rather quick acquaintance, only objective factors can be observed. So even if a man or woman had a preference for wealth and status, family commitment and health, the only thing that they would be able to remotely surmise would be health—to the extent that sickness shows up on the person's physical appearance.

Since it was not specified, I'll make the following assertions: the women were more likely interested in wealth, status, family commitment, health and physical appearance; the men were primarily interested in physical appearance and health; both men and women were interested in physical appearance both for aesthetics and as a proxy for health, but men more so.

As you will find in the upcoming chapters, women are not only interested in men's physical appearance and health in regards to protection (i.e. a muscular badass) and DNA transfer (higher-testosterone men positively impact offspring health), but are also interested in family commitment, wealth and status (provision of resources to ensure a "nest" to safely raise offspring). Men's primary drivers have to do with physical appearance as this relates to the ability to bear healthy, attractive children. The reasons for these preferences are grounded in our evolution.

EVOLUTIONARY BIOLOGY REFRESHER

CHAPTER SUMMARY

○ Fossil records indicate that for most of human existence, hominids (humans and human-like beings) coexisted in hunter-gatherer (foraging) communities. It was in these communities (in the "wild") that most of the evolutionary adaptations occurred.

○ Gender roles in foraging communities were extrapolated to be largely egalitarian, though while both men and women had equal weight in decision making, their duties were relatively differentiated. Men mostly engaged in hunting and military activities and women mostly engaged in child-rearing and gathering activities.

○ Males both cooperated and competed to gain access to females and in the process maximized the benefit of the females' survival and survival of their offspring.

○ Women and men have both conflicting and overlapping biological imperatives. Women maximize human survival through mate "quality" (Bateman Principle) and men through mating "quantity" (Coolidge Effect).

○ Current times are still considered "Neolithic" which was when humans started to live in one place with larger communities and participating in agriculture. As a result, the current social norms are heavily based on this method of subsistence, although human biology and social adaptation are heavily "Paleolithic".

CHAPTER 2

EVOLUTIONARY
BIOLOGY REFRESHER

Paleolithic and Mesolithic Era

About 5 million years ago (MYA), prehistoric hominids, split off from other pre-human ape species and began their own evolution. The existence of the famous "Lucy" (*A. afrensis*) coincided with the first use of fire around 3 to 4 MYA. Since then, many pre-human hominid species came into and out of existence. One of the most notable pre-humans, and relatively recent (with regards to evolutionary time) hominid species, *Homo* ["*H.*"] *Erectus*, had the longest evidenced existence (about 1.8M years). The era of *H.Erectus* began about 1.9 MYA until 143 thousand years ago (KYA).

According to the Smithsonian Institute, *H.Erectus* are the oldest known hominids to have body proportions (height range from 4'9" to 6'1" and weight range from 88 to 150 lbs) akin to that of modern humans, signaling life adapted to living on the ground with ability to walk/run long distances. *H.Erectus'* range was in Northern, Eastern and Southern Africa, and Western and Eastern Asia. There also exists evidence that their brain size almost doubled between 1.8 MYA and 700 KYA. The biggest change in brain size (correlated with climate change) occurred about 1 MYA. [2]

Although it's evidenced that use of stone tools began a little before 2.5 MYA, the first major innovation in stone tool technology occurred about 1.76 MYA consisting of large cutting tools akin to hand axes and cleaters. It is suggested that the tools helped *H.Erectus* survive changing climates. Evidence of campfires also occur during the *H.Erectus* era. The functions of the hearths appear to be multifunctional: cooking, social interaction, warmth, and to keep away predators. Evidence that H. Erectus ate meat and tubers conclude that H.Erectus lived a foraging or hunter-gatherer lifestyle. In addition to innovation and utilization of complex tools, there is also evidence that H. Erectus was involved in coordinated hunting activities and cared for infirm and/or weak companions—indicating higher social inclinations [3].

As a result, H.Erectus represents one of the widest dispersals of early humans in hominid evolutionary history and it is probable that H.Erectus lead to the emergence of later hominid species, such as our own (*H.Sapiens*). There is also the high probability that *H.Erectus* coexisted with other early hominid species. At about 143 KYA, towards the end of its era, *H.Erectus* likely coexisted with our own *H.Sapiens* and there is speculation that *H.Sapiens* emerged from *H.Erectus* and mated with H.Erectus.

The Smithsonian Institute makes the claim that *H.Sapiens* emerged about 200 KYA and then around 100 KYA became the anatomical modern humans as we exist today [4]. However, there is also evidence that our species emerged even earlier on, about 350 KYA [5].

The point of introducing the aforementioned evolutionary segue is to present the evidence that, like *H.Erectus, H.Sapiens* foraged and used stone tools with the premise that social customs and norms were built around the biological need to reproduce. Stone tools and fire were commonplace and evolutionary boons to hominids.

I surmise that the main difference between us and our more distant hominid ancestors is that everything about us was smaller except for the larger cerebral cavity. One conclusion drawn was that, to survive more climatic change, early humans had to evolve bigger brains to solve the bigger problems that come with survival [6]. Prehistoric humans made and specialized stone tools into a variety of smaller complex tools, including but not limited to: fishhooks, harpoons, bows and arrows, spear throwers, sewing needles and other composite tools. As a part of their foraging diet, humans spent a large percentage of time gathering plants and hunting and/or scavenging animals. Humans were collecting and cooking shellfish about 164 KYA and making specialized fishing tools around 90 KYA.

Foraging and Social Structure

While there is limited evidence on H.Erectus' social structure except for what can be ascertained from archaeological and paleogenetic findings (i.e. H.Erectus coordinating hunting activities and caring for infirm and/or weak companions), it is more feasible to extrapolate what social life was like for early humans by looking at modern humans who still engage in foraging.

Dr. Alyssa Crittenden, a behavioral ecologist and a research fellow in the Department of Cellular & Molecular Medicine and the Center for Academic Research and Training in Anthropogeny (CARTA) at the University of California, San Diego, has worked with the Hadza foragers of Tanzania since 2004. Crittenden's research interests include life history theory, allomaternal investment, the ontogeny of prosocial behavior, the evolution of childhood, the human diet and the sexual division of labor. According to Crittenden:

> Like almost all other hunter-gatherer groups, the Hadza have an egalitarian social structure...Labor and food are shared between related and unrelated camp members. Hadza women have a great amount of autonomy and participate equally in decision making with men...The Hadza that reside in the bush, approximately 300 people, collect roughly 95% of their diet. Their diet, which is extremely well balanced, includes a wide variety of plant foods (e.g. tubers, berries, fruits, legumes, nuts, and seeds), small to large sized game, a great number of bird species, and the larvae and honey of both stingless and stinging bees...Women typically forage in groups and target plant foods, while men tend to hunt solo or in a pair and focus on hunting and honey collection. . Children also forage and are able to collect almost half of their daily caloric intake by the time they reach middle childhood. Children tend to focus on resources that are relatively easy to collect (e.g. berries, fruit, nuts) and are located close to camp [8]

Though it appears that Crittenden's focus regarding egalitarianism is heavily weighted in execution (i.e. regarding decision making for the group), I would like to turn a focus to the risks and rewards of foraging. The purpose of this is to highlight how much of an individual risk a person makes for the benefit of the group's survival.

Men, often tasked with hunting, would appear to put more bodily risk on the line. Hunting puts men in direct competition with other African bush carnivores, like lions and leopards. In addition, should the men be hunting bigger game, like horned ruminants, it's possible for the hunter to become the hunted as the game goes after the men in defense. Although the Masai are a semi-nomadic primitive group (also located in Tanzania), they have a patriarchal structure [9]. The Masai do not collect 95% of their diet like the Hadza, as their primary livelihood revolves around herding cattle. However, the Masai raise men to be "warriors" who are tasked with the protection of the people, at their personal expense.

The parallel here is that while both men and women contribute great value to the survival of the group, the personal risk of life and death often falls on the man, whether it is military in nature or hunting. While a similar argument of personal risk can be made for women who must give birth in primitive conditions, childbirth probably occurs at its most frequent on an annual basis while hunting/protecting the tribe are daily endeavors. While the execution of egalitarianism lies in the decision-making processes, the division of labor itself is based on gender.

Gender Roles and Evolution

"Sexual dimorphism" is a reference to characteristics, in addition to sexual organs, that differentiate males from females of the same species. While duties in hunter gatherer societies are gender based, researchers make the claim that the degree of sex-based differences, or lack thereof, are what differentiated humans from their primate relatives. Sexual dimorphism has implications for mating systems and social behavior as indicated by a scientific article that analyzed the 3-million-year-old *Australopithecus afarensis (A.afarensis,* the same species as "Lucy") [10].

According to the article, *A.afarensis*, had only slight to moderate levels of dimorphism and these levels persisted well into the emergence of the genus "*Homo*" (of which humans belong). The article also indicates that the degree of sexual dimorphism determines the ferocity of male competition for mates. The takeaway is that the higher the level of competition, the lower the level of cooperation. Modern day humans exhibit approximately 15% dimorphism while other hominid primates like gorillas and orangutans exhibit upward of 50% dimorphism. These levels have implications on how male cooperation in a group affects group survival.

The article references utilizing analysis of living nonhuman primates and humans and their behaviors. For example, a comparison between baboons and chimps show that the baboon dimorphisms are high, males are fierce towards each other and cannot tolerate one another and therefore, it is implied that baboon males lead a solitary existence. This is contrasted by chimps in that while they exhibit aggressiveness towards each other, males are generally tolerant of each other and they exist in multimale groups. Therefore, it is implied that chimps have lower levels of dimorphism than baboons.

Analysis of *A.afarensis* deduced that *A.afarensis* had lower levels of canine (sharp teeth) dimorphism than chimps, however, there were body size dimorphisms. They equate this to characterization of *A.afarensis* as a multimale, cooperating kin group with strong male competition. This is a system that highly benefits females as they can not only both choose the most viable male to reproduce with, but it also indicates that the "losers" would also cooperate within the social structure to ensure survival of offspring that aren't even their own. Which has implications in the female *"dual mating strategy"* that will be examined later in this text. Paraphrasing the article, *A.afarensis* had a monogamous rather than polygamous mating system, indicating a higher level of male paternal investment. In conclusion, early hominids were very human-like in social behavior.

The Neolithic (Agricultural) Revolution

The foraging, or hunter-gatherer, mode of subsistence was the primary mode of subsistence until the end of the Mesolithic period about 10 KYA, that was replaced with the spread of the Neolithic Revolution [7]. The Mesolithic period, a transition between Paleolithic and Neolithic eras, is largely focused on the transition that humans were making between foraging to farming. The Masai tribe is a good proxy for modern Mesolithic life as they live a hybrid foraging and cattle herding strategy. Geographic origin also plays a role as most Mesolithic paleo-archeology emphasizes Europe in this era and geography in sub-Saharan Africa is often referred to as "Epipaleolithic".

The Neolithic era is believed to have occurred around 10,200BC and 8,800BC (around 12 KYA to 11 KYA) and is also referred to as the Agricultural Revolution. In this era, humans began to live in one area and/or settlement and human population grew heavily from farming. The establishment of towns and cities from groups and clans flourished.

While there are eras in between Paleolithic and Neolithic that are often referenced regarding the types of tools and technologies prevalent, for the purposes of social structure, the major difference between the Neolithic and Paleolithic eras pertains to the contrast of a farming and settlement lifestyle vs a foraging and nomadic lifestyle. While hunting and fishing were still prevalent in the Neolithic era, humans primarily subsisted on farmed food and domesticated animals. This method of subsistence persisted until modern times

Biological Imperatives

With new wave commentary on gender politics and how heterosexual males are born with privilege because they are born with a penis, it is easy to overlook that history and by extension, prehistory, has been a hostile environment for men without means. The narrative of the male privilege birthright ignores that men of lower status had very difficult and possibly unfulfilling lives, from the biological and societal perspectives of building a family and having successful offspring. In addition, mainstream focus is heavily gynocentric and while gynocentric foci helped the human race to be as successful as it is, it is not representative of egalitarianism, which researcher Crittenden praised in her assessment of Hadza foraging tribes in its purest form.

In biology, success is determined by the ability to procreate and pass on genes. Nature benefits from increased competition (only the hardiest of the species survive), and genetic diversity (the ability of a male to "disseminate insemination"). These biological factors may conflict with sociological views of success, like men and women competing for the same jobs, a man who does housework, or a woman who is a breadwinner, etcetera.

An online ABC News article, "Genetics Suggest Modern Female Came First" [11] written by Maggie Fox, outlines how geneticists were able to determine the emergence of the first male, or "Adam" and the first female, or "Eve", using two aspects of human DNA: Y chromosomes for men, and mitochondrial DNA for women. Only men have Y chromosomes and women pass on mitochondrial DNA from generation to generation virtually intact. It was estimated that a man who lived about 59 KYA is the ancestor of all men, "Adam" and a woman who lived 143 KYA was the first "Eve".

The approximately 80-thousand-year gap between the appearance of the first male and female is likely is due to two primary genetic bottlenecks for the Y chromosome, and by extension, men. First, the instance of one tribe/clan/group conquering another, the successful tribe gets to mate with all the women in the conquered tribe in addition to their own. The "losers" genes go, for all intents and purposes, into genetic extinction. Second, it could be happenstance that a man would have only daughters, and this will also cause his Y chromosome to go into absentia. This speaks to differing sexual strategies (women's primary focus on quality vs. men's focus quantity, for genetic diversity) and biological imperatives between men and women. These strategies/imperatives often conflict with one another.

BATEMAN'S PRINCIPLE

The Bateman Principle: the "rod and reel" of female sexual strategy

Angus John Bateman was an English geneticist who was notable for studying sexual behavior in fruit flies. Bateman was able to infer from his observations that the number of offspring fathered by a male increased with the number of females he inseminated [12]. In contrast, the number of mates a female fruit fly had did not affect the number of offspring she was able to produce. It was surmised that the "limiting factors", of male and female fruit flies, were the number of pairings and the number of eggs produced, respectively.

Bateman contrived three principles following this observation:

1. Males show greater variance in number of offspring than females

2. Males show greater variance in number of sexual partners than females

3. There is a stronger relationship between Reproductive Success (RS) and Mating Success (MS) among males than females.

RS refers to offspring being successfully brought into the world and MS refers to the ability of a male to be accepted by a female mate. The commonsense notion here is that the more females a male mates with, the higher the chance to have viable offspring and contribute to genetic diversity. Therefore, we can conclude the following:

> **Ova are more reproductively "expensive"—the cost to the female of producing a single ovum is higher than the cost to the male to produce a single sperm cell.**

With regards to human behavior and sexual selection, Bateman's Principle was expounded upon by Bob Trivers, an evolutionary biologist [13]. In 1972, Trivers proposed that post-zygotic (after birth—from infancy) parental investment (i.e., feeding young, defense from enemies/predators) was heavier in females than males, rendering females the "choosier" sex and the males the more competitive sex.

Females invest more in rearing offspring to adulthood

Imagine for a minute that you are a pre-historic woman and you live in a time before the modern niceties we currently enjoy. There's no military, law enforcement, grocery stores, brick and mortar buildings, and (gasp) no internet or smartphones. On top of all that, you're seven months pregnant, and have seen a lot of carnage in your day: like saber-toothed tigers and giant boars tearing at the flesh of a fresh kill or dead carrion. You realize that if any of those animals turned their attention towards the toddler at your side, you'd be in for a circus of horror. Eating your live little one might give you the time to escape and give birth to the baby inside of you, only for a "wash, rinse, repeat" cycle to occur. How would you psychologically cope?

The Bateman Principle covers the idea that since females bear the highest cost pre- and post-birth of offspring, it follows that it was tantamount for the female human to pick the strongest, most fit human male to procreate with. In a world without condoms and Nuvarings, you better be sure that before "Og" lays the smackdown, he is the baddest muthafucka with a club and boulder; because If he's the Kevin Hart type, he'll hide behind your booty and run at the first sign of danger.

All jokes aside, the importance of the Bateman principle is that the millions of years of evolution have hardwired females, who take the greatest risk from pregnancy, to pick the cream of the crop males to survive. This lays the groundwork for the concept of hypergamy that was mentioned previously. The Bateman principle governs the female sexual strategy with regards to mate selection—a "rod and reel" (catching what they want and throwing back what they don't want) approach.

> **Females generally use a "rod and reel" approach to mate selection, ensuring that the mate fits the criteria required to maximize offspring survival. Female imperative: mate quality.**

The Coolidge Effect: "the wide-casting net" of male sexual strategy

The "Coolidge Effect" coined by Frank A. Beach [15], behavioral endocrinologist, refers to the phenomena whereby males in an animal species display renewed sexual interest and/or vigor with new females even though previously sexually satisfied by an original female partner. This effect is said to have two purposes—one, genetic diversity through the insemination of multiple females, and two, mate recognition.

The interesting thing about the Coolidge Effect was the repeated reinvigoration of males (in the initial experimental case of rats) to copulate with new female mates even past the point of sperm production [15]. Male rats were able to achieve erection, but ejaculations produced little to no sperm.

> **Males take a "wide-casting net" approach to mating, using variety to fulfill genetic diversity. Male imperative: mate quantity.**

Since biological reproductive success for males/females depends primarily upon mate quantity/quality, therein lies a conflict of interest between the two strategies. Evidence from the Bateman principle suggest that there is an inverse relationship between frequency of mating and rejecting available partners ("choosiness"). This falls along the line of economic reasoning: the more abundant something is, the cheaper its price. To summarize, here is a brief table outlining human biological history:

TABLE 1.	Human Biological History			
From	**To**	**Approx. duration (years)**	**% of Total Time**	**Item**
3.25 mya*	Present	3.25 M	100	Existence of all hominids
1.9 mya	143 kya	1.8 M	55	Emergence and existence of Homo Erectus
1.8 mya	0.2 mya (200 kya)	1.6 M	49	Foraging was major mode of subsistence
1.76 mya	Present	1.76 M	54	First innovation of stone tools and evidenced use of fire
1.25 mya	Present	1.25 M	38	Brain size of Homo Erectus doubled
350 kya**	Present	0.35 M	11	Emergence of H. Sapiens
11 kya	Present (0.011 mya)	11 K	0.34	Neolithic Era—Farming then living in cities

*mya = million years ago
**kya = thousand years ago

All the behaviors related to foraging and hunting—our "primal" biological instincts—comprise approximately 99.66% of hominid existence, as culture is formed around climate. It is only in the 0.34% slice of hominid existence that we began farming and living in cities and displaying cultural behavioral norms consistent will living in large groups and staying in one place. If we want to be extra conservative and want to only look at the emergence of homo sapiens as a starting point for measuring human behaviors, then 11/350 = 3.14% of the time our behaviors were consistent with living in one place/in cities and farming culture and 96.86% of the time our behaviors were consistent with nomadic hunting and gathering culture. Therefore, wouldn't a reasonable person expect our tendencies, when it comes to our biological urges, to be at least 96.86% hunter gatherer and 3.14% Neolithic? I make the reasonable assumption that we are much more led by biology that relates to our foraging ways of life than our farming ways of life. And it is by our farming ways of life that most monotheistic religions were founded. The first emergence of monotheistic religion was recorded to have occurred in Egypt around 14th century BCE—

that's only 3,319 years ago—whereas we have been Neolithic for 11 thousand years. All the "rules" of the way individuals should live their lives (especially with regards to religions like Islam, Judaism and Christianity) all fall well within this time frame and are rules that many of the laws that exist in the United States of America today are based on. Therefore, there will be an inherent conflict between our biology and what is socially acceptable.

CHAPTER SUMMARY

○ As an extension of the conflict of male and female "mate-maximizing" behavior and rapidly changing social norms, men bear the brunt of seemingly "irresponsible" and "wanton" behavioral traits.

○ Two experiments, one conducted in Japan and the other in Britain determined that female attraction to males is hormone based, and changes depending on where she is in the menstrual cycle. The preferences oscillated between men with a more masculine or feminine appearance, as dictated by the effects of testosterone on male secondary sex characteristics.

○ Women face a tradeoff between cooperative "nesting" men who provide direct resources to maximize offspring survival; and more "disagreeable" and "aggressive" men who supply superior genes to enhance the survival of offspring.

○ Male social behavior, often correlated to testosterone levels, demonstrate "Alpha" and "Beta" qualities. However, this can be expanded upon to allow for wider gradations in male behavior especially because humans have an incentive to survive in groups and have changing social roles over time.

○ The net result is that the men that are likely to provide the best genetic material are the least likely to have long-term "nesting" interest; and the men who are cooperative and more likely to provide the long-term benefits are less attractive to women in the short run. As a result, women have found using a "dual" mating strategy can maximize their offspring survival.

CHAPTER 3

CADS AREN'T DADS: THE DUAL MATING STRATEGY

WESTERN CULTURE (U.S., U.K., Australia, and Canada) largely has roots in monotheistic dogma. This dogma promotes monandry/monogamy which entails two people being physically intimate with each other at the exclusion of all others. While these precepts can promote nuclear family units and decorum governing how sex should be handled in society, it is not consistent with the cyclical changes in preferences of various types of men by women based on hormonal patterns.

"There is increasing evidence that changes in women's hormone levels during the menstrual cycle affect their social perceptions and preferences... [and there is] evidence that women's preference for masculinity, apparent health and self-resemblance in faces change systematically during the menstrual cycle..." [40]

"Alpha Fucks, Beta Bucks (AFBB)", and the more suitable for work: "Alpha Lays, Beta Pays" is the theory that a woman tends to choose the "bad-boy"/thug types of guys in her youth and to "settle" for nice guys/"balding accountants" as she approaches the end of her fertility age. Is the AFBB phenomena real, or is it just an acronym made up by misogynistic basement dweller virgins?

In humans, concealed ovulation and limited visual similarity between offspring and their fathers can result in uncertainty of paternity. Such uncertainty, coupled with converging evidence for cyclic changes in female sexual behavior and preference for

male characteristics, suggests that female mating strategy need not be entirely exclusive... [natural selection] might have favored human females who pursued a mixed mating strategy under some ecological and social conditions. Women with a long-term sexual partner are more likely to have extra-pair copulations in the follicular [high risk] phase of the cycle than during the luteal [low risk] phase or menses. A female might choose a primary partner whose low masculine [more feminine] appearance suggest cooperation in parental care ("long-term" preferences are unchanged across the menstrual cycle) but occasionally copulate with a male with a more masculine appearance when conception is most likely [high risk follicular phase]. [Women] accrue benefits from polyandry while maintain the advantage of ostensive monandry. [41]

Two experiments, one conducted in Britain the other in Japan, found women to be overall attracted to slightly feminine faces, but this inclination changed based on the menstrual cycle.

Japanese Study

39 women with an average age of 21 who were <u>not</u> taking oral contraceptives were shown different faces of men at different points in their menstrual cycle. Two main ranges in their cycle were noted: the high conception risk ("high risk") phase which occurs between the end of menstruation and ovulation (also the "follicular" phase), and the low conception risk ("low risk") phase which occurs after ovulation and before the onset of menstruation (also the "luteal" phase). The women were then asked to select the faces that they considered attractive. These faces varied between being altered to varying degrees of masculinity and femininity (20 to 40 percent). They also asked the women if they were in a monogamous committed sexual relationship with a male partner. The study found that women preferred faces that were more masculine in the high-risk phase than in the low-risk phase and in addition, trends showed that women in a committed relationship already preferred faces that were more masculine overall. This study showed the probability of conception (and the British study too) affected the preference of masculinity in male faces. [40]

British Study

In a study similar to the Japanese study, 65 British women whose menstrual cycle and oral contraceptive information were previously ascertained, averaging 20 years in age, were allowed to alter the facial shapes of the men from 50% feminized to 50% masculinized. Afterwards, they were asked to choose the most attractive faces for a "long term" committed relationship or a "short term" sexual relationship. The responses (based on attractiveness choices) were averaged over the high risk and low risk periods. For women not on oral contraceptives, conception risk (whether high or low risk) interacted with the type of relationship desired. Short term sexual relationships and more masculine faces were preferred during the high-risk phase, whereas preferences remained unchanged when women judged attractiveness for a long-term relationship. Women taking oral contraceptives did not display any cyclic changes in facial shapes. [40]

The following themes can be surmised from the experiments above:

1. When chances of pregnancy are higher, women tend to be more attracted to masculine attributes

2. Women already engaged in committed relationships tend to be attracted to masculinity overall (outside of their partners)

3. When it comes to short-term sexual relationships (what can also be termed as "hookups"), women prefer more masculine faces

4. When women take oral contraceptives there is no change in facial preference (i.e., meaning the tendency was toward slight femininity in the face).

Reasons and Benefits for AFBB

According to one article, there are two types of benefits that a woman can get from mating: direct and indirect.

Direct benefits are benefits that directly accrue to the mother (i.e., social support and structure of family and friends of the partner, material supports such as financial resources, etc.) [40]. Direct benefits are often sought out during the luteal phase and during pregnancy or when the body is preparing for pregnancy when women show stronger preferences for characteristics in a partner that are beneficial to her such as social and material support.

Indirect benefits can be interpreted as having benefits that do not directly accrue to the mother (i.e. the baby from a coupling benefits by having a stronger immune system, and being a "healthy baby", but it doesn't directly help the mother in care giving). Indirect benefits come with the territory of having a highly masculine partner during the high-risk phase of the menstrual cycle [40]. "[The changes in female preferences during the menstrual cycle] stem from a range of items, including but not limited to maximizing the likelihood that offspring inherit strong immune systems or increasing the likelihood of successful pregnancy [40]". In addition to having a strong immune system (which is an indirect benefit to the mother) the above statement also mentions the "increasing the likelihood of a successful pregnancy", which goes into the dimension of resource provision. Recall that once the woman is out of the ovulation and follicular phases, she is in the luteal phase or pregnant. At this point, more cooperative attributes are desired which, from the experiments, suggest a more feminine type of male demeanor.

It can be said that one aspect of "successful pregnancy", as evidenced in the article is heavily social in nature, which states, "[women in the luteal, low-risk phases] promote affiliation with individuals who will provide support and care during pregnancy" [40]. This "support and care" suggests a higher level of parental investment and, for all intents and purposes, can be translated into "providing resources" (i.e., time, money, living arrangements, social networks, etc.). This is done after the fact (the woman is already pregnant and needs support to ensure the pregnancy is successful).

The risks of obtaining high genetic quality

The primary issue is that the mating behaviors that lead to pregnancy are often not the same mating behaviors that provides long-term direct benefits to help the baby thrive. Alimony and child support laws work to minimize the risk that pregnant woman go without a provider. In older times, if a man walked out on his family and was the sole provider, the wife and children risked starving to death, being ostracized and wearing the "pauper" label. In current times it appears as the pendulum has swung in the other direction, but I digress—that is a follow up topic to be addressed in a later volume.

The tradeoff is that masculine men who display characteristics of good immunity/health are not usually the type of men who will "nest" and play the father role—rearing and providing resources for offspring—not in the dual model presented by the sources evidenced. Or in other words, "cads aren't dads".

Consider the following three statements:

"Men's facial masculinity is positively related to their long-term health and circulating testosterone level" [40]

"Masculine traits in men are thought to signal greater heritable immunity to infectious disease and lesser willingness to invest in partners and offspring compared to men with more feminine traits." [40]

"[Men] with masculine faces are ascribed more negative personality characteristics (e.g. untrustworthy, cold personality) and are more dominant than men with relatively feminine faces [40]."

The first statement and the first half of the second statement state that the more masculine the man is, the healthier he is generally, and the more likely to pass these traits on. The second half of the second statement and the third statement speak on the disposition of such a man and that he's less likely to *invest* in rearing the offspring and is less likely to be trustworthy and cooperative, hence, not making a good "partner" in the sense of a partnership being a team to raise the child. Therefore, the question that might arise is: "If women knew that they are less likely to secure paternal investment from a masculine man and that the cost is potentially going without a provider, would they still procreate with them?"

Society instinctively "knows" that women are more likely to procreate with such a man and have provided workarounds in the form of child support laws for the unmarried and add alimony laws for the married so that the alphas/cads will bear the costs. Alimony would also affect provider men too, since hypergamy would have it that most women would date/marry "up". In modern times, it can be argued that alimony affects women too, as their earnings growth has steadily outpaced men's in the past decade (the data is found later in the text in the "Racial Hypergamy" section). However, societal attitudes would have most men forgo alimony, at the behest of being shamed.

How women employ the AFBB strategy

Finally, consider the following suggestions in the source articles:

> If men with good genes…require a considerable amount of mating effort to obtain, or if there are tradeoffs between good genes for immunocompetence and other desirable qualities (such as willing ness to invest in their offspring or partner), it would benefit women to modulate their mate preferences depending on their probability of conception [40].

Women may maximize the possible benefits of their mate choices by being more open to short-term relationships with masculine men around ovulation. When fertility is highest...[women] generally report being more interested in socializing with men around ovulation than at other times...[women] report greater frequency of sexual fantasy about men other than their primary partner around ovulation than during the luteal phase of the cycle.

Enter the "Gamma" Male

Dominance and quality as a parent are attributions made at opposite ends of the continuum relating to facial masculinity and each might be associated with costs and benefits to reproductive success. A preference for males with a more masculine appearance might confer benefits for offspring in terms of resistance to disease but confer costs due to potentially decreased paternal investment [41].

What the quote just said, in a nutshell, is that the more masculine a man, the less likely he is to "stay put" (make a parental investment), and herein lies the female dilemma. It seems that on one end of the spectrum is a cad and the other end of the spectrum is a dad, what if it could be a goldilocks zone somewhere in the middle? Enter the "Alpha/Beta" Square:

TABLE 2. Alpha and Beta Traits	
Alpha Traits: Yes Beta Traits: No **"Alpha Male"** **(Bad Boy/Thug)**	Alpha Traits: Yes Beta Traits: Yes **"Gamma Male"** **(Married with Game)**
Alpha Traits: No Beta Traits: No **"Omega Male"** **(Loser/Basement Dweller)**	Alpha Traits: No Beta Traits: Yes **"Beta Male"** **(Nice Guy/Beta Male "Provider")**

This square introduces two other elements to the mix: Gamma and Omega males. It goes a little deeper than the Alpha/Beta dichotomy. If I have not mentioned previously, the society we live in makes it costly for a man to wantonly have offspring, and the barriers set up (child support/alimony) make a market for different types of men to enter (hence our discussion about men being able to provide as separate from their ability to protect—the "protection" part has been outsourced to law enforcement). Essentially, this square breaks down men's roles and their worth as greater society sees it regarding children and women. Alpha traits have to do with pure aggression and "douchebaggery", and Beta traits have to do with duty to family and homebody-ness. As I make my descriptive paragraphs, you'll get the gist.

Let's go counterclockwise around the square, starting with the Alpha, who needs no real introduction. The chiseled-jawed, dimple chinned, lean and muscular, warrior skulled six-foot-tall man is the thing of cinematic action heroes and in real life. The Alpha is the one who is genetically primarily desired by women. His challenge is being able to rein in his aggression, lest it put him in jail. Therefore, the majority of the Alpha men walking around free are ones who are smart/wise enough to know when to be aggressive. By making themselves known in the "fuck with me at your own risk" way, they deter other males who would usurp their positions. Since Alphas are desired by many women, they are not forced to commit to any one woman; and their actions, at times no matter how reckless are often given carte blanche by females in society up until the point that it hurts her—badly. It's like the desire to be able to have a dangerous animal do one's bidding. All is fine and dandy until the animal turns on the owner—we know the stories. A woman who gets with a guy with a known propensity for violence (she may have "sicced" him on other men as well) and is an asshole, but for some reason, she thinks that she can harness that power on her behalf. Until one day he turns around and kicks her ass, then all of a sudden, he's an "abuser". Or the desire to get a known promiscuous man to "hang up his hat", that backfires because, guess what, that's his nature. The term "Fuckboy/i" is a term invented by females frustrated that they can't get an Alpha to be faithful (he's the male "equivalent" of a "THOT").

Being an Alpha is something that is also time-dependent, as you will see in later chapters regarding "Depreciation and Time Erosion" of market value. Or like Wesley Snipe's character Monroe Hutchens said in the movie *Undisputed*, "Someday, every fighter loses. Sooner or later, somebody comes along and they got your ticket. Too old, just wasn't your day, whatever the reason is. In the end, everybody gets beaten. The most you can hope for is that you stay on top a while." The Alpha is eventually either done in by another Alpha, or time and broken relationships wear him away, or he becomes a Gamma.

Below the Alpha is his polar opposite, the Omega. The Omega is known for never standing up for himself and has no physically desirable traits to women as far a society is concerned (he does not have the ability to provide or protect and is not desired for DNA). Often disparaged as a "basement dweller", he usually recluses into his own digital world that allows him to escape the harsh dichotomies and judgements of this society. I surmise that in the olden days Omegas were those "Boo Radley" types. Not all Omega males will stay Omega—by doing things like sticking up for themselves, they get the grit to move into Beta territory (because he won't be genetically inclined for Gamma). But if they don't stick up for themselves and let a little steam off, it may turn disastrous for wider society if they someday explode and it catches others—people who had nothing to do with their torment—in the wake. Just like for the Alpha male, people are surprised to learn about the results of bullied males who "all of a sudden" load up their automatic weapons and start spraying the masses. It has only become in the last 5 to 8 years or so that attention has been drawn to stop the bullying; not out of the "goodness" of our hearts, but because of the aforementioned consequences. It the past, greater society accepted that it was normal to bully people they considered "weird" okay.

If an Omega harnesses his talent in a non-contact domain, he can become a *de facto* Alpha in that domain. Take the writer of *The Game of Thrones*: he might have been considered Omega in the past, but when his books hit paydirt and the productions became realized, his status shot up. The Omega, like the Alpha, has no responsibilities to women (except maybe his mom if dude is living at home) but for different reasons. The Alpha because he has so many women that he doesn't cater to a single woman, and the Omega because he is not desired by women, and therefore is not put in a position to be responsible to them.

Adjacent to the Omega is the Beta. In the Alpha/Beta dichotomy, the Beta is often given the Omega role—a pushover and the opposite of Alpha. The social structure of humans allows multiple gradations of social roles to occur because of the inherent nature of humans to survive in groups. Recall that the previous statement, "H. Erectus was involved in coordinated hunting activities and cared for infirm and/or weak companions –indicating higher social inclinations" [3]. Therefore, allowing for a "get in where you fit in" has allowed humans to not only survive, but thrive.

In that regard, the Alpha/Beta relationship is akin to CEO/COO relationships, whereby the CEO sets the vision for the organization and the COO carries out the day-to-day operations in concordance with that vision. In this sense, Beta is only concerned with carrying out and maintaining the status quo. Beta likes certainty in outcomes—and therefore gets a bad reputation for being a pushover—because he likes what works already and doesn't want to rock the boat, whereas Alpha is all about pushing the envelope and making dynamic changes. However, the Beta can turn Gamma in a situation where Alpha abuses his authority to the point where maintaining the status quo would be so detrimental to his situation that staying in the shit is worse for him than taking a risk to change it. These are the *Breaking Bad* situations where somebody who is usually considered a Beta decides to "nut up" because he has virtually nothing to lose for attempting to change the situation.

Finally, the Gamma male constitutes the "goldilocks zone" between the Alpha and the Beta. The Gamma male takes significant necessary risk—but makes the calculated decisions of a Beta. Alphas usually wing it with gut instinct—which usually gets them where they need to be—but they take losses which may be unnecessary. This is where Gamma gains ground. Gamma uses his Beta traits to determine the risk/reward aspect of a decision, but then, once the decision is made—and this is the important part—he acts with the intention of carrying out the plan. Therefore, the difference between Gamma and Beta is the willingness to take action, and the difference between Alpha and Gamma is the willingness to assess whether he can benefit from taking action. It is said that Gamma is the point at which an Alpha has learned from his mistakes and has toned down/kept his "wild" side at bay. Say, for example, a guy who started barfights but who now has a family will think twice about whether he wants to risk the societal consequences of starting a fight in a bar. It is also said Gamma is the point at which Beta decides to "man up" (I hate that phrase because it is often used in a sexist way by females towards men, but it's the best one I can come up with) and not let people fuck with him any type of way. As a result, the Gamma male would likely be the optimal choice for a woman who wants a man with Alpha qualities (the person may or may not come with the exact "look") for aggressiveness and masculinity but it being balanced with a sense of responsibility (read "paternal investment") and commitment.

CHAPTER 4

THE DEADBEAT
DAD ARGUMENT

"And although most men are ho's, he flows on the down low 'Cause I never heard about him with another girl"

~ Salt n Peppa "Whatta Man"

Women Mated More "Successfully" than men

An article written by Megan Fox for CBS news entitled "Genetics Suggest Modern Female Came First" [11] has, at its center, genetic analysis of DNA samples from the Y chromosomes of more than 1,000 men and mitochondrial DNA, which women seem to pass down virtually unchanged from mother to daughter, determined that the genetic "Adam" was a man who lived in Africa around 59,000 years ago, whereas the genetic "Eve" lived 143,000 years ago.

The article explains this gap with the reasoning that women are better at passing on their genes than men and that fewer men participated in reproduction than women did. The article offers two real-world reasons for the "shortened male genetic legacy". The first is the instance of one tribe conquering another, where the males in the dominant tribe get to mate with the women in its own tribe plus the ones they conquered. Referring to the practice of polygamy, the article states, "a few dominant males get to marry and have children and the rest see their genes consigned to the rubbish heap of posterity." The second reason is that pure chance, such as a man having only daughters, prevents his Y chromosome from being passed down to the next generation.

In my opinion, the article's tone is disingenuous—it appears to take the stance that women were better at passing down genes because they "mated" with the conquering tribes of men. This mating practice would make women the receptacles of the genes of the men conquering and therefore passive, not active, initiators of the human mating ritual. I do agree with the fact that, while women and men tend to be born around the same rate over large numbers of people, in practice they have not paired up on a one-to-one basis, and dominance hierarchies among them played a significant factor in who got to mate. Humans live longer now in the post-modern era than they did in the prehistoric era, and there would be no mathematical basis, especially considering the strides made in technology and education, that men and women could not pair off one-to-one, or roughly one-to-one. Coupled with the increased flourishment of women, and diversity in roles, there is no logical basis for hypergamy in the post-modern age.

Are men more promiscuous than women?

In 2002, there were about 4 million live births at an average of 2 births per woman [16]. The "Human Sex Ratio (HSR)" (average number of boys to girls born give or take and subtracting "intersex" *de minimis* estimates) is roughly 1 to 1. Applying this knowledge, a "quick n' dirty" calculation shows:

$$\frac{4\ Million\ avg\ births}{2\ births\ per\ woman} \approx 2\ Million\ women\ giving\ birth$$

If we disregard the combined biological effects of the Bateman principle and Coolidge effect, in a "perfect conservative fundamentalist world", where each man and each woman paired off and created these babies (and raised them together, to boot), we would have 2 million women and 2 million men having 2 children each, which comes to a total of 4 million births; 2 million men should have sired, leave any extraneous circumstances (i.e. artificial insemination, "sperm jacking", or "stealthing"), the 4 million live births that year. However, according to a WebMD article, a national survey was conducted on the number of children sired by men, the results were as follows:

"Among men who took the survey, 17% reported fathering one child, 16% reported fathering two children, and 14% reported fathering three or more kids" [17a].

One way this can be interpreted is that about 47% of men are siring all the offspring. Remembering the HSR is one to one, 2 million women means 2 million men born. Extrapolating we get:

$$2 \; Million \; Men * 47\% = 940,000 \; men \; siring \; children$$

Instead of 2 million men siring offspring, it's 940,000 men siring them. So, now we have 940,000 men fathering 4 million children with 2 million women.

From this reasoning alone, this proves the 80/20 rule and the research that was conducted prior: **not all men are selected to mate**, and of the ones that do, most of them are having more than one child. Other reasons for not coupling (i.e. sexual orientation, life of celibacy) and the fact that every coupling doesn't result in live birth (i.e. some women will have miscarriages and/or abortions) will result in a skew in the number of men and women having children together. To summarize:

TABLE 3. Men and Child Fathering Behavior [17a]

Percent of Men Fathering Children	Number of Men siring per child (based on 2 Million men)	Number of Children Fathered per man
17%	340,000	one child
16%	320,000	two children
14%	280,000	two or more children
47%	940,000	all children fathered (17%+16%+14%)

The data above is taken from the US in March 2002 to 2003 and, according to words in the article, there were 61 million "men" age 15 to 44 (it behooves me to note that when it serves society, boys under 18 can be called "men"—maybe they should have said "sexually mature males" but I digress). Looking at the above percentages, the trend is a decrease in the percent of men siring multiple children as the number of children fathered per man increase.

While the distribution of children to fathers is specifically unknown, based on relative percentages to the 47% of all children fathered, it is 64% likely that the 4 million kids born in 2002 were fathered by men who have two or more children ((16+14)/47 percent). Since the average number of children per woman is two, the 36% of men who fathered only one child are "sharing" their child's mother with another man.

To dig a little deeper, on the chance that any one man would be fathering children with multiple women throughout his lifetime, I stumbled upon the "Child Trends" website, which had this to say: "A 2006 [Child Trends] study estimates that 15 percent of men, or more than one in seven, will father children with more than one woman by the age of 40" [17b].

If we assume data is rather consistent over time (there's about a 3-year difference between the WebMD and the Child Trends studies), we can conclude:

$$(\% \; of \; men \; fathering \; multiple \; children)$$
$$* \Big(1 - (\% \; of \; men \; fathering \; children \; with \; multiple \; women)\Big)$$
$$= \% \; of \; men \; fathering \; multiple \; children \; by \; one \; woman$$

Plugging in the data from our combined analysis we have:

$$(16\% + 14\%) * (1 - 15\%) = \% \; of \; men \; fathering \; multiple$$
$$children \; by \; one \; woman$$
$$26\% = \% \; of \; men \; fathering \; multiple \; children \; by \; one \; woman$$

Regarding the propensity for a woman to have multiple men sire her multiple children, a 2011 article by NBCnews.com made the following claim: "one in five of all American moms have kids who have different birth fathers, a new study shows. And when researchers look only at moms with two or more kids, that figure is even higher: 28 percent have kids with at least two different men" [17c]. This data came from a study conducted by Cassandra Dorius who, at the time, was a postrostral fellow at the University of Michigan Institute for Social Research. Her study took data from 4,000 American women interviewed at least 20 times over a 27-year period. We can assume that the women who were interviewed in the study were 14 to 22 years old when the study began, because Dorius' study references women 41 to 49 years old [17e]. This makes it a good proxy for comparison since the data presented earlier regarding men's, or rather, sexually mature males' "seed-spreading" behavior.

When the article made the claim that 20% of American women had kids by different birth fathers and 28% of American women having kids with at least two different men we can safely make the assumption that the 28% figure includes the 20% figure, because "at least two different men" and "had kids by different birth fathers" entails that there be *at least* two men minimum. Therefore, we can scrap the 20% figure from the analysis and look at the 28% figure.

The article also had information regarding the racial distribution of women with multiple birth fathers, stating that 59% of them are Black, 35% are Hispanic, and 22% are White. So, it follows that a rational person would assume that the 28% figure quoted across all the American women is an average of the aforementioned racial percentages. Therefore, Census data can be used to approximate the percentages, if we assume that both Dorius' data regarding the 4,000 women and the Census' 40 to 49-year cohort is normally distributed. Here's what we get:

TABLE 4. Racial Distribution of Multiple Baby Daddies

	Race	Black	Non-Hispanic White	Hispanic	Total
	Population in Thousands				
A	Number of women in U.S. 40 to 49 years [17d]	2,923	14,219	3,072	20,214
B	Percent with multiple baby daddies [17c]	59%	22%	35%	
C = (A x B)	Total number of women with multiple baby daddies	1,725	3,128	1,075	5,928
D = C/(5,928)	Weight	0.29	0.53	0.18	1.00
E = (B x D)	Weighted Percent	0.17	0.12	0.06	-
F = Summation of all the weighted percents in item E	Weighted average percent of American women (Black, White and Hispanic) with multiple baby daddies	35%			

The average number is closer to 35% than 28%, but for shits and giggles, we can also assume that the article didn't mention Asian and Native American women either because the 4,000-woman cohort didn't have Asian and Native American respondents, or, their numbers were politically unsatisfying. Regardless, we can humor that and average the Census percentage and the article's claim and agree to a compromise of 32%.

Now if we combine the estimations that 26% of men father multiple children by one woman versus 32% of women have multiple fathers to their children, and that researchers' (Crittenden's) claims that women "mated" more successfully than men, we can logically assume that the average woman has sex 6% more often than the average man. So can men, as a group, really be more promiscuous?

CHAPTER SUMMARY

○ Anywhere people of the opposite sex engage in social activity is a sexual marketplace. As of late, online platforms have made gathering in virtual social activity ubiquitous, ergo the many dating apps allow people to meet and communicate with potential mates.

○ Biologically, fertility drives sexual value of the human female and virility drives the sexual value of the human male. Both are time-based phenomena, generally with the younger the potential mate, the higher the value, all else equal.

○ As people began to live in groups and specialize in different skill sets, the ability of a man to provide was not limited to what he could hunt, but what he could trade for. This gave him more leverage to be a suitable mate. As societies formed governments, privately initiated acts of violence were sanctioned, making the role of protection one of the collective directorates rather than individual agendas. However, the innate desire for the *ability* of the man to protect is still there and factored into assessment of his virility.

○ The aspects of male and female value on an ordinal scale of minimal to maximal value, is usually known as a "10 scale" or "Decile Scale", but can be any range of numbers with prespecified values. Theoretically everybody has *some* value and generally *nobody* is perfect. As a result, numbers approaching 0 on the minimum end and 10 on the maximum end can be used in lieu of 0 or 10 (although it's not uncommon for "1 to 10" to be used where 1 is the absolute lowest and provides some value—which acknowledges the fact that everybody has value, even if minimal).

CHAPTER 5

SEXUAL
MARKETPLACE
VALUE (SMV)

"Wherever you go, there you are."

~ Unknown

Introduction to the marketplace

For the purposes of this book, the "sexual marketplace", is a place whereby interactions between the sexes, generally for the purposes for having sex and/or sexual relationships, take place.

The words "sexual marketplace", which include "sex" and "marketplace" is covered by Webster's Dictionary's definition of "sex" with regards to biological sex and sexual activity, up to, and encompassing the act of sex itself and the motivations thereof. Although Webster's definition of the "marketplace" used terms like "the everyday world" as the market itself (to which I emphatically concur), I intend to focus in on the smaller pockets where social activity takes place. [18]

From online apps like Tinder, Plenty of Fish (POF), and OK Cupid, to bricks and mortar eating/drinking/entertainment places and religious places of gathering are some of the largest sexual marketplaces. Anywhere people congregate a sexual marketplace is formed, and you are being "marked to market" (i.e., your Sexual Marketplace Value (SMV) is being assessed) each time you visit one of these places.

From cradle to grave, there is no escaping the sexual marketplace or having one's SMV assessed—as the wise phrase goes: "wherever you go, there you are". Sex is one of the primary drivers of human behavior and it doesn't stop whether one is married, single, divorced, widowed, a senior citizen, visiting a foreign country, attending school, etc. In fact, we have a slew of buzzwords related to the exchange of male and female value. Phrases like "she's out of your league", "stay in your lane" or "know your role". Are vice-signaling terms to indicate, usually to a male, that the female he wants to give attention to has a marketplace value much higher than he can reckon with.

The Bateman Principle and Coolidge Effect conflicts are the drivers of sexual marketplace dynamics. In any market, there are determinants of demand. You can think of a certain style of dress that, when endorsed by a famous person, can come into style overnight. One particular instance, but not directly analogous to this, was the rising popularity of skateboarding gear in the early 2000's among black youth. In the 90's in the D.C. area, I recall common black youth thinking wallet chains, torn off wide-leg jeans and skateboarding shoes as things that *bammas* wear. Fast-forward to the early 2000's when the Neptunes, Lupe Fiasco, and Pharell Williams wore the skater style, it gained traction. Finally, when Lil' Wayne started rapping about DC shoes (no relation to the city of Washington D.C.), black kids everywhere were wearing skateboard apparel and shopping at Pac Sun, even if they had no idea of what an "ollie" was.

Now imagine two dark-skinned black men, the same in every way (height, education, temperament, etc.), except one of them has green eyes, and the other one has brown eyes. The green-eyed black man can fetch a higher SMV because having green eyes among dark-skinned black men is rare, and the rarer a commodity is, the more in demand it becomes and, thus, the higher it's price.

Commensurately, we could think about the market for Chinese women. Asians are the smallest minority in the US by numbers (about 5.1% of the total US population in 2012), and therefore they are "rare". Thus, in the US, Chinese women (a subset of Asian women) would have a higher SMV than in China, where there is practically nothing but Chinese women. As a result, men and women must make decisions on which qualities matter to them and their values. There have been several determinants that are known to be valued by either sex and I will list them here. Keep in mind that these are theories and take a stab in the dark based on the limited research contained therein for your reading entertainment.

Determinants of Sexual Marketplace Value

While a lot has changed in terms of technology and innovation from the human race in the past, an article in Science Daily found that human mating preferences are rather primitive irrespective of the fact that we consider ourselves to be socially evolved [19]. Cognitive scientists from the University of Indiana conducted an experiment that ascertained that men are attracted to beauty and women often traded beauty for security and commitment. It also found that females followed the patterns of most mammals, being the choosier of the two sexes. The experiment conducted was a speed-dating session with 46 adults assessing themselves on evolutionarily relevant traits (i.e. self-assessing their market value) which included items such as physical attractiveness and health (which is akin to "looks and athleticism"), present and future financial status (which is akin to "money and status") and parenting qualities (which can be considered a status-like category because investment (time and money) in raising offspring usually comes with a positive future outlook (which suggest a positive return on said investment).

The participants claimed that their motivations were to find someone like themselves but, once the speed-dating began, men and women played out their evolutionary cues. Men going for more attractive women and women drawn to the men who were wealthier and secure. In addition, when asked if the male/female participants wanted to see the female/male counterparts again, the male wanted to see 1 in 2 women again versus women only wanting to see 1 in 3 men again. This experiment simply reconfirms the *Bateman Principle*.

What men biologically value in women (fertility)

Fertility can be regarded as equivalent to youth and beauty (for the appearance of fertility). One major biological driver behind men's demand for women is the demand for fertility—innately for child-bearing purposes. Certain characteristics, which are indicators of fertility, like healthy hair, skin, and nails, wide hips, and full breasts (regardless of size) attract men to women. While the definition of attractiveness changed over time, it is no surprise as to why Marylin Monroe and Jennifer Lopez, generations apart, have had similar levels of sex appeal and similar shapes. Sir Mix A Lot's "I Like Big Butts" and Queen's "Fat Bottom Girls", are examples of two completely different music eras and cultures exalting a curvy (not equivalent to "obese") pear-shape as a sexually appealing shape for most men. A pear-shaped body is also healthier according to some sources [20].

While some men may like thinner women and others bigger, the overall shape and proportion is what conveys the fertility message. Simply because a woman looks "fertile" doesn't mean that she is. Since humans didn't really live that long after puberty before the modern age, the outward appearance of health was evolutionarily more tied to actual health.

Non-Growing Follicles (NGF)

Besides reproductive hormones, the human ovarian reserve can be used to estimate the level of fertility of females from birth to menopause. The human ovary normally contains a specific number of non-growing follicles (NGF) whose population declines with the progression of age. This decline can be used to model female fertility. In this case, a chart of % NGF remaining is reconstructed from a study conducted by Wallace & Kelsey, who attempted to model the age-related population of NGF from conception to menopause [21]. The following is *a* derivative of the original Wallace and Kelsey chart which shows the relationship between %NGF remaining and age [appendix note 2]:

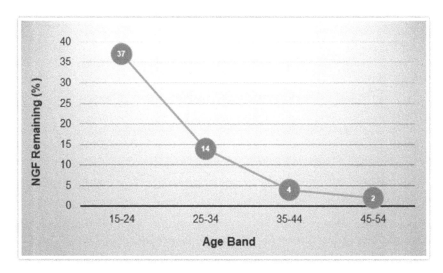

Figure 12. NGF Remaining (%)

As we can see, the younger a woman is the more likely to be fertile, all else held equal. Based on biological urges to mate and procreate, age has a negative effect on demand since it has a negative relationship to fertility. For the purposes of later comparison, I have rebased [appendix note 1] the %NGF Remaining graph to the age of 15 = 100, to show how all subsequent values index to the initial age:

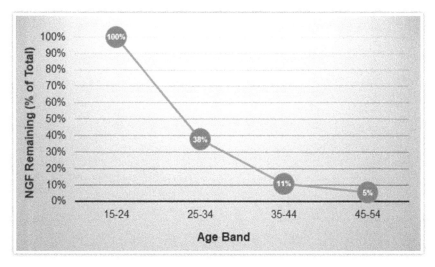

Figure 13. NGF Remaining – 10 Year Average (%, Rebased)

What women biologically value in men: A protector and provider (virility)

In the hunter gatherer tribes and semi nomadic tribes like the Masai (as mentioned previously), it is not uncommon for men to protect the homesteads of the tribe. In addition, hunting is another way that men foraged. Women also played a role, as well as children, by gathering berries, discerning between which were good and which were poisonous to eat, but men had the burden of bringing most of the nutrition in the tribes by hunting. What would make a more agile and good hunter? And protect the tribe? Testosterone.

In some men, testosterone levels remain high throughout life, but in most they begin to decline at about age 40. Unlike the precipitous drop in hormones that women experience at menopause, however, the decline is gradual, averaging just 1% a year. This drop is imperceptible at first, but by age 70, the average man's testosterone production is 30% below its peak [22].

The following graph shows the relationship between free, bioavailable testosterone and age [23a]:

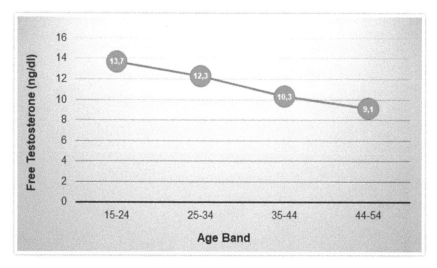

Figure 14. Free Testosterone (ng/dl)

Free Testosterone

Muscles allow the human body to perform work. Before I build my case on why testosterone is a factor in being able to protect and provide (especially in a more primitive setting) I'll briefly answer the opposition and acknowledge that being muscular does not guarantee the performance of work. However, I would argue that the probability of *successfully* performing work is higher with muscle. The hormone testosterone plays a vital role in male development.

> **Testosterone has many direct effects on the male anatomy and metabolism. It is responsible for the deep voice, increased muscle mass, and strong bones that characterize the [male] gender... The hormone also has crucial, if incompletely understood, effects on male behavior: It contributes to aggressiveness, and it is essential for the libido (sex drive), as well as for normal erections and sexual performance. Testosterone stimulates the growth of the genitals at puberty and it is responsible for sperm production throughout adult life. [22]**

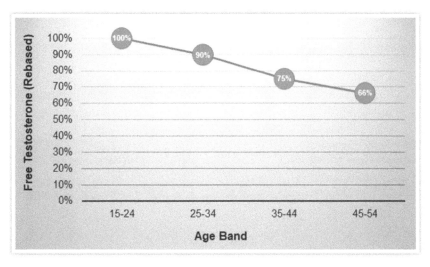

Figure 15.   Free Testosterone – 10 Year Averages (Rebased)

The above graph is rebased for easier comparison with the 15 to 24-year range = 100 [appendix note 3]. Like fertility, virility, which is based on free testosterone rates in men indexed from their teens to their early twenties, declines over their lifetime. The biggest drop in free testosterone occurs as one is going from the 25 to 34-year range to the 35 to 44-year range. Which confirms/reiterates the Harvard source.

Male and female biological factors comparison

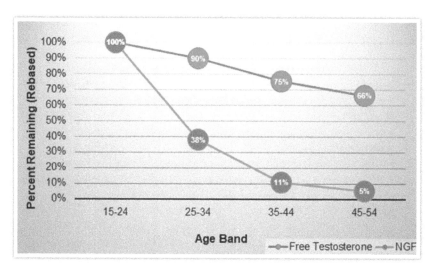

Figure 16.   Free Testosterone vs. NGF Remaining (%, Rebased)

The mean indicator for female fertility decreases at a faster rate than male virility. This differential is more pronounced as time goes on:

Age range	Free Testosterone	%NGF Remaining (Rebased)	Growth Differential from Base Year
TABLE 5. Male Female Biological Factors Comparison			
15-24	100.0	100.0	0.0
25-34	89.8	37.8	52.0
35-44	75.2	10.8	64.4
45-54	66.4	5.4	61.0

Based on the averages, biologically, and considering legality, it would best for females to produce viable offspring in the 18 to 24-year range. Males can produce throughout their lives, but for comparative purposes, we'll stop here at 54. While a woman can maximize peak virility by choosing a man in the 18 to 24-year range, she may want to choose a man in the 25 to 34-year bracket, because, as you will see later, his earnings would be at a higher point. Alternatively, a man might want to choose a woman in the 25 to 34-year range who may have a higher level of maturity, but yet still fertile. In addition, the 25 to 34-year time range minimizes the differential in biological value.

Breakout of the "Provider" Role – Violence Monopoly

German sociologist and political economist Max Weber authored a work entitled *Politics as a Vocation* whereby he defines an effective government operating within various jurisdictional boundaries as a "state" and this state is only as effective insomuch as it has a monopoly over the legitimate use of physical force. Violence is another way of interpreting physical force. Weber, in a nutshell, summed up two conditions for a state to exist: a territory (read legitimate boundary) and the monopoly of the legitimate use of violence within that territory. All *legitimate* use of physical force where a state exists is derived from granted permissions from that state [24].

Therefore, we can conclude that if physical force exists without the state's permission, the action is either illegitimate or, if ubiquitous, the community is not a "state" or is a highly ineffective one. One situation that comes to mind are the conditions in Somalia, whereby various territories are controlled by different warlord clans. Since violence is not controlled by one source there, Somalia, as far as Weber's definition is concerned, is not a state, but the various territories run by warlords can suffice as de facto states even if they have no written constitution.

Extending this logic to foraging communities (communities that humans were a part of for the lion's share of their existence), it is likely to be the case that protection of a tribe/clan and family (as families are microcosms of communities) would go hand and hand with the ability to provide sustenance. It is also likely that the people who used physical force to acquire food (hunting) are likely to use physical force to protect their communities. This is akin to the popular lore of post-apocalyptic homesteads, where military (violence turned outward) and law enforcement (violence turned inward) are run by the same groups of people.

In modern-day society with rule of law, the protector and provider roles are separated—provisions are made through productivity and trade and protection is generally given by the legal governing body of that jurisdiction. While the innate biological drivers for women to select men based on the ability to protect as well as provide are still there, in a practical sense the protector and provider role is separated in modern times and the demand for provision can be supplicated with income (rather than hunting a kill etc.). As a result, I measure of the ability of a man to provide in the modern age by his income.

Median Income over time

To show income patterns over time, I created a cohort out of Census median income data starting from 1977 until 2016 to illustrate a man's lifetime earnings from 15 to 54 [25a]. I did this by taking the range of Census data on median annual earnings of men in each age group during a different time range and "linked" them together [appendix note 4]. For example, I assumed that to follow a 16-year-old over a ten-year timespan, his income would be initially extracted from the 15 to 24 age range in 1978 ($12,334 in 2016 dollars) and then later in the 25 to 34 age range in 1988 ($40,552 in 2016 dollars) at the age of 26. Repeating this logic and applying it to age ranges up to 45-54, the entire graph of such a cohort would appear like this:

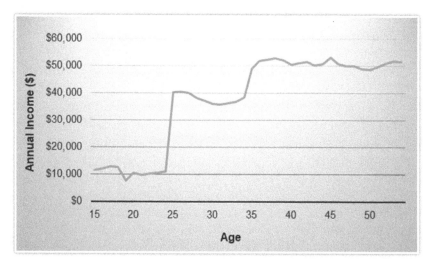

Figure 17. Men's Lifetime Income Profile (2016 Dollars)

There are two weakness to this technique. First, the cohort that the assumed ages are extracted from provides an average of all of those in that group. As a result, the median income value for the 16-year-old in 1978 is also averaged in with individuals 15 through 24 in the first grouping, and later at the age of 26, his income is averaged with 25 through 34-year-old individuals in the second grouping. Second, we cannot tell if the same people in either grouping consistently provided Census data. For example, some of the individuals in the age 15 thru 24 cohort may not have showed up in the 25 through 34 cohort, and vice versa. But if we assume that some of the people who answer Census surveys tend to do so over time, this provides a good common-sense view of what a man's income looks like as he ages. When we average the year to year changes in ten-year increments, we get this:

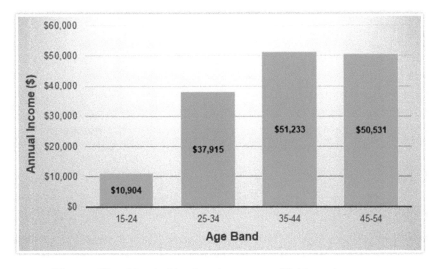

Figure 18. Men's Median Income – 10-Year Averages (2016 Dollars)

A quick look at this graph shows what is expected – a man earning less as he starts his career—later to become a master of his craft. He then maximizes his earning potential at an older age. Things level out from there. If I were to extend the analysis, we'd see his earnings drop as he nears the retirement ages (55 to 64 and 65 to 74) as we'd expect to see him take more leisure time and work fewer hours. I used these particular age bands to make them comparable to the NGF% and Free Testosterone rebased graphs. Here is a rebased version:

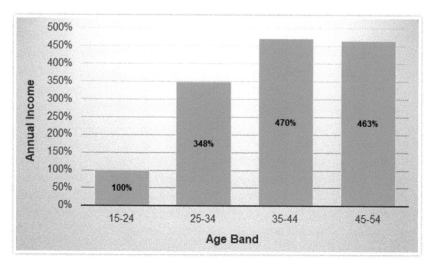

Figure 19.   Men's Median Income – 10-Year Averages
(2016 Dollars, Rebased)

We can see that peak earning potential for a man based on this cohort is in the 35 to 44-year band. This presents an interesting problem for a woman attempting to maximize her choice in men because peak free testosterone is in the 15 to 24-year band (for legal purposes 18 to 24, if she is 18 or over).

Combined Value (Modern Age Value)

Since virility declines slower than fertility, a man at any given age has a relatively higher biological value index on average than women in his age group, especially as the age cohort gets older. While this is a biological/biochemical truth (comparing average levels of testosterone and NGF), demand for women at any age is going to be determined by *more than just biological factors alone*. In this post-modern era, the only example that comes to mind that separates age and fertility would be clinics that provide in-vitro fertilization and/or egg freezing/use of surrogates. This is not so with men. However, when the effect of income and testosterone are averaged together ("protect and provide") a man can greatly enhance his biological value [26].

TABLE 6.	Male Attributes (Composite)		
	Protect (Virility)	Provide	Protect and Provide
Age range	Free Testosterone	Median Income	Combined Value (Average)
15-24	100.0	100.0	100.0
25-34	89.8	347.7	218.8
35-44	75.2	469.8	272.5
44-54	66.4	463.4	264.9

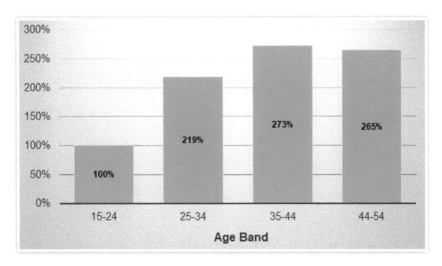

Figure 20. Combined Value – 10-Year Averages (Rebased)

When comparing the average combined attributes of men and women, their attributive differential that was illustrated in Figure 20 is larger:

TABLE 7. Male Female Attribute Comparison

Age range	Combined Value (Male)	%NGF Remaining (Female)	Growth Differential from Base Year
15-24	100.0	100.0	0.0
25-34	218.8	37.8	181.0
35-44	272.5	10.8	261.7
44-54	264.9	5.4	259.5

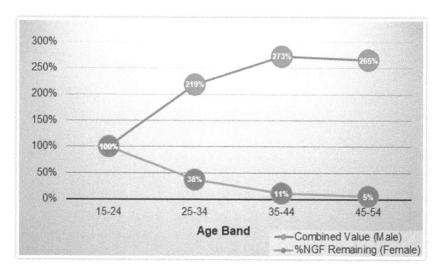

Figure 21. Combined Value vs NGF Remaining (%)

The above graph shows the difference in biological value per age group, per the previously suggested variables. All else held equal, a man is likely to have more biological value than a woman of the same age/within 10 years of his age after 25. If a man and a woman of the same age after age 25 get together, this difference in value could be considered the "raw" (pardon the pun) level of hypergamy.

An online article in the *Independent* took research from a Finnish University journal that revealed:

that the youngest age men claim to be attracted to remains the same no matter how old they are i.e. a 40-year-old man would still consider a relationship with a 22-year-old woman when he turns 50 and 60 …[research] confirmed that women have a much narrower age range, preferring male partners who are either older than them or close to their own age [25b].

The reason that men prefer younger women was explained by the lead author of the study in terms of basic evolutionary theory: "natural selection has probably shaped men's sexual strategies to include a particular interest in highly fertile, young women, but because women, in many cases, are pickier with respect to sexual partners, most men could not find a partner unless their sexual motivation would be more inclusive" [25b].

These findings coincide with the biological values presented—men going for fertility and women going for men who are older. While they did not directly mention why women went for older men, I propose that their reasons fall in line with provider value theory, or it could be the older man who can hold his own alongside the younger, as it has been quoted: "Beware of an old man in a profession where men usually die young".

Mother Nature's Cruel Joke

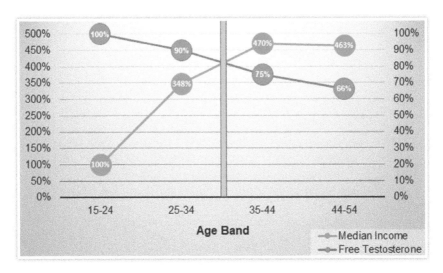

Figure 22. Male Paradox

By graphing each of the male attributes on its own axis and comparing them, it exposes the bitter sweetness of a man's existence in a post-modern society. When the average man is young, he has a lot of energy but a low level of discretionary income. As this man gets older, his income increases, he builds capital, but he finds that his "spunk" is dwindling. This is the crux of the "Male Paradox" illustrated above and demarcated by an equilibrium "crossover" point (orange vertical line), where a man's ability to protect and provide are both equal. This occurs in the 25 to 34-year range. Rule of law, improvement of sanitary conditions, advances in healthcare, and adequate financial systems in developed nations have afforded many people an increase of life. Gone are the days that a person died because they stepped on a rusty nail. To the left of the crossover point, is all-night clubbing, drinking till you puke, and Ihop pancakes, but still maintaining erections harder than Chinese calculus. To the right of this point, is pea knuckle, parcheesi, show re-runs, Carnival Cruises and "early-bird" specials at Denys. Ole Uncle Elroy can use some of that income to purchase pills and potions from the medical industry to help him "keep up" with his "sugar bae".

The Quarterback (QB) and the Wide Receiver (WR)

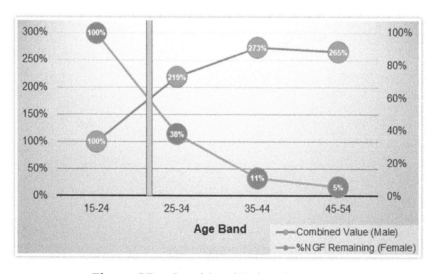

Figure 23.   Combined Value Crossover

When %NGF is graphed against its own axis and compared with the male Combined Value, the crossover point becomes an "equilibrium age" at which men and women can provide optimal value to each other. Here, the age range is between the 15 to 24 and the 25 to 34 range. Combining the age ranges, we'd get a 15 to 34 age range with the crossover point being at the median location, which would yield an average age of 24.5.

To the right of the crossover point, men's values are relatively higher than women, and men would benefit from choosing a younger woman. Woman to the right of the crossover point may feel they are not getting attention from men their own age.

To the left of the crossover point, women's values are relatively higher than men's and they could benefit from choosing an older man. At this point, they might look at guys their age as physically attractive but "unpolished" and "immature" and might look to benefit from the experiences and stability that a higher income can provide.

These relative crossover points provide interesting clues and information for both women and men, but especially for women who are looking for a long-term relationship for the purposes of raising a family. If likened to American football, the woman is the QB who must throw her "football" (display her value/accept an offer) to the man who is the WR (makes an offering of value). The WR is on the field with a cornerback covering him and tons of distractions (i.e., other women in the field). The potential for a completed pass and touchdown (a successful LTR) entails many challenges, this is why in football, well-timed long-range passes are the most awe-inspiring plays—because it speaks to the chemistry between the QB and WR.

One might notice that a seasoned QB always throws the football where the WR is projected to end up, never to where his WR is, lest the football be intercepted. Therefore, the name of the game for women is to project where the man is headed, rather than trying to get him when he lands there.

Multidimensional Analysis (SMV Determinants)

Since there are more factors than just income and biological factors that drive choices in the Sexual Marketplace, a more comprehensive explanation (while not a panacea) is needed. Therefore, I put forth, based on internet randomness and trolling, the "LAMPS" and "VCLAW" methods of valuation which can be tied to rankings to determine various factors that can add "depth" to mate selection.

Relative Importance Concept

Since modern humans have different preferences based on personal values and environments, the relative importance of each of the attributes mentioned below (i.e. LAMPS) are going to vary between individuals and within groups of individuals, i.e. ethnic groups/cultures. From my personal experience, Chinese women place a heavier priority on money and status and Black women place a heavier priority on looks and athleticism. This doesn't mean that looks and athleticism aren't important to the former, and money and status isn't important to the latter. It's just that their relative environments determine the qualities/characteristics that would best help them to survive.

If you think about China, all of the dynasties, rebellions, famines, bandits, and the high-power distance that people have (small middle class) and their adherence to law, a wealthier person would be able to take care of family better. Remember that money and status change based not only on personal efforts, but in governments (one's money can be determined by a large extent to the ability of either themselves or the government to protect the creation and growth of that wealth). Anecdotally, I have seen Americanized Chinese women tend to have a slightly different value system, still embracing wealth (money), but willing to trade off between looks and athleticism as well (more on tradeoffs later).

Also, anecdotally, Black American women often inhabit areas where the strongest guy is the one who is the most likely to survive/thrive as most of the income earning on average has been done by either manual labor, or brought in through athleticism (athletes), aggression (gangs) and aggression-related activity (rappers who rap on violence). As a result, physically stronger men ("show 'em that you ain't no punk") were valued higher. In addition, the beauty standard by which the United States is associated with gravitates towards a European beauty standard. Traits that are more European often, due to the tribal nature of humans, enable one to have a better chance of survival. A microcosm of this can be seen in the Black community whereby Black Americans (people of African ancestry that have lived in the US for generations since the 1800s) with European features—hair that tends to be more wavy, green eyes, and light skin, often get preference over traditionally sub-Saharan African features (wide noses, darker skin, kinkier hair).

Alluding to the anecdotal comparison of values between Chinese women and Black American women—also applying this standard to men—the relative importance of traits is, for lack of a better term, "subconsciously" calculated. It is very rare to find a man or woman to have maximum value across all attributes of their nature: a person who rates high in the looks category often doesn't have to be conscientious, as people who see this person or want to have sex with this person will often assist in completing their tasks subconsciously with the hopes of being able to mate with them. Thus, people with "personality" or who are "down to earth" are often people who are not a 9 in looks. It follows that if one values both good looks and a conscientious demeanor, there is a tradeoff between those qualities. In this text, we will refer to them as "Relative Importance Weights", w_i, where the $0 < w_i < 100\%$ and the i represents the attribute that it is judging (i.e., Looks, Money, Status).

How women value men: Looks, Athleticism, Money, Power, Status (LAMPS)

The LAMPS approach to Sexual Marketplace Value (SMV) takes a multifaceted approach to capture the various factors that make a man sexually marketable and generate demand from women looking to make a heterosexual monogamous coupling.

Originally and frequently called "LMS" (ignoring athleticism and power), online forums and discussions have evolved to include athleticism and power as they are indicators of the degree to which males exhibit the ability to protect and the ability to lead a tribe. We now delve into each of the attributes separately, to give some clarity.

LOOKS

"LOOKS" IS A SIMPLE catchall phrase that regards physical attractiveness that generally stems from genetics—attributes which can only be altered by surgery. It also implies that the alterations change the underlying structure of the person's physique. Things like nose size/shape, eye color, bone structure (for height), implants (like chin and breast and calf implants) and symmetry, are just a few things that can alter looks.

Some of variation in looks also is affected by "nurture" rather than "nature". A person who has contracted Bell's Palsy may end up with a droopy face had they not contracted the disease. A person who looks like a tennis ball is jutting out of their neck, later finds they have Goiter from lack of iodine in the diet. To the degree which a person cares for themselves (eating proper nutrition, dental care, and for the most part avoids drugs and alcohol, or does not make it a regular part of their lives) constitutes the degree of control a person has over looks.

Income is another important part, since people with means have access to healthy food and hygienic practices and tend to live in environments that are not heavily polluted. People with good income can afford to maintain their health through nutritional and environmental means and likely are less stressed because they can do so. They also create an environment that promotes their health, has good security and law enforcement, etc., which leads to the next point.

Trauma comes from accidents and intentional happenings. A good-looking person can be horribly disfigured in a fire, car accident, or explosion, a natural disaster like a hurricane can easily send shards of glass that could turn a cabbage patch doll into a garbage pail kid. Fights can leave jaws and noses broken, orbitals cracked, and teeth missing, along with other cuts, contusions and abrasions that, if it reaches deep enough can cause structural damage can alter a person's looks (hence Biggie Smalls' phrase "when I hit ya, I split ya to the white meat" (the 'white meat' is the fascia that gives muscles integrity)).

Finally, age, or the natural attrition/depreciation of one's physical body (jump forward to "depreciation and value erosion" for depth on this): things that used to be up are either drooping down because of the law of gravity or because the proper facilities are not working to "get it up". This is a category of age that cannot be avoided. It can be mitigated through lifestyle factors but it cannot be avoided. The takeaway is, aside from factors outside of one's control, the degree to which one "looks good" is largely something that is gifted by genetics.

There are two proxy measurements that I will use to calculate the magnitude of looks which will be denoted by "L" and be a value from 1 to 10. The first, using the "New Golden Ratio" [27b] (to calculate Face Length Percentages (FLP)), and the second using men's Waist to Hip Ratio (WHR) [38a].

New Golden Ratio

The "Golden Ratio" is approximately 1.62, and per Wikipedia, is defined as "two quantities are in the **golden ratio** if their ratio is the same as the ratio of their sum to the larger of the two quantities [29a]." Google/ Wiki it for a deeper explanation. Based off of this ratio, it has also been discovered by researchers that there is an optimal level of facial attractiveness. The conclusion was derived from comparisons of faces with identical facial features (i.e., the picture of the same person) but altered distance between various points on the face (i.e., the distance between the eyes and mouth). The findings resulted in finding optimum attractiveness when the vertical distance between the eyes and mouth is about 36% of the face's length and if the horizontal distance between the eyes and mouth is about 46% of the face's width. This was coined the "New" Golden Ratio [27b]. A more complete calculation discussion of this can be found in the appendix [appendix note 5]:

Calculating the Golden Ratio based on Face Length Percent (FLP)

$$FLP = Face\ Length\ Percent = \frac{Distance\ from\ eyes\ to\ mouth}{Distance\ from\ hairline\ to\ chin}$$

Based on the above formula, here is a table of values:

TABLE 8. Abridged New Golden Ratio Table		
Face Length Percent (FLP)	Percentile	L_{FLP} (Looks ranking based on FLP)
0.10	0%	0.00
0.12	8%	0.77
0.14	15%	1.54
0.16	23%	2.31
0.18	31%	3.07
0.20	38%	3.84
0.22	46%	4.61
0.24	54%	5.38
0.26	61%	6.15
0.28	69%	6.92
0.30	77%	7.68
0.32	85%	8.45
0.34	92%	9.22
0.36	100%	9.99
0.38	92%	9.22
0.40	85%	8.45
0.42	77%	7.68
0.44	69%	6.92
0.46	61%	6.15
0.48	54%	5.38
0.50	46%	4.61
0.52	38%	3.84
0.54	31%	3.07
0.56	23%	2.31
0.58	15%	1.54
0.60	8%	0.77
0.62	0%	0.00

Based on this formula, a person with a FLP of 40% (0.4) has an L value of 8.45 on the 10 (Min/Max) scale.

Knowledge Check

If the distance between Jake's eyes and mouth is 4 inches and the distance between Jake's hairline and chin is 8 inches, what is his what is his ranking based on facial appearance?

Men's Waist to Hip Ratio (*WHR*)

> The WHR is gender specific. Women tend to have a lower WHR compared to men. Until the beginning of puberty, the relationship between waist and hip is almost identical in boys and girls (nearly 0.9). Later, the influence of estrogen causes the pelvis to grow in women. This results in the typical female fat distribution where fat accumulates in the buttocks and upper thighs, causing the WHR to deviate from 0.7. In males, the hip in proportion to waist remains larger (the ideal is here 0.9) [28a].

WHR has often been used to determine female proportions for attractiveness, which lead to the "coke bottle" or "pear shape". It has also been determined by the World Health Organization (WHO) that it is a measure of health as well.

Men's WHR is also a factor in how he appears to have a "V" shape. Ladies, picture the guy at the beach with the beer gut versus the lifeguard whose "streamlined" shape makes him appear to also live in a marine habitat. While a more appropriate measure of the V shape may be shoulder-to-waist (circumference around shoulders divided by waist circumference) ratio, there is no related health metric associated with it. As a result, WHR will determine relative health, outline appearance and, as you will see, will be combined with the New Golden Ratio to determine the magnitude of looks (L).

While aestheticians have determined the optimal male WHR to be 0.9, based on WHO's health recommendations, a WHR below 0.9 constitutes a low disease risk [28a]:

TABLE 9.	Male Waist to Hip Ratio Categories		
From	**To**	**Disease Risk (Men)**	**Notes**
Below	0.95	low	Optimal at 0.9 (for aesthetics); WHO says less than 0.9 healthy, start at 0.88 to be just below threshold
0.96	1	moderate	
1.1	Above	high	1.0 and higher increased disease risk; but start at 1.1 since it doesn't include 1—and should be higher than women's minimum threshold

Based on the above table health aspect, I used a WHR of 0.88 to be a "Weight Ranking for Men" (WRM) (of 9.99 (optimum) and since a male WHR above 1 is considered high disease risk, I used a WHR of 1.1 to be an WRM of 0.5 (minimum). Based on this, we have the following formula [appendix note 6]:

$$L_{WHR} = -43.136(WHR) + 47.95$$

Where the WRM is the ranking based on men's WHR.

TABLE 10.	Values of L based on WHR		
WHR	**L_{WHR} (looks based on WHR)**	**WHR**	**L_{WHR} (looks based on WHR)**
1.10	0.5	0.98	5.5
1.09	1.0	0.97	6.0
1.08	1.5	0.96	6.5
1.06	2.0	0.95	7.0
1.05	2.5	0.94	7.5
1.04	3.0	0.93	8.0
1.03	3.5	0.91	8.5
1.02	4.0	0.90	9.0
1.01	4.5	0.89	9.5
1.00	5.0	0.88	9.99

According to this, a man with a WHR of 0.97 has an L value of 6.

KNOWLEDGE CHECK:

- If Jake has a WHR of 0.89, what is his L value based on WHR?

Relative importance weights of sub-attributes

In this section, the Face Length Percent (FLP) and men's Waist-to-Hip Ratio (WHR) were both factors used to determine "L" for looks. What this means is that when a woman looks at a man and thinks to herself "He looks good", she's looking at his FLP and WHR and "subconsciously" giving him a score. Mathematically, men's looks ranking is a function of FLP and WHR:

$$Looks\ Ranking\ (L) = f(L_{FLP}, L_{WHR})$$

For simplicity the additive model incorporating what percent of importance (relative importance) the woman gives FLP and WHR will determine how FLP and WHR affect the Looks Ranking (L):

$$L = (w_{FLP}) * L_{FLP} + (w_{WHR}) * L_{WHR}$$

Since all percentages add up to 100% or 1, we know that

$$w_{FLP} + w_{WHR} = 1\ or\ 100\%$$

Since there are only two variables, if we know one, we know the other:

$$w_{FLP} = 1 - w_{WHR}$$

Supposed Jake approached Janet to ask her out, and body shape is relatively important to Janet 20% of the time when she judges a man's looks. How relatively important is a man's facial proportions to Janet?

Using the above formula

$$w_{FLP} = 1 - w_{WHR}$$

$$w_{FLP} = 1 - 20\%$$

$$w_{FLP} = 80\%$$

Facial proportions are important to Janet 80% of the time.

How important is We can assume that Jake probably has visible abdominal musculature (abs), but if abs are important to Janet 20% of the time (Jake's $w_{WHR} = 0.2$ or 20%) the value of Jake's abs in determining his looks are only $9.5 \times 0.20 = 1.9 = L_{WHR}$.

KNOWLEDGE CHECK:

- Using what we learned about Jake from the last two knowledge checks, and Janet's preferences, what is Janet's overall opinion of Jake when it comes to his looks?
- Hint: Use the following formula:

$$L = (w_{FLP}) * L_{FLP} + (w_{WHR}) * L_{WHR}$$

ATHLETICISM

"**A**THLETICISM", REGARDING OUR THESIS, refers to the appearance of and ability to perform work that results in enhanced survival. This is influenced by genetics but can be developed as well. The phrase 'work that enhances survival' refers to defense of oneself and others (can he "fight") and employment that an athletic build would be a boon to, like military and/or law enforcement, fire fighter, paramedic, construction worker, auto body mechanic, farmhand and mover.

While the WHR gives an outward appearance to body frame, bodyfat % [28b] can be an indicator of the appearance of athleticism. A person with an imposing muscular appearance is a person that most people are not likely to mess with. While muscularity is not always a sign that the individual can perform work that enhances survival (i.e., he's "swole", but he can't fight), it is a good indicator since lower body fat usually equates to higher levels of testosterone and higher testosterone, all else equal, would tend to increase the vigor and virility of the man in question. Therefore, being athletic does not necessarily mean that the person has the skills to perform a physical task but is more likely to be ready to adapt to a physical task should it be presented.

There are many ways to measure body fat%—the most accurate is the hydrostatic or "dunk" test, whereby a person is weighed on a scale and then weighed underwater and the differential between the two weights is considered fat (since muscle is denser than fat) and that number is divided by the scale weight to determine body fat%. But the most common are the calipers or "pinch" test and the bioelectrical impedance test. I am tempted to delve into this here since I have a fitness background, but I must stop short for brevity. If you are interested in finding your own body fat%, pick a method that works for you. I decided to use a source from a Fitness city Blog [28c] which is just about as good as using official sports medicine books with regards to straightforwardness. The data is translated here for analysis:

Body Fat Percent		Men			
From	To	Range	Category	Notes	Athleticism SMV Rank Range (Arbitrary)
below	5	N/A	Health Risk	Check with doctor increase body fat	0.1 to 1.99 (give 1.5)
5.1	8	2.9	Ultra-Lean	Elite Athlete level	8 to 9.99
8.1	12	3.9	Lean	Lower than most and excellent for health	6 to 7.99
12.1	20	7.9	Moderately Lean	Generally acceptable for health	4 to 5.99
20.1	30	9.9	Excess Fat	Excess accumulation of fat	2 to 3.99
30.1	above	N/A	Health Risk	Check with doctor to decrease body fat	0.1 to 1.99 (give 1.5)

TABLE 11. Male Body Fat Categories

I ascribed arbitrary athletic-based SMVs in the end field and attempted to break the categories in a somewhat normal distribution. The two outlying fields I decided to rate at 1.5 with equal vigor. While it's more likely to see a person with excess levels of fat that poses a health risk than too little, in a world of people who don't eat for days, possibly because of a sickness or drug habit, and people who eat for days on end, possibly because of a sickness or drug habit (addiction to food being the drug), they are both equally unhealthy, regardless of the relative prevalence. For the slice in the middle, which comprises most people (SMV's of 2 to 9.99), there is a graph in the appendix [appendix note 7] that demonstrates the relationship between Athleticism SMV and bodyfat:

The rankings in the above graph are tied to upper and lower bounds of the different categories that relate to bodyfat%. The relationship is clear—the higher the bodyfat%, the less athletic and the lower the SMV based on the Athleticism "A" Value. There will be a little tidbit on how to construct regression-based graphs later in the book.

From our original trendline equation to find SMV based on bodyfat%, the following relationship is established:

$$Athleticism\ Rank\ (A) = -4.458lnBF\% + 17.239$$

Where "A" is the 10-scale "Athleticism Rating", and based on this relationship, I constructed the following table. Here are some values of BF% at a given SMV:

TABLE 12. Rating based on Body Fat Percent	
BF%	AR
42.7	0.5
38.2	1.0
34.2	1.5
30.5	2.0
27.3	2.5
24.4	3.0
21.8	3.5
19.5	4.0
17.4	4.5
15.6	5.0
13.9	5.5
12.5	6.0
11.1	6.5
10.0	7.0
8.9	7.5
8.0	8.0
7.1	8.5
6.4	9.0
5.7	9.5
5.1	9.99

According to the above table, a guy with 11.1% bodyfat has an SMV of 6.5.

Exceptions to the Rule (of Law)

There are frequently exceptions to the bodyfat% and "ability to enhance survival rule". Kyuzo Mifune, judo master, was 5'2" and weighed 100 lbs. at 40 years old, fought a 6', 240 lb sumo wrestler, subsequently slamming the sumo using *sumi otoshi*. Woe be a muscular brawler who happened to drunkenly stumble into UFC's Roy "Big Country" Nelson and assume that Roy was an easy target because he doesn't appear muscular. The same can be said of Eric "Butterbean" Esch, named the "king of 4 rounders" because he ended his opponents within 4 rounds.

The important thing to note is that while Mifune, Nelson and Esch don't appear athletic, their athleticism has a known value. They have all earned money in the martial arts, and can deter/vanquish opponents. On the other hand, outwardly athletic underwear model, Tyson Beckford, has no record of using his athleticism for combat. He derives value from his athleticism through modeling and acting.

This is where we come to the point of apparent athleticism (displayed for looks) versus real athleticism (actual ability). In a land of law and law enforcement, and in a higher status area, apparent athleticism wins, because aside from self-defense, use of athleticism to inflict bodily harm (violence) is prohibited by law. As a result, Mifune, Esch and Nelson, would likely command a lower SMV than Beckford. Contrarily, in a post-apocalyptic scenario, the Mifunes, Eschs, and Nelsons of the world would thrive.

Athleticism can be developed (nurtured) to a great degree. Proper diet (especially what not to eat) and exercise (especially weight training) can change an individual's body composition over time. The primary goal is for a man to have access to free testosterone which, with the proper diet, is released from its globulin prison to be bioavailable. Genetics (nature) also play a huge role in bone density and body type and, thus, if the preferred athleticism is displayed through a certain body type, say "tall and lanky", then an equally lean person with a "short and stocky" body type would not be considered a la mode.

Like with looks, trauma caused by accidents, mayhem, violence etc., can negatively impact athleticism through the direct injury to bones and muscles and other important tissues and organs. Also, injury of the legs (which provide mobility and the ability to perform athletically and do most forms of cardio) detract from the body indirectly. An injury can also lower the morale and cause a man to have a "fuck it" attitude about personal maintenance. But, as long as the man draws breath, he has an opportunity to work on this aspect of value. Like looks, athleticism is affected by age, because the body composition of muscle is dependent on free testosterone levels, which decline over time. Therefore, we tend to see older men with more body fat than younger men. While this can be mitigated, it will not remain the same over time.

KNOWLEDGE CHECK

- Chad has an SMV of 8 based on Athleticism. What is his bodyfat % (use table above)?
- If Chad goes keto and lowers his bodyfat by 11.25%, what will his new SMV be?

MONEY

"Money…is the key to all problems, if you don't believe that, then you wait till they solve them"

~ Vanilla Ice, "Ice is Workin' It"

THE TANGIBLE AND INTANGIBLE currency that is liquid and is ready for use, for the purposes of this text, is "Money". The important part is that it is liquid—for liquidity gives the appearance of abundance and opulence and can be a display of value in the sexual marketplace.

Women's subconscious desire for money stems from the ability to participate in experiences that money can buy, like shopping, traveling to distant places, and partaking in activities (i.e. like jet skiing in the Bahamas or wind surfing in Aruba).

A miserly "Cheap Pete" type of person is less likely to have this experience because the money he has is tucked away, not for current and spontaneous use. Living way below their means to acquire money for money's sake—to have the pleasure of counting it—may not seem like a full and enjoyable life for a woman he's interested in, because it is not being used *on her*. In addition, hoarding may signal a lack of confidence to take the necessary financial risks to make life exciting.

A person who just won the lottery, for example, could go live a wild lavish life, throwing money around to experience many of life's pleasures, but, putting luck aside, without the proper guidance, these people face the possibility of squandering their fortunes to live in the short term. Since no one knows how long they will live, the spectrum of risk goes from "live only for today" versus "save everything for the future".

Many women have been hooked on flamboyant men who spend money wantonly in the short term—only to find out that it was ill-gotten. This is where money and status diverge. Money does not bring long-run status. A man's occupation speaks more to his status and the prospect of being able to maintain a quality of life, which in turn can be used to estimate surpluses and shortages into the foreseeable future.

It is the war between the spendthrift and the miser. In the short term, people often enjoy the spendthrift because, in that moment, he is showing everybody a good time. But when the music stops and the vomit is cleaned up off of the floor and the cum rags are tossed in the hamper, there he stands in the midst of his megalomania wondering what next "high" to chase. This is not a sustainable way of life—maybe for someone who knows they don't have a long time to live—but this way of daily living may lead one down the road to long-term decay (jump forward to the section on "depreciation and value erosion" to delve deeper on this).

The miser, on the other hand, lives dead in the present moment to live for some future date—as if secretly trying to project out when he's going to die, save money right up until the time they know it would happen soon, and then start spending it. People don't really enjoy misers in the present moment, but would put up with a miser if they know that they are in the miser's will—such is the way of the busty blonde gold-diggers of the past—in a symbiotic, long-game relationship. In between these two extremes, the spendthrift and the miser, exists a man with good sense enough to show a good time without breaking the bank or being cheap.

With regards to "nature", money can come from inheritance. Someone can be born into money. The ownership of capital is what separates the wealthy from the poor. Money can, while it is projected in the form of liquid assets in the present, be the result of a huge nest egg or family business generating the passive income that allows a person to spend extravagantly in the present moment without worrying about the future.

If you're not born into money, with the "nurture" aspect, it can be acquired with good business acumen/prospects, education, and good fortune. It can also be lost through bad business deals, publicity, and legal battles.

Money as a physical tangible asset can be lost through external/environmental happenings, which include but are not limited to: theft (physical or non-physical robbery), natural disasters like fire and flooding, extortion, computer glitches, etc. Money depreciates over time if not invested. Therefore, if it is not spent or put to use wisely, one risks squandering the money in the present moment.

How much money is "a lot" of money (Scalar Attribute Rating)

The value of money is relative to its purchasing power and the economy in which it operates. Consider the Ibbotson chart where you can see the value of $1 throughout different points in America's history, from lows like The Great Depression to pre-Y2K, post-dotcom Silicone valley highs. Everyone knows their favorite great auntie, pinching pennies with long, wrinkled E.T. fingers, reminiscing about when soda "usta costa qwota"; or the foreigner who laments how expensive it is in her new chosen place of residence as compared to "back home" –money's value changes over time and place.

Putting time value aside for now, a reasonable person can determine how much money is a lot of money based on the highest and lowest amounts of money stock (money) in the area. If one has more money than average (higher than the median in a normally distributed model), then that person, for all intents and purposes, has a "lot" of money. IRL, people who have more money are better able to multiply it through income additions and/or compound interest. As a result, money stock is not normally distributed. However, for simplicity, I will assume that money is normally distributed, and use a linear model to determine a man's value on a Min/Max scale based on highest and lowest values in a given physical location [appendix note 8]:

Scalar Attribute Rating (SAR) =

$$Rating_{max} + (Xvar - Var_{max}) \cdot \frac{(Rating_{max} - Rating_{min})}{(Var_{max} - Var_{min})}$$

Where

$Rating_{Max}$ = *highest rating on the scale (i. e. 1 to 10) for population*

$Rating_{Min}$ = *lowest rating of attribute*

Var_{Max} = *highest real world variable amount*

Var_{Min} = *lowest real world variable amount*

$Xvar$ = *variable amount in question*

The above formula and conditions are used to "transform" or translate a real-world variable into a rating on the 10-scale based on information regarding the highest and lowest scores for that variable. For example, if in a certain region, the largest Certificate of Deposit (CD) amount is $100,000 and the lowest is $10,000, and we're estimating on a scale of 0.1 to 9.99, how would we rate someone who had a CD amount of $63,000, we'd do the following:

$$\frac{(9.99 - 0.1)}{(\$100,000 - \$10,000)}(\$63,000 - \$100,000) + 9.99 = Money\ Rating\ (M)$$

$$M = 5.92$$

As you can see, a person with $63,000 is a little better than average. A 5.92 rating means that the person is in the 59th percentile with regards to money holdings.

KNOWLEDGE CHECK

- Generous Jerry has $400,000 in the bank. The bank manager pitching Jerry on their CD offerings told him that the largest average daily balance is about $2,000,000, and their lowest is $13,000. What is Jerry's Money rating on a scale of 1 to 10?

- Now let's take the case of John E. Bwai, who has $300,000 in his Ameribux bank account. The largest bank balance at Ameribux is $500,000. If John is considered a 6 on a scale of 0.5 to 10, what is the minimum bank balance at Ameribux?

"I have the power!"

~ He Man

IN 2011, RAPPER 50 Cent made $10M telling his then 3.8M followers to buy stock in a company that he partially owned; the company had significant holdings in Glaceau, the producer of Vitamin Water [30a]. His influence was able to secure him a deal that the average person would be very hard-pressed to find.

In 2019, a Cosmopolitan article addressed the Advertising Standards Authority (ASA)'s guidelines that anyone who had more than 30,000 social media followers is considered a celebrity and is subject to certain rules [30b].

The gap between 30,000 and 3.8M is larger than 0 and 30,000, so while I don't care to delve into measurement methods here, it is easy to see why I consider "the ability to influence and/or impose your will on others", as "Power".

A person with power may not have high status. Post-modern organizational theories have made a point of separating management from leadership. In a nutshell, this theory defines a manager is someone who performs organizational objectives efficiently and a leader as someone who has the vision of where the organization goes and the directive to realize that vision. A leader can be a manager and may or may not have the official power to impose organizational sanctions on employees (i.e., demotion, termination, suspension, etc.), but the main point is that the leader is able to get people to follow them.

Leaders often "lead from the front", that is, they set an example by doing what it is they require of their followers to do and are in the proverbial trenches with them. A person of power can have low status. Think of the neighborhood community activist organizer, or the local gang leader. They may have low societal status, but their character ability to inspire and/or strike fear in the hearts of followers causes them to be formidable force.

It is possible that, with regards to "nature", genetics such as serum testosterone levels can affect whether or not the person has an aggressive and or imposing disposition and is willing to take risk with not only themselves, but with other people's assets. As testosterone is affected by age, it may either affect leadership through reduced vigor, or, if the mind is sharp, age could result in the leader being more of a tactician and using economy of motion and wisdom in decision making.

Power can be usurped by a more aggressive party or, like in *Jurassic World*, Chris Pratt's character screams "New Alpha!" when a monstrous genetically engineered dinosaur cause the raptors that have obeyed him for so long to turn on his crew.

Power can also be stripped from a non-aggressive party when the person in power is seen as unfit to lead due to loss of mental clarity/emotional stability. This happened in the 2009 *Star Trek* where Zachary Quinto's Spock, who was the current captain of the USS Enterprise, had been pushed into an emotional corner by Chris Pine's James T. Kirk, and he snaps and beats up Kirk in front of the crew. Afterwards, Spock relinquishes his position because he was "emotionally compromised". Kirk, as second in command, usurps power.

Environmental factors that influence power are numerous—a breakdown or restructuring of a civil order could cause shifts in power. For example, a resource crisis or pandemic whereby a large number of people are displaced may cause a rupture in modern day governmental structures and cause factions of people to fend for themselves and create new social hierarchies. Examples are post-apocalyptic TV series' like *The Walking Dead* where people team up in clans and communities to survive a zombie outbreak. The Scalar Attribute Rating (SAR) technique from appendix note 8 can be used to calculate varying levels of power on a given maximum and minimum scale.

KNOWLEDGE CHECK

- Danali Trux has 20,000 social media followers. A recent survey regarding social media influence states that the minimum number of followers on average is 10 and the maximum, which makes on a celebrity, is 35,000. On a scale of 0.1 to 10, what is Danali's Power/Influence rating?

- Danali's subscriber base has now grown 20%, and a recent survey showed that the minimum average follower count is 20. If Danali's Power/Influence rating is a 6 on a scale of 0.1 to 9.99, what is the maximum number of subscribers to make one a celebrity?

STATUS

"Nigga didn't give a fuck about my status. Now that I'm at this, I'm loc'd out and livin' lavish"

~ Spice 1 "Jealous Got Me Strapped"

A POSITION HELD IN A socioeconomic hierarchy that affects one's social mobility in said society, for the purpose of this book, is "Status". Status, by nature, can come with inheritance and/or association with people, but it doesn't necessarily imply power.

Take King Norodom Sihamoni of Cambodia for example. Despite being ambassador to the UNESCO and known for being a cultural ambassador to several European nations, he is held in scrutiny for his apparent lax attitude towards prime minister Hun Sen, who has been said to be running a dictatorship under Sihamoni's watch. Sihamoni's criticized inaction have led many to label him a "puppet king". In this instance, it is easy to see the difference between status and power. Sihamoni's title, and hence status is higher than Sen's, but Sen's power is higher than Sihamoni's.

One of the most detrimental blows to status comes from loss of reputation. Take, for example, in *The Game of Thrones* when Cersei Lannister, part of the ruling family of Kings Landing, briefly had her political power usurped by a pope-like character called the High Septon who made her parade naked through the ghettoes of her kingdom. She was then jailed until loyal followers released her. Her status was reduced to a prisoner in what was once her kingdom.

Loss of mental clarity/stability can cause a person's status to be suspended, if honorably, by a "forced" resignation. Take in the movie *Crimson Tide*, Gene Hackman's character was relieved of duty by Denzel Washington's character over the controversy of whether or not to follow an incomplete order dictated by higher authority.

With regards to environment, a change in systems can cause a change in status. A high-ranking official loses their status in the event that the system or government that gives them that status becomes null—either by end of term or coup d'etat.

Since, on many levels, education dictates occupation and occupation dictate an industry title, I will use earned income as a proxy for status here. I will assume a person's W2 income is a direct reflection of their job title and, hence, status. Use the SAR rating formula from appendix note 8 can be used to calculate varying levels of status.

Suppose Sam Mule lives in a town where the maximum average annual income is $500,000, the minimum is $25,000, and Sam earns $300,000. If Sam is being judged on a Min/Max scale of 0.1 to 9.99, what is his rating (within 2 digits)? Use the variable scalar transformation formula to solve:

$$\frac{(9.99 - 0.1)}{(\$500,000 - \$25,000)} (\$300,000 - \$500,000) + 9.99 =$$

$$= Income/Status\ Rating$$

$$5.83 = Income/Status\ Rating$$

Sam is considered a 5.83 on a scale of 0.1 to 9.99.

KNOWLEDGE CHECK

- Suppose Sam Mule lives in Bumfukegypt where the maximum average annual income is $500,000 and the minimum is $30,000. Sam is considered a 7 on a scale of 0.5 to 10 with regards to his status by way of his annual income. What is Sam's current annual income?

VIRTUOUSNESS

"Don't move too fast, remember patience is a virtue"
~ Juvenile "Gone Ride with Me"

I N MARK MANSON'S BOOK *The Subtle Art of Not Giving a Fuck,* he talks about the tradeoff between variety (number of different new exciting people) and substance (growing with and learning with one partner and forsaking others to allow for more personal growth and development). The ability to foster self-control over one's appetites, especially for sex, is the mark of a virtuous person. Running with the sexual restraint piece, Miriam Webster.com defines "virtuous" as "having or showing high moral standards" and that it "archaically" refers to a woman's chastity. For the purposes of this text, we will attempt to quantify the number of sexual partners that optimizes female value in the eyes of a male seeking a partner long-term.

An article in the Huffington Post entitled "New Study Claims People Who've Had More Sexual Partners Report Unhappier Marriages" [31b] commented on a study from "The National Marriage Project", which used research from Galena K. Rhoades and Scott M. Stanley, two professors from the University of Denver. The professors used relationship data of 1,000 unmarried Americans ages 18 to 34 from 2007 to 2008 to come to the following conclusion: People, especially women, who have had multiple sexual partners before getting married, report unhappier marriages later on.

After tracking 418 people who got married within 5 years of the study (I'm assuming from 2012 to 2013), the professors delved deeper to see what factors, notably the participants' sexual history, played a role in marriage quality. Rhoades and Stanley used four of the 32 items on a measurement called the "Dyadic Adjustment Scale" (DAS) [31a]. The DAS is a self-reported assessment of relationship adjustment that is based on research of over 1,000 published studies on relationship satisfaction (dissatisfaction) and contains sample data of 218 married and 94 newly divorced people.

Here's what they found:

1. 23 % of participants who *only* had sex with their spouse before getting married reported higher quality marriages versus those who had other past sexual partners as well.

2. 42% of people who lived with a romantic partner other than future spouse reported "no" to higher marriage quality (35% did report "yes" to higher marriage quality)

Based on participants and their findings, they wrote, "we further found that the more sexual partners a woman had had before marriage, the less happy she reported her marriage to be" [31b].

The professors theorized that "more experience may increase one's awareness of alternative partners." This is akin to psychologist Barry Schwartz's "Choice Paradox" whereby the more choices a consumer is aware of, the more dissatisfied a consumer becomes with a single choice because they aware of alternative options.

When this paradox of choice comes to sex, it takes humans into a whole different territory of risk and reward. It's not like going trick-or-treating in a neighborhood and having a whole lot of different candy to choose from. An unknowing trick-or-treater risks getting nasty little "Sweet Tarts" or those "Bazooka Joe" bubble gums that taste like a solid form of Pepto Bismol. For the unknowing woman, she runs the physical risk of multiple known STDs, ones that aren't known (NGUs), bacterial vaginosis, and HPV. She runs the risk of an unwanted pregnancy and, if she doesn't carry to term, miscarriage and abortion, all of which, I propose, can be emotionally taxing. In addition, there's the emotional risk of multiple broken pair-bonds. And here's where the road gets rocky.

Earlier in the text when I spoke on the *"Dual Mating Strategy"* it referred to different biological imperatives. While, over the generations, men and women have had different emotions towards sex, being more liberal in the post-modern times and more conservative going backward, one thing has always held true: women have easier access to sex. It might not be sex with a Chris Hemsworth or a Michael B. Jordan, but if they really were "feindin'" they could go out on the town and hook up with the first guy who hit on them who had good oral hygiene and a decent job. Men don't have that kind of power. Which brings us to a little-known rule of thumb that is often not mentioned in today's day and age: **women are the gatekeepers to sex and desired men are the gatekeepers to commitment.**

The originally known statement says that "men are the gatekeepers to commitment" but I added "desired" because of hypergamy. The bar is always raised on the male standard. A woman decides when and where sex is going to happen—and a man decides when he decides to commit his resources to a given woman. Making a resource commitment as mentioned in the *Dual Mating Strategy* section, is him making a paternal investment. This is more than sex; this is him sharing and garnering resources for her to potentially help with the successful raising of offspring. I, ironically, posit that virtuousness can be seen as a trait in a man if, and only if, he is desired by women.

It doesn't take much effort for a poor man to go on a fast, but a man who is used to eating all different types of exotic food—a well-traveled man of means—would find a fast more challenging. As a result, a sexually "loose" woman's male equivalent is a man who "loosely" commits his resources to every woman he encounters—a man who is a "relationship whore".

The challenge after poking around a little bit was trying to find the "optimal" number of sexual partners that would minimize female detachment. I assume this would also maximize male desire to commit. While a man may not be able to physically tell if a woman had a lot of partners, he could emotionally tell based on her ability to emotionally bond with him. This is something that is different for every man/woman but, is generally found that more partners, especially for women, equals more detachment. The function governing virtuousness must invariably decrease as the number of partners increase, right? It's not that cut and dried.

I posit that the optimal number of sexual partners to make a woman's virtuosity score 9.99 would be somewhere between 2 and the average number that women currently claim they sleep with. Based on anecdotal evidence, most western men who only intend to be with one woman, don't want virgins. It is only the rare and the religious that you will find wanting to have a virgin. I'm not going to make a value judgement on that, but the point is, most men don't want to teach the woman to do everything. They want the woman to have already come off of her training wheels. This would require her to have had a couple of sexual partners—her first time may usually be awkward and she might not be sure of herself. She needs a few experiences to learn her body and to discover what she likes and how to make herself cum.

So, a virgin would not be a top-score, but the distribution is not symmetrical. Most men would rather have a virgin than a woman who has had, say,100 sexual partners. If we assumed a normal distribution, and the maximum number of sexual partners women have on average are 100, then the mean/median would be 50 (a 5 on the 10 scale). Of course, in reverse, that would put 100 at the score of almost zero (0.01) and the virgin at almost 10 (9.99). But something "feels" a little peculiar about a distribution like that. As a result, I posit a special case here where we have an "inverted V" shaped rating schedule:

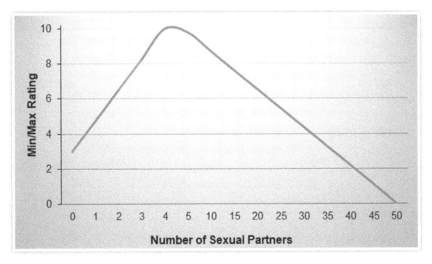

Figure 24. Calculated Rating for Number of Partners

The assumed notion above is that a virgin would rate as a 3, a woman with 3 partners would rate as a 10, and a woman with 50 partners, for all intents and purposes would rate as almost 0. The following piecewise linear distribution that I have constructed is a special case of the SAR from appendix note 8:

If $Xvar \leq Var_{Mid}$:

$$\text{Virtuousness (V)} = \frac{(SMV_{Max} - SMV_{Mid})}{(Var_{mid} - Var_{min})}(Xvar - Var_{mid}) + SMV_{Max}$$

If $Xvar > Var_{Mid}$:

$$\text{Virtuousness (V)} = \frac{(SMV_{Min} - SMV_{Max})}{(Var_{max} - Var_{mid})}(Xvar - Var_{max}) + SMV_{Min}$$

Where:

$Xvar$ = number of sexual partners, and

($Vvar$, SMV_{Mid}) = first data point on "inverted V"; the number of partners that are neither optimal nor sub-optimal

(Var_{Mid}, SMV_{Max}) = second data point on "inverted V"; the optimal number of partners associated with the highest rating

(Var_{Max}, SMV_{Min}) = third point on "inverted V"; the suboptimal number of partners that garners the lowest rating

For example, LaDauna has been with 12 guys. Where she's from, guys who are interested in long term monogamous relationships have the opinion that 4 partners is the optimal number and 30 partners is sub-optimal. On a scale of 0.1 to 9.99, what is LaDauna's rating in their eyes?

Answer: Since 12 partners is more than 4, we will use the second piecewise equation, and thus:

If $Xvar > Var_{Mid}$:

$$\text{Virtuousness} = \frac{(SMV_{Min} - SMV_{Max})}{(Var_{max} - Var_{mid})}(Xvar - Var_{max}) + SMV_{Min}$$

$$\text{Virtuousness} = \frac{(0.1 - 9.99)}{(30 - 4)}(12 - 30) + 0.1 = 6.95$$

LaDauna would get a 6.95 Virtuousness rating.

KNOWLEDGE CHECK

- How would LaDauna's rating change if she had 3 partners and a virgin is considered a 7 on the scale of 0.1 to 9.99?
- If the men became more liberal in their views and considered 50 partners sub optimal and 6 partners optimal, considering LaDauna had 12 partners and the scale rating stays the same, what would be her new rating?

CONSCIENTIOUSNESS

THIS ASPECT OF VALUE is somewhat hard to quantify as it is highly psychological. Online trolling of Jordan Peterson's talks has yielded that conscientious people tend toward overall long-term life success, as conscientious people usually follow through on what they say they are going to do. In one of his lectures, he disclosed that helping non-conscientious patients is one of clinical psychology's major challenges. Since goal setting is a tool to effect behavioral change, lack of conscientiousness nullifies the effects of goal setting.

In one of his lectures, Peterson describes that conscientious people are often "self-disgusted" and are in constant course correction so they don't fall to the bottom of societal dominance hierarchies (i.e., the social "ladder") and that their tendency to move toward the completion of goals causes them to stabilize their environment, making their life more predictable. This results in the conscientious person being "less miserable" rather than "happy" which, because of the asymmetry of humans, places more weight on negative outcomes than positive ones (look up the coin toss experiment) and can be an enormous boon on their mental stability.

Further research points out that conscientious people tend to be systematic, thorough and detail oriented—and if their job success requires conscientious behavior, this can be a plus. However, a "darker" side of conscientiousness—when taken to the extreme—can leave the overly conscientious person perceived as hesitant, worrisome, slow, perfectionist, and hard to please/demanding.

In terms of the value, it would bring from a female partner, it would be the tendency to lean towards non-neuroticism and level headedness and diligence. Finishing what is started and being able to follow from a premise. This is especially good in constructive criticism and disagreements, whereby the woman "fights fair"; only using the elements of the disagreement to dispute her position rather than using outside elements and/or emotional "below the belt" blows (i.e., "you probably think that way because your mother was a runaway").

Conscientious people tend to deduce cause/effect relationships and avoid disaster primarily by their ability to "read the signs". Conscientious people are aware of the company they are surrounded by. If they are in a low-income, distressed place, they don't flaunt or flash jewelry or wealth. They also don't get black-out drunk around people that they do not know/trust on purpose, because the outcome could be deleterious to their health and well-being. Conscientious people perform regular car maintenance—when the oil light comes on, they get their oil changed—even though the car can "go" more miles.

A reoccurring theme of conscientiousness has to do with goal setting and completion. Therefore, I'll use the following measurement:

$$Goal\ Completion\ Ratio\ (GCR) = \frac{Items\ or\ goals\ satisfactorily\ completed}{Total\ Items\ or\ goals\ set}$$

$$GCR * 10 = Conscientiousness\ Rating\ (C)$$

KNOWLEDGE CHECK

- Amanda Hugginkiss just successfully lost 10 lbs. in accordance with her New Year's resolution. Over the past 10 years, she has made the same resolution, but only successfully reached her goal six of those years. What is her current conscientiousness score?

LOOKS

T HE SAME PRINCIPLES THAT we used earlier for the looks attribute for men will be used here, especially because the study that gave the Thurstonian Attractiveness variable weight in this book is a study that used female faces to determine the New "Golden Ratio" [27b]. Since the Golden Ratio, mentioned in appendix note 5 above, is a ratio, the relative sizes of men's and women's faces will not matter. Refer to Table 8 to get the looks rating for the knowledge check. Here is the basic formula:

$$FLP = Face\ Length\ Percent = \frac{Distance\ from\ eyes\ to\ mouth}{Distance\ from\ hairline\ to\ chin}$$

In addition, in the section *"Dual Mating Strategy"*, the general preference of women is for faces that tend to be more feminine (except during periods of ovulation) and they feel feminine faces are more trustworthy etc. Since men are much more visual and, when it comes to the average importance of looks, men would likely place more weight on that attribute than women.

To the degree looks are a representation of healthful practices (i.e., skin, teeth, hair) this may also be a sign of fertility as good-looking skin is associated with youth. Therefore, that which makes her appear younger also makes her appear more fertile.

KNOWLEDGE CHECK

- Renee has looks rating of 6.92 and the distance from her eyes to mouth is 3 inches. What is the distance from her hairline to her chin?

AGE

WHILE WE HAVE DEMONSTRATED that fertility declines with age [21], we assume, regarding consenting adults, the minimum sexual marketplace age is 18 (social expectations and shaming also play roles on age differentials and human choices). While there are different "age markets", all women of legal age affect the SMV of the collective participants in a market. Another assumption is that 21 would be preferred to 18, since the person can legally drink alcohol, and places that serve alcohol are usually considered a socially acceptable place to gather. Up until about 25, would be prime, so you would possibly see SMV rise from 18 to 22 (as woman becomes more mature, but not ripe). Then, between 22 to 25, you may see a leveling off (also depends on how she treats her body—i.e. too much drinking, smoking, drugs, etc.), then a gentle decline from 25 to 30, a heavier decline from 30 to 35, then a more pronounced decline past 35 (almost dropping rapidly).

In the truest of the variable, age is a function of time, but to keep things simple, we'll assume that people inherently know this when they choose an age value. Age is also a factor in the ability to recover from illness and childbirth. Younger isn't necessarily always better, depending on goals, as a lot of post-modern people tend to forgo having children. Regarding maturity, below a certain age, women might not be prone to a long-term relationship and may value variety of experience over stability.

Based on data from the Wallace and Kelsey graph the following abridged table was constructed from appendix note 2:

TABLE 13. Age Ranking	
Age	*Rebased to Age 18 = 10 for Age Ranking
15	n/a
20	8.37
25	5.34
30	3.01
35	1.62
40	0.93
45	0.46
50	0.46
55	0.46

As a result, you can see that a 35-year-old, with regards to NGF% remaining, would get a ranking of 1.62.

KNOWLEDGE CHECK

- Patty is 25 years old. According to Table 14, what can her age rating be estimated as?

WEIGHT

OR THIS TEXT, "WEIGHT" will not just refer to physical pounds, but also weight distribution (BMI and WHR), which is the measure to how one "carries" one's own weight.

According to the National Academy of Sports Medicine (NASM), Body Mass Index (BMI) is a person's weight in kilograms divided by the square of height in meters. A high BMI can be an indicator of high body fatness. BMI can be used to screen for weight categories that may lead to health problems, but it is not a diagnostic of an individual's health condition. Therefore, the table below summarizes the "disease risk" that individuals may have at varying BMIs:

TABLE 14. Body Mass Index (BMI) [30c]				
From	**To**	**Disease Risk**	**Classification**	**Notes**
below	18.5	Increased	Underweight	Throw out
18.6	21.9	Low	Acceptable	
22	24.99	Very Low	Acceptable	
25	29.99	Increased	Overweight	
30	34.99	High	Obese	
35	39.99	Very High	Obesity I	
40	greater	Extremely High	Obesity II	Throw out

From this table, I made assumptions using the Body Mass Index classifications of obesity ($BMI_{overwight/obese}$) and acceptable weight ($BMI_{acceptable}$) and derived two formulas [appendix note 9] and a table based on the formulas that calculate the "Body Weight Rating (BWR)" based on the female BMI:

TABLE 15.	BWR based on BMI		
BMI	**BWR**	**BMI**	**BWR**
39.99	0.5	24.99	5.0
38.33	1.0	24.35	5.5
36.67	1.5	23.71	6.0
35.00	2.0	23.07	6.5
33.34	2.5	22.43	7.0
31.67	3.0	21.79	7.5
30.01	3.5	21.15	8.0
28.34	4.0	20.51	8.5
26.68	4.5	19.87	9.0
25.00	4.99	18.60	9.99

KNOWLEDGE CHECK

- If Monica's BMI is 24, what is her BWR?

Weight Distribution piece

Earlier in the text, we extrapolated on ideals of shape of males and females, noting that the closer a man was to a WHR of 0.9, the more ideal the waist and deviations away from this ideal were commensurate with decrease in attractiveness.

Anecdotally, in male circles, it has often been the case that women of differing weight levels were considered attractive as long as the proportion of fat on their body was distributed in a certain manner—in other words—"how the weight is carried". In the 90s, "Lil' Kim" got the nickname "Queen Bee"—the etymology of which not only was a nod to the importance of the queen bee in a bee colony to be the most valued and sexually mature—but ironically the proportions of the bee—the thorax of which pales in comparison to the abdomen. This creates the appearance of femininity in nature, as the queen bee's sole role to be the reproducer of the hive and she is faithfully protected by the worker bees in her employ. Like the queen in a bee hive, Lil' Kim's bodacious hips eclipsed her waist. The result: a "hourglass" or "pear" shape that is comparable to many that fit attractiveness ideals:

Devendra Singh, researcher specializing in attractiveness, carried out numerous investigations in the waist-to-hip ratio in the nineties. He discovered that all winners of the "Miss America contests" from 1920 until the 1980`s had a WHR between 0.72 and 0.69. He also found that playboy's models WHR was between 0.71 and 0.68. For decades the ideal waist-to-hip ratio was consistently 0.7, despite the changing body weight of these models. Thus, in spite of their different weight classes, the beauty icons Marilyn Monroe, Sophia Loren, Twiggy and Kate Moss all had at least one thing in common - a WHR of about 0.7 [29b].

Here is a summary table of disease risk associated with the WHR:

TABLE 16.	Women's Disease Risk Based on WHR		
From	**To**	**Disease Risk**	**Notes**
Below	0.8	Low	Optimal at 0.7 (for aesthetics);
0.81	0.85	Moderate	WHO says less than 0.85 healthy
0.86	Above	High	1.0 and higher increased disease risk

Using a similar linear method to the one for the male WHR above, I calculate the female Body Shape Ranking (BSR), using methods in appendix note 9. Here are a table of values below based on the above formula:

TABLE 17.	Women's WHR		
WHR	**BSR**	**WHR**	**BSR**
1.00	0.5	0.84	5.5
0.98	1.0	0.83	6.0
0.97	1.5	0.81	6.5
0.95	2.0	0.79	7.0
0.94	2.5	0.78	7.5
0.92	3.0	0.76	8.0
0.91	3.5	0.75	8.5
0.89	4.0	0.73	9.0
0.87	4.5	0.72	9.5
0.86	5.0	0.70	9.99

KNOWLEDGE CHECK

- If Monica's WHR is 0.79, what is her BSR?

Weight Ranking

Using relative importance, we can average the WBR and the WRW to come up with an overall ranking that is based on weight. These factors both encompass the BMI, which is like a weight to height ratio, and the WHR, which is a waist to hip ratio. Combining the two is a proxy for the "volume-mass" of a woman's body:

$$Weight\ Ranking\ (W) = w_{BWR}(BWR) + w_{BSR}(BSR)$$

KNOWLEDGE CHECK

- If Quintavious is a man who cares about how much a woman weighs 20% of the time and his main focus is her "coke bottle" shape, accounting for 80% of what he finds attractive; and sees Monica in the mall, what will his perception of her overall ranking for "W" be?

LMS, LAMPS, VCLAW and LAW

Earlier I mentioned the pluses and minuses of using "LMS" vs "LAMPS" that LAMPS provide more depth and LMS is more relevant in a modern society. LMS also has another benefit—the fewer variables there are, the easier it is to compute. So, for ease of calculations, I will often refer to LMS (Looks, Money, Status) as to what women value about men and for what men value about women, I'll shorten "VCLAW" to "LAW" (Looks, Age, Weight).

VALUATION TECHNIQUES

CHAPTER SUMMARY

○ The concept of "Expected Value" is the commonsense notion that a person observing a series of independent outcomes on the same subject can make an inference on what the next observation will be by averaging what was previously observed.

○ Relative importance is the concept that people give the observations different weight based on personal biases or other reasons. Thus, if one is told that DWI arrests occur on Thursday evening because there are more police and because there are more happy hour specials on Thursday, the personal bias of the individual will determine which of these reasons has heavier "weight".

○ Applying the concept of Expected Value to Sexual Marketplace Value (SMV), the many attributes of men and women can be combined based on the relative importance of each of those attributes to the observer. This aspect of calculation considers different qualities matter differently to different people. A number on the Min/Max scale between 0 and 10 can be calculated taking all the different attributes into account.

CHAPTER 6

VALUATION **TECHNIQUES** (ATTRIBUTIVE)

Expected Value Theory

The valuation of SMV is based on probability theory and statistics. The concept of "Expected Value (EV)", which is the average of a variable's observed values in an experiment, is the cornerstone to this theory. EV is important because it is the best guess a reasonable observer would make about an unknown value based on previous experience. A reasonable observer would often assume the expected value of x, or ($E[x]$) to be a truism (be equal to x) over many observations; or $E[x] = x$.

Imagine that you have coffee Monday through Friday across the street from an office building and you notice a woman in a red dress exiting the building Monday through Thursday according to the following schedule:

TABLE 18. Lady in Red Timetable	
X = Day	Y = Time
Monday	5:05 PM
Tuesday	5:00 PM
Wednesday	5:15 PM
Thursday	5:20 PM
Friday	**?**

What time on Friday should we expect to see her exit, or in other words, what is the Expected Value of Y? First, we'd reframe the time stamps so that the minutes would reflect being in proportion to the hour by dividing them by 60. In other words, 5:30 PM = 5.5. Using this logic, we have the following:

TABLE 19. Transformed Schedule		
X	Y= Time	Y' (transformed Y)
Monday	5:05 PM	5.08 PM
Tuesday	5:00 PM	5.00 PM
Wednesday	5:15 PM	5.25 PM
Thursday	5:20 PM	5.33 PM
Friday	**?**	**?**

Then, we'd average all of the transformed Y' values by adding them all up and dividing by the total number of observations: (5.08 + 5.00+ 5.25 + 5.33)/4 ≈ 5.17. Therefore 5.17 is the transformed value that equates to the time we expect to see the lady in red appear. To get the actual time, we multiply 0.17 by 60: 0.17 x 60 = 10.2 ≈ 10. So, we should expect, more or less, to see the lady in red to exit the office building around 5:10 PM:

TABLE 20. Predicted Schedule		
X	Y	Y'
Monday	5:05 PM	5.08 PM
Tuesday	5:00 PM	5.00 PM
Wednesday	5:15 PM	5.25 PM
Thursday	5:20 PM	5.33 PM
Friday	**5:10 PM**	**5.17 PM**

Most statisticians use the average, or expected value, to predict the future based on historically observed data (i.e., the best guess we have of how something is going to present itself tomorrow is how it has presented itself over time).

This aspect of expected value is called the "simple" average. A simple average assumes that each event in the series (the times we see the lady in red Monday through Thursday) has an equal chance, or probability of occurring. Since there are only four observations, the probability of occurrence is ¼ or 25%. We would get about the same answer if we treated the transformed variables as such:

TABLE 21.   Schedule with Probability

			A	B	C = (A x B)	D = Σ (column C)	E = D's last two digits * 60
X = Day	Y = Time	Y'	Probability (weight)	Probability Shares	Total	Friday's Expected Time
Monday	5:05 PM	5.08 PM	0.25	1.27		
Tuesday	5:00 PM	5.00 PM	0.25	1.25		
Wednesday	5:15 PM	5.25 PM	0.25	1.31		
Thursday	5:20 PM	5.33 PM	0.25	1.33		
Friday	**5:10 PM**	**5.17 PM**			**5.16**	**5:09:36 PM**

From this, we see that the Expected Values can also be conveyed as a weighted average. A weighted average is simply an extension of the simple average we used above, where the probabilities are not equal to each other (in this example, they are for simplicity). All probabilities, or chances, must sum up to 100% or 1, because assuming we've covered all bases, we've reached 100% chance that the outcome is what we predict. I used the additional seconds indicator with the same method I arrived at minutes (by multiplying the converted figures to the right of the decimal by 60 since there are 60 seconds in a minute), to show how close it is to the minute (if rounding to the nearest minute, it becomes 5:10 PM). Assume the following about the appearance of the lady in red:

TABLE 22. Scheduling with Probability (Revised)

		A	B	C = (A x B)	D = Σ (column C)	E = D's last two digits * 60
X = Day	Y = Time	Y'	Probability (weight)	Probability Shares	Total	Friday's Expected Time
Monday	5:05 PM	5.08 PM	0.20	1.02		
Tuesday	5:00 PM	5:00 PM	0.30	1.50		
Wednesday	5:15 PM	5.25 PM	0.15	0.79		
Thursday	5:20 PM	5.33 PM	0.35	1.87		
Friday	**5:10 PM**	**5.17 PM**			**5.18**	**5:10:48 PM**

What this says is that on Thursday, there is a 35% chance that the lady in red will exit the building at 5:20 PM. By changing the probabilities, we get a different average but still somewhat close to it. In fact, without going into statistical rigor, about 68% of the time there should be a deviation of time roughly ± 0.14 around the simple average (5.17). What this means is that if our observations of the lady in red are a normal, regular occurrence, 68% of the time, she should exit the building between approximately 5:02 PM (5.03) and 5:19 PM (5.31).

KNOWLEDGE CHECK

- Biff works at the construction site in the wee hours of the morning. Depending on traffic, he gets to the site according to the following schedule:

TABLE 23. Schedule Example

X = Day	Y = Time
Monday	4:59 AM
Tuesday	5:03 AM
Wednesday	**?**
Thursday	5:19 AM
Friday	4:44 AM

If each day *nothing out of the ordinary* occurs, when can we expect him to be to work on Wednesday? Fill out the following table to help:

TABLE 24. Schedule Example (Transformed)		
X	**Y**	**Y' (transformed)**
Monday	4:59 AM	4.98 AM
Tuesday	5:03 AM	5.05 AM
Wednesday	**?**	**?**
Thursday	5:19 AM	5.32 AM
Friday	4:44 AM	4.73 AM

Now, suppose that getting to work is easier on Monday and Friday, but harder on Tuesday and Thursday. Biff arrives on Monday and Friday with a 30% probability and on Tuesday and Thursday is 20% probability What is Biff's estimated arrival time Wednesday? Fill in the blanks.

TABLE 25. Example Schedule with Probability					
			A	**B**	**C = (A x B)**
X	**Y**	**Y'**	**Probability (weight)**	**Probability Shares**	
Monday	4:59 AM	4.98 AM	30%	?	
Tuesday	5:03 AM	5.05 AM	20%	?	
Wednesday	**?**	**?**			
Thursday	5:19 AM	5.32 AM	20%	?	
Friday	4:44 AM	4.73 AM	30%	?	

Expected Sexual Marketplace Value

Going back to our rankings that we got from our attributive variables (LAMPS, LMS, VCLAW, LAW) we can apply those arbitrary rankings to the theory of expected value to analyze how value weighs, or relative importance determine how men and women rate each other on a 10 scale in the sexual marketplace. This framework offers a multidimensional approach to valuation, not just including physical appearance, but other attributes that women and men both see and value in each other. The purpose for introducing the expected value theory is twofold:

1. To provide a mathematical basis for the weighted average
2. To provide the logic that a reasonable person makes the best guess given the information provided.

The General Conditions are:

> **Postulate 1**: The Expected Sexual Marketplace Value (SMV) should be equal to the actual SMV of a given sex:

$$E[SMV_j] = SMV_j$$

Where:

$$j = m \text{ or } f \text{ (male or female)}$$

> **Postulate 2**: The Expected SMV is equal to the weighted attributes therein:

$$E[SMV_j] = \sum_{i}^{n} w_i * i$$

Where:

$$j = m \text{ or } f \text{ (male or female)}$$

$i = ith$ attribute (i.e. "M" for "money" or "V" for "virtuosity" etc.)

w_i = the realive importance weight the observer places on i,
and $<0 < w_i < 1$; and $\sum_{i}^{n} w_i = 1$

$E[SMV_j]$ is the weighted average of the attributes of a given sex. The "i" values are the specific attributes (i.e., Looks, Age, etc.) that will be rated on a Min/Max scale (often 1 to 10, but can have other "goalposts"). So, if you give the person a 5 for looks and a 7 for money on a scale of 1 to 10, then $i = 5$ for looks, and $i = 7$ for money.

The "w_i" values, as mentioned earlier, determine the relative importance the observer (a man/woman observing a woman/man) places on each specific attribute in "i". The fact that the weights must total 100% or 1 implies preference tradeoffs. In other words, this takes into account tradeoffs made between choosing one attribute over another. Someone who holds looks as very important would have a higher weight attached to that attribute and, thus, would have to have lower weights attached to other attributes less valued.

Let's assume there are 5 attributes (like in LAMPS theory) and we expand Postulate 2, then we have:

$$E[SMV_j] = \sum_{1}^{5} w_i * i =$$

$$E[SMV_j] = w_1 * 1 + w_2 * 2 + w_3 * 3 + w_4 * 4 + w_5 * 5$$

Let's assume that all of the attributes, 1 through 5, are equally weighted, that is:

$$w_i = w$$

Then we'll have:

$$E[SMV_j] = w * 1 + w * 2 + w * 3 + w * 4 + w * 5 =$$

$$E[SMV_j] = w * (1 + 2 + 3 + 4 + 5)$$

Intuitively we know that = 0.20 or 1/5, since there are 5 attributes and they're each being multiplied equally, and $\sum_i^n w_i = 1$. What we've done is essentially turned our weighted average back into a simple average by giving each observation the same weight. Thus, our answer above would be

$$E[SMV_j] = .20 * (1 + 2 + 3 + 4 + 5) =$$

$$E[SMV_j] = .20 * (15) = 3$$

Which is just like saying "add up all the numbers and divide by the number of numbers", or our simple average: $\frac{(1+2+3+4+5)}{5} = 3$

"LAMPS" Model: How Women Value Men (Looks, Athleticism, Money, Power, Status)

$$E[SMV_M] = (w_L)L + (w_A)A + (w_M)M + (w_P)P + (w_S)S$$

$$Where\ 0 \leq L, A, M, P, S \leq 10$$

$$And\ \{0 < w_i < 1|\ \sum_i^n w_i = 1\}$$

Remember that in this book, this assessment may "regress" to "LMS" for ease of calculation and a more superficial approach, such that

$$E[SMV_M] = (w_L)L + (w_M)M + (w_S)S$$

"VCLAW" Model: How Men Value Women (Virtuousness, Conscientiousness, Looks, Age, Weight)

$$E[SMV_F] = (w_V)V + (w_C)C + (w_L)L + (w_A)A + (w_W)W$$

Where V, C, L, A, W are nonnegative values greater tha zero and less than or equal to 10.

$$And\ \{0 < w_i < 1 | \sum_i^n w_i = 1\}$$

Remember that in this book, this assessment may "regress" to "LAW" for ease of calculation and a more superficial approach, such that

$$E[SMV_F] = (w_L)L + (w_A)A + (w_W)W$$

KNOWLEDGE CHECK

- Johnny sees Katie and gives her a 7 on looks, a 6.7 on age, and a 5 on weight. Johnny says that looks are important to him 40% of the time and weight is important to him 30% of the time. What is the expected SMV of Katie?
- Katie thinks Raymond's overall SMV is 7.45. If she gave him an 8 on looks, 6 on money and a 6.5 on status. Looks are important to her 70% of the time, and status is only half as important to her as money, what percent of the time is status important to her?

LAMBDA (THE HYPERGAMY FACTOR)

CHAPTER SUMMARY

○ The Hypergamy Factor, also called "Lambda" or goes by its symbol "λ", determines the degree of difference between male and female value based on market conditions. The closer it is to 1, the more likely a man and woman will be "on each other's level".

○ In any market, the value of a man/woman is determined by the average rating they get from other women/men in their market.

○ A person's market value is dependent upon who finds them interesting ("you are who likes you"). Therefore, a person's SMV can be "backed out" of the average SMVs of the people who are interested in them.

○ A person with an unjustified price premium results in "overpricing" themselves and/or "pricing themselves out" of a market. The price premium can come from many sources, including but not limited to, false beliefs about oneself and the one's market, family, time and location.

○ Long-term and short-term pricing strategies differ, but major conflicts occur when a person is disingenuous about their relationship duration preference; usually resulting in unwanted consequences to the longer-term relationship seeker.

CHAPTER 7

THE **HYPERGAMY FACTOR:** LAMBDA (λ)

WHEN THE HYPERGAMY FACTOR, lambda, is equal to 1, we have the condition that the male and female SMVs are equal ($\lambda = 1 \mid SMV_M = SMV_F$); hypergamy is non-existent and the man and woman can be said to be "equally yoked". As λ approaches 0, theoretical "infinite" hypergamy sets in, and the only being who would be able to meet her criteria would be a non-human entity with humanoid features (i.e., a god). This would be akin to an immaculate conception, where a woman could give birth independent of male existence. A $\lambda = 0.5$ is a woman who choses men who bring twice the value of what she brings or more. The degree of hypergamy dictates the size of λ [appendix note 10]:

TABLE 26. Abridged SMV/Lambda Table

Hypergamy factor (lambda)	Average Male SMV based on Lambdas	Female SMV (rounded)
0.985	1.0	1.0
0.854	1.8	1.5
0.810	2.5	2.0
0.783	3.2	2.5
0.763	3.9	3.0
0.747	4.7	3.5
0.734	5.4	4.0
0.724	6.2	4.5
0.714	7.0	5.0
0.706	7.8	5.5
0.698	8.6	6.0
0.691	9.4	6.5
0.685	10.0	7.0
0.822	9.1	7.5
0.876	9.1	8.0
0.907	9.4	8.5
0.930	9.7	9.0
0.947	10.0	9.5
0.961	10.0	10.0

KNOWLEDGE CHECK

- Use the "Abridged SMV to Lambda Table" to answer the following questions:
- Suzy the Sumerian has an SMV of 4.5. She's interested in Bobby the Babylonian, who has an SMV is 7.
  1. What is the average male SMV equivalent based on Suzy's SMV?
  2. What is the average highest SMV of women who are attracted to Bobby?
  3. Is Suzy less or more likely to be treated well? Explain.

Problem Set

Connie Cro-Magnon, Holly Hunter-Gatherer, Hadley Homo-Erectus are at a party. Their lambdas are 0.76,0.82, and 0.79, respectively. In walks Nathan the Neanderthal and they agree that he has a 7.7 in looks, 6.6 in money, and a 5.5 in status. They know that looks and money matter to them equally and that status matters to them 40% of the time.

What is Nathan's SMV?

What are the SMVs of the women assuming their lambdas accurate? Which of the women is the *most* likely to date Nathan?

The "Yoke" of Hypergamy

There is a biblical concept of being equally/unequally "yoked" like oxen to a cart. I think it is mentioned in Corinthians when it speaks on not being "unequally yoked" with "non-believers". This recalls a cart with two oxen that are strapped to it—one with longer yoke/reins than the other. I assume that this condition would have the cart go off of the "straight and narrow" path, as one ox may pull one way, and the other pull in the other direction. I surmise the interpretation—when dealing with others—is be wary of keeping company with people who are going in a different direction than you.

The point of this section is not to critique the Bible, but to discuss the "yoke" itself. And for the purposes of this book, the "yoke" is the degree of value that men and women bring to the table in their coupling. The "yoke" is hypergamy.

I addressed hypergamy as a concept above, but here I will put it in a theoretical mathematical framework. But, for the purposes of this book, an equally yoked couple would bring equal value to the table and, thus, their expected values should be the same:

$$E[SMV_M] = E[SMV_F]$$

Therefore, the following condition would exist

$$(w_L)L + (w_A)A + (w_M)M + (w_P)P + (w_S)S =$$
$$= (w_V)V + (w_C)C + (w_L)L + (w_A)A + (w_W)W$$

Or superficially,

$$(w_L)L + (w_M)M + (w_S)S = (w_L)L + (w_A)A + (w_W)W$$

But hypergamy won't allow that to happen per the *Bateman Principle*. Hypergamy ensures that the male's expected value is higher than the female's ($E[SMV_M] > E[SMV_F]$) so it is reasonable to assume that $E[SMV_F]$ is a proportion of $E[SMV_M]$. This proportion will be referred to in this text by the following names "lambda", "hypergamy", "hypergamy factor", and is symbolized by the Greek letter λ. And the relationship is such that:

$$\lambda(E[SMV_M]) = E[SMV_F]$$

And the condition that $0 < \lambda \leq 1$

And since we expect actual values to equal expected values, we have

$$\lambda SMV_M = SMV_F$$

KNOWLEDGE CHECK

- In the previous knowledge check, we dealt with Katie and Raymond. Based off Raymond's value of 7.45, if $\lambda = 0.82$, what is Katie's expected sexual marketplace value?

ACTUAL VALUE MODELS

"What you think about me is none of my business"

~ unknown

The Court of Public Opinion

In 1971, the United States of America came off of the "gold standard" whereby every currency note issue was backed by gold, presumably housed at Fort Knox. Afterwards, the value of the US dollar was determined not by gold but by the "full faith and credit" of the United States government—whatever that means to you. Essentially, the dollar is only as good as what it is believed to be. This is a type of "top down" approach. Being backed by gold was a "bottoms up" approach—the value of the dollar was based on the fundamental supply and demand for gold.

Another analogy to this top down vs. bottom-up approach is how real estate prices are contrived. A bottom-up approach would be to look at how much the house is worth, based on financial parameters such as how much can be reasonably asked for rent and determine based on this cash flow how much the house can generate and therefore derive its value. A top-down approach would be to look at all similar-styled houses—in square footage, and in the same location and see what they're selling for, then the price of the house in question can be derived within a stone's throw of that figure.

In the Sexual Marketplace, the "court of public opinion" occurs on two fronts—one, where a group of people of one sex assign a price/value to a person of the opposite sex, and two, data is observed regarding the SMV of the interested party(ies) towards the opposite sex and assigning a value accordingly.

Mob Behavior: Female/Male Group Valuation

There are four girls at a bar, numbered 1 through 4. A good-looking guy spots them and is particularly interested in girl number 3. Will he get her? Suppose their average market Lambda is 0.8, Here's the table for the analysis:

A	B	C = B/Σ(B1:B4)	D	E = (D x C)
Girl	**SMV**	**Weight**	**Opinion of Guy** **(based on LMS)**	**Share**
1	5	19%	10.0	1.92
2	6	23%	9.5	2.19
3	7	27%	9.0	2.42
4	8	31%	7.0	2.15
Male SMV = **Σ (E1:E4)**	**8.69**			

TABLE 27. Market Value Based on Female Group Opinion

In this example, we use the weighted average as we have previously. This time, the weights are applied based on the woman's SMV. The higher the woman's SMV, the more weight her opinion carries with the group and, thus, influences group opinion. According to the table, the guy is above average looking as determined by the group of girls. Girl 1 thinks he's a perfect 10, and girls 2 and 3 (the one he's interested in) think he's pretty hot themselves, giving him a 9.5 and 9 respectively. Surely, girl 3 would date him because she thinks of him as a 9, right?

It's highly possible that if she were alone that she would date him but, since she's a part of a group, the opinion of the group creates the market condition that his *market* SMV is 8.69.

If she thinks he's a 9, and her SMV is 7, then we can back out her personal lambda:

$$\lambda SMV_{M,girl\,3} = SMV_F$$

$$\lambda 9 = 7$$

$$\lambda = 0.77$$

The group opinion lambda is

$$\lambda SMV_{M,group} = SMV_F$$

$$\lambda 8.69 = 7$$

$$\lambda = 0.81$$

Remember as lambda decreases towards 0, hypergamy increases. An increase in lambda means a lowering of market expectation. The group lambda ends up being lower than Girl 3's expectations, killing her desire for him. The alpha female (Girl 4) throws a monkey wrench in Girl 3's plans because she rated him as a 7. Acting on her own, girl 3 might have enjoyed a relationship with a guy who exceeds her expectations but, because of "groupthink", she let the mob make the decision for her.

One reason this could be is that over millennia humans have evolved as a social species that survive in groups and, thus, relying on this instinct has got us from the stone age to where we are today. Though, not without deleterious effects—losing people to mobs because of racism, or wars, or innocent men going to jail without fair trial, or the "witch hunt" that caused so many women to be burned at the stake at the accusation of witchcraft in early American history. As the numbers go, they are those who have "fell through the cracks" or who were the "broken eggs" used to make the societal omelet.

Market Data: You are who likes you

Imagine a woman threw on her best duds and, with a hot cup of cocoa, sat down to create an out-of-this-world Tinder profile. She gets likes by guys 1 through 4. Assuming the market lambda is 0.8, this is how we can interpret the data:

TABLE 28. Market Value of Female Based on Interested Men

A	B	C	D = (B x C)	E = B / Σ (B1:B4)	F = (D x E)
Guy	SMV	Market Lambda	Translated Female SMV	Weight	Shares
1	6.3	0.8	5.04	0.23	1.17
2	7.1	0.8	5.68	0.26	1.49
3	5.9	0.8	4.72	0.22	1.03
4	7.8	0.8	6.24	0.29	1.80
Female SMV = Σ (E1:E4)	5.48				

Based on the guys who like her, weighted by their SMVs, we find the woman is a 5.48 on a 10 scale—given the market lambda. If the lambda goes up (expectations of women become lower in the general market—bringing each guy's value up), then so will her SMV.

Actual Value Weighted Analysis

The above two valuations are rooted in the fundamental that the SMVs of males and females are interdependent [appendix note 11]. Just like the value of a house is affected by the houses that surround it. Especially in the first example, where a perfectly suitable mate is turned away. This happens because the "mini market" or the friends that were around girl 3 had a greater effect because they were in closer proximity. Just as a value of a house is more affected by the houses on the same block or in the same development more than they are affected by other houses in the same municipality that are not in the same immediate area.

KNOWLEDGE CHECK

- Nathan the Neanderthal, Cody Cro-Magnon, and Harry Homo Erectus, whose SMVs are 8, 7, and 6 respectively, are all interested in dating Foraging Franny. The market lambda is 0.77 ($\lambda = 0.77$). What is Franny's SMV?
- Which one of the guys would Franny most likely date?

Pricing Premiums

Imagine a house with all the "bells and whistles". Maybe it comes equipped with solar panels, water filtration system, a dumb waiter, "energy-star" appliances, and items that make living in the house easier than if it didn't have those amenities. The person(s) who would benefit from buying such a house are in the market for those amenities, but do not have the skill or time to procure and install of the items in question. Therefore, they would buy the house at a premium, getting the amenities and saving themselves time.

With regards to the sexual marketplace, a person who has a market premium (asking price greater than market value) would be someone with the qualities that the opposite sex person wants and is willing to put up with the competition and expectations of that person and the other costs that come along with them.

People who carry unjustified market premiums often find themselves "priced out" of a market until they either cave and *lower* their expectations or *increase* their value to justify the price they are asking. The sub-sections below list a few examples of biases that cause pricing premiums.

"Overpricing" Oneself

One common mistake both men and women make is that they may price themselves based on what they value/believe are good values versus what the market says the value is. The man/woman who makes the statement that he/she deserves a relationship because he is a "nice guy" or she has her PhD is an example of this.

For the man, he is valuing himself on what he values in a woman (being a "nice guy" would fall under conscientiousness) versus what the woman sees is the value in him. He is assuming that being conscientious is something that women value in men. While I'm sure there's nothing wrong with being conscientious for the sake of conscientiousness, it does not necessarily follow that women equally value that attribute.

A woman who believes that because she has earned a PhD that it makes her more desirable of a catch to all men is in for a rude awakening—if not in the near term, in the long term. Having a PhD is not necessarily a bad thing, as long as it does not affect the degree to which she respects others if they don't have one. But the point is, since she values education (which for men, falls under status), she's giving herself a value based on male value attributes.

What ends up happening from the above scenarios, is that they end up "tacking on" an extra attribute that doesn't belong to them

Recall our initial conditions:

$$E[SMV_M] = (w_L)L + (w_A)A + (w_M)M + (w_P)P + (w_S)S$$

$$E[SMV_F] = (w_V)V + (w_C)C + (w_L)L + (w_A)A + (w_W)W$$

But with the false value pricing we have:

$$E[P_M] = (w_L)L + (w_A)A + (w_M)M + (w_P)P + (w_S)S + (w_C)C$$

$$E[P_F] = (w_V)V + (w_C)C + (w_L)L + (w_A)A + (w_W)W + (w_S)S$$

Where P_j = the price of j= male or female

Substituting the market values into the price equation, we have:

$$E[P_M] = E[SMV_M] + (w_C)C$$

$$E[P_F] = E[SMV_F] + (w_S)S$$

We can see that the prices have a "premium" included which are caused by a false belief of value. They have, in essence, increased the price of the product without increasing the value determined by the market.

KNOWLEDGE CHECK

- Mesolithic Mary just got her PhD in Paleontology. She's so excited because the increase in her income has allowed her to accumulate a bank balance that puts her asset holdings in the 70th percentile of people in her region. When looking for a man, education is important to her 30% of the time and she would consider a guy with a PhD an 8 on the status scale. The amount of money a man has in the bank is only important to her 20% of the time. If you ask most guys, they will say she's average. What is Mary's ESMV and Expected Price? What market level of hypergamy would allow Mary to get away with her price? What does that mean in layman's terms?

A FACE ONLY A MOTHER COULD LOVE

Familial Bias

"A face only a mother could love" is a saying that means that a person is unattractive to the extent that only their mother could love them—the fallacy is that the statement assumes that mothers unconditionally love all of their offspring. A mother is likely to be biased towards the appearance of her offspring if none other than the simple fact that she is either in part or the whole reason why her offspring appear as they do. Therefore, unless she is truthful to herself about how she or her bloodline is relatively unattractive (with respect to the "Golden Ratio" and societal expectations of beauty), she may either add a premium to the market value of her child (usually the son) because she sees qualities that she thinks others don't, or she is secretly cheering in the stands for her son to have her opportunity to "breed out" and, for lack of a more congenial statement, "get some of that ugliness out of the family".

The familial bias can also occur in the opposite direction, putting a discount on their child's appearance if the child is attractive but, because the parent behaves in a dysfunctional manner—including but not limited to jealous competition and emotional abusiveness—can say and/or do things to wound the child's self-esteem. What I call the "I ain't shit, so you ain't never gonna be shit" mentality (a la the movie *Juice*). The child may then go out into the world offering themselves to people who are way below their market value because of this.

IT AIN'T TRICKIN' IF YOU GOT IT

Time Biases

Another example of bias that occurs may be enacted because of what I call "time loop" bias. This can come from parents, but usually comes from older people towards younger people. Trapped in a time loop, the older people will think about what they value in a mate and project that onto the younger person in the present day.

For example, a young man performing a protective/caregiving function like helping an elderly woman to lift something heavy or cross a busy street may elicit from her a reaction of "you'd be a good young man for my granddaughter". Not knowing that her granddaughter may have a completely different value system/perception of value than she does. The granddaughter might want to have a friend in a guy like that, but may not see him as an object of sexual affection—as there are other factors and criteria that she may have. In addition, a man doing things for a woman in the elderly woman's time when women depended on men for necessities is a good quality to the old woman, but to her granddaughter, she may feel she doesn't need a man do to those things for her, and instead, has another perception of what qualities are valuable to her.

Another time bias is an age market bias. Humans have a natural tendency to deteriorate over time. As a result, younger people will have a higher SMV than older people, all else equal. Even when adjusted for wealth, a younger person still has relatively more potential to become what the older person is and more. Therefore, older people often see younger people as more attractive and without being in the same sexual marketplace as the younger person, are unable to ascertain the value younger person A to younger person B. To them, A & B might look like a cute couple.

This happened to me in the past. An older woman saw me walking around with another woman a few years younger than me in the building. The old woman thought that the young woman and I were dating. When I explained to her that we weren't, she mentioned that we would be a cute couple. I had no qualms about it because I was attracted to the woman, but the young woman didn't have the same feelings about me. Therefore, I put thoughts of dating her out of my mind and moved on mentally. We were still cool and hung out together, but nothing "extra" came out of our friendship.

One last time bias that I have encountered revolves around what I call "time warp" bias. This happens when a person has been out of the dating market for some time and, based on a past perception of value, carries on as if they can get the same value they received in a previous time.

This usually happens to older people who, in their heyday, operated along certain established norms (i.e., traditionalism, chivalry etc.) and, in a time past, secured a relationship that was based on those previously accepted norms. Then for whatever reason—a divorce or being widowed—the person finds themselves "back on the saddle". Often times, a person re-experiencing the sexual marketplace after being gone will behave like a newborn fawn—legs buckling under the weight of social pressures and eyes wide shut in the headlights of the Mac Truck of rejection. But there are those who often flamboyantly behave as if they were bringing the 80s back—and thinking that they have the "moves like Jagger".

For men who behave this way, they may have a rude awakening when they discover themselves always spending money on their younger mate. For women, they are rudely awakened to younger men not wanting to spend the night or commit after having sex.

Location Bias

Another bias occurs because a person may move from one market where they had a higher value into another market where they have a lower value. The sexual economics of location are dealt with in the next book, but for now, the concept is a person seen as "exotic and rare" in one marketplace, is in their ancestral country of origin, a dime a dozen.

Take Superman, for example. He's the shit on Earth because he can fly, has X-ray vision, and is solar powered, blahsy blahsay, but on Krypton, everybody can fly, has X-ray vision, etc. Lois Lane would have had a field day on Krypton.

Regardless, the phenomena of men moving across sexual marketplaces to maximize their value is not unheard of. Men are better off when they go to a place where they are the rare/exotic and/or meet the hypergamy standards there. Among Black Americans, there is a running joke that Black American women vacation in Jamaica and Black American men vacation in Brazil/Dominican Republic due to this phenomenon, but when they take a cruise they both eat fried catfish and drink white Zinfandel.

Women are more likely to overprice themselves than men because men deal with rejection head on and have direct data as consequences of their actions and/or inactions about their current stature in life. In America, it is culturally taboo and viewed as bullying to directly tell a woman information that can be perceived as negative about herself. As a result, women do not often have the real data with which to make decisions about their value. However, there are some suppositions, like the gaining of weight, that women are made aware of changes in their perceived value.

Many years ago, Kristie Alley had a TV show whereby she was lamenting on how her dating life was going to change after her drastic weight gain. To which one of her supposedly gay African American advisors in her entourage exclaimed: "black guys like ample booty". This was an acknowledgement on two fronts: one, of hypergamy, more specifically racial hypergamy (which I deal with toward the end of the book), and two, an acknowledgement that Kristie's market value had declined because of her weight gain.

Problem Set: Calculating Valuation based on live public opinion

1. If the sum of the SMVs is 28, and the weights of Girl 1,2,3, and 4 are 14%,21%,29% and 36% respectively, find the SMV of each girl (y variable) rounding to the nearest whole number:

TABLE 29. Example SMV		
A	**B = C x Σ (C1:C4)**	**C**
Girl (x variable)	**SMV (y variable)**	**SMV Weight**
1	?	14%
2	?	21%
3	?	29%
4	?	36%

$$\sum SMV_s = 28$$

2. If Guy 1 has an SMV of 8 and Girl 2 wants to date him (he approaches her alone), what does her λ have to be?

3. If Guy 1 approaches Girl 2, who thinks Guy 1 is an 8. Girl 2 is in a group with Girls 1,3, and 4, and their opinions of Guy 1 are 10, 9, and 8.5 respectively, what is Guy 1's SMV based on these opinions?
4. If the market λ = 0.7, which girls will date Guy 1?

Calculating Valuation Based on Dating Site

Samantha is excited; she just setup her OK Cupid profile and is ready to start dating. There are 4 guys that "slid" into her inbox DMs. She ascertains the following information about the guys based on their profile pic and other data:

TABLE 30.   Example SMV Calculation

A	B	C = B/ Σ (B1:B4)	D = (C x B)
Guy (x variable)	SMV (y variable)	Weight	Shares
1	7.00	?	?
2	7.25	?	?
3	7.50	?	?
4	7.75	?	?

1. Finish the table, rounding to 2 decimal places
2. What is Samantha's SMV based on the guys that are interested in her if the market lambda is 0.65?
3. If Samantha's lambda goes up to 0.8, what is her new SMV?
4. When Samantha's hypergamy factor (lambda) goes up, does she become more or less picky?

Pricing Issues: Short Term vs Long Term Mating Strategies

Both men and women have a twin mating strategy for short term and long-term coupling (although we focused only on the female twin mating strategy above). I postulate that when facing a choice about a woman he'd like to share resources with (i.e. a home with raising children), he'd be more discerning in choosing attributes that go beyond the superficial.

For men, the choice between long- and short-term mating would show up in what he feels is important—or in the relative importance weights. A lower total relative importance on items of substance like virtuousness and conscientiousness and characteristics that have to do with bearing and raising offspring like age and a higher relative importance on more superficial items like looks and weight may signal a short-term strategy. In addition, a lower relative importance on looks would help to reduce competition.

For women, like men, in the short term to get their rocks off, would likely go strictly for the "DNA heralding" men that appear to have high testosterone, favoring a higher relative importance on looks and power (which together generate charisma) and a lower relative importance on athleticism, money and status (ability to protect and ensure long-term stability).

For this discussion of long-term relationship qualities, the total combined relative importance weights to fewer desirable short-term attributes are "restricted", and the more desirable long-term attributes are "unrestricted". As a result, **a woman's successful long-term mating strategy holds athleticism, money, and status together (unrestricted) more important than looks and power together (restricted),** as looks and power are short-term attributes. **For men, a long-term strategy requires that virtuousness, conscientiousness, and age together (unrestricted) be more important than looks and weight together (restricted).** The main point of this section is that regardless of what people say they want in a relationship; you can always tell where their values are by what is important to them (i.e. their relative importance weights).

Let the sum of the restricted relative importance weights be less than the sum of the unrestricted relative importance weights:

$$\sum w_{restricted} < \sum w_{unrestricted}$$

Also, remember the caveat that all of the weights add up to 1 or:

$$\sum w_{restricted} + \sum w_{unrestricted} = 1 \ or \ 100\%$$

$$\sum w_{unrestricted} = 1 - \sum w_{restricted}$$

Plugging this back in, we have

$$\sum w_{restricted} < 1 - \sum w_{restricted}$$

Gathering like terms

$$\sum w_{restricted} < \frac{1}{2}$$

Assuming a long term relationship preference, attributive weights that are less valued (restricted) must, as a total, have *less weight* than the more valued (unrestricted) ones. For this to be true, the sum of the restricted weights must be less than 50%.

Take, for example, a male long-term nesting mating strategy where he values V, C and A but devalues L and W. Therefore, the restricted weights are w_L and w_W and the unrestricted weights are w_V, w_C and w_A. And the claim that w_V = 20%, w_C = 20% *and* w_A = 15% holds true because $w_L + w_W$ must be 45% and 45% is less than half.

Now, if the claim was made that he has a long-term strategy but w_V = 10%, w_C = 10%, w_A = 10% this could not be true since w_L *and* w_W = 70%. Looks and weight mean more to him than he led on and he's not really looking for a long-term strategy but a short term one.

One of the biggest issues in dating usually occurs when one party or the other "masquerades" their strategy. Here are a few scenarios:

Person A wants a long-term intimate relationship but pretends to be short term.

This can happen for a few different reasons:

As a passive/reactive strategy, Person A doesn't want to "scare off" the other person, especially in the post-modern "hookup" culture. Person A doesn't want to seem "needy" and, in a non-committal culture, Person A may think that if they start a short-term relationship it could lead to a long-term one without putting the "burden" of having the other person decide whether to commit or not. Person A is essentially undervaluing his/herself and/or overvaluing the other person.

Person A may take an aggressive/proactive strategy, "test driving" the other person to see if that person is a good "fit". Anecdotally, I've seen this occur mostly if Person A is a woman and the other person is a man. This happens usually because Person A is not completely sold on the guy and thinks that there won't be too much of a loss if it doesn't work out since she can easily bail out.

This can backfire if the guy, understanding and either accepting it to be short term, or being a true short-termer himself, demonstrates value that was not previously known to the woman and, upon discovering this value, she switches (unbeknownst to him) to the first reason— either not trying to scare the guy off, or realizing her intentions. This often ends up in a relationship stalemate because if the guy chose her for a short-term strategy, it's because he truly is short term and this often ends up disappointing the woman. A short-term person has no incentive to change their actions if they are with a long-term person because the expectancy that the relationship will not last is built into the short-termers valuation of said relationship.

Finally, Person A may not be sure if he/she desires a long-term relationship or may think that he/she doesn't deserve one. People who are long-term who masquerade as short term often suffer greater because their expectations of what the relationship would or could be will not be realized if they are with a true short termer.

Person B only wants a short-term physical relationship, but pretends to be long-term

People who masquerade as long term but who are short term may want to get something from the other person who operates under long-term principles. Anecdotally, I have seen this more frequently in men towards women for the purposes of getting sex. The woman may tell him that she only will have sex with a long-term partner and he may be either so infatuated with her that he will lie about his intentions for the promise of sex, or it could be a challenge, a type of "forbidden fruit" especially in the case that certain belief systems (i.e. religious dogma) are the source of the woman not wanting to be sexual in the short term.

To people who are pretending to be long term, they can only do it for so long until patience wears thin and it becomes only a matter of time before they disappoint their long-term partner. This strategy only works clean if their partner is either a short term who is pretending as well or a long term who is open to "test driving" initially. In the case that they either both dissolve the relationship, or they find value in each other and continue, would be a "win-win".

Problem Set: Long- or Short-Term Relationship?

Stephanie tells her friends that she wants a long-term committed relationship. So far there are two guys who have expressed interest in being with Stephanie (and their attributive qualities are known to Stephanie)—Jake and Biff. Fill in the highlighted blanks in the table to help you answer the questions:

TABLE 31. Long-Term Relationship Score Example					
	A	B	C	D = (A x C)	E = (B x C)
Looks	8	5	?	?	?
Athleticism	6	7	?	?	?
Money	6	8	?	?	?
Power	8	5	?	?	?
Status	7	9	?	?	?
Sum of Restricted weights (Looks and Power)	?		Sum of restricted shares	?	?
Sum of Unrestricted weights (Athleticism, Money, Status)	?		Sum of unrestricted shares	?	?
Jake's SMV (Sum of all his Shares)	?				
Biff's SMV (Sum of all his Shares)	?				

If Stephanie places *equal importance* on each of the attributive values, fill in the table's blanks. Is Stephanie serious about having a long-term relationship? Do Jake and Biff fulfill the requirements for a long-term relationship? Who is better fit for a long-term relationship, Jake or Biff? Who is Stephanie likely to choose?

If Stephanie's relative importance weights change to the following, fill in the table and answer the questions:

TABLE 32. Long-Term Relationship Score Example					
	A	B	C	D = (A x C)	E = (B x C)
Looks	8	5	0.20	?	?
Athleticism	6	7	0.10	?	?
Money	6	8	0.20	?	?
Power	8	5	0.35	?	?
Status	7	9	0.15	?	?
Sum of Restricted weights (Looks and Power)	?		Sum of restricted shares	?	?
Sum of Unrestricted weights (Athleticism, Money, Status)	?		Sum of unrestricted shares	?	?
Jake's SMV (Sum of all his Shares)	?				
Biff's SMV (Sum of all his Shares)	?				

Based on the information in the table, is Stephanie looking for a long-term relationship?

Which man is better suited to enter into a long-term relationship with Stephanie? Why?

If Stephanie says she wants a long-term relationship, but dates Jake, what is likely to happen?

If Stephanie's relative importance weights change to the following (fill in the table to answer the questions):

TABLE 33. Long-Term Relationship Score Example					
	A	B	C	D = (A x C)	E = (B x C)
Attributive	Jake	Biff		Jake's Shares	Biff's Shares
Looks	8	5	0.15	?	?
Athleticism	6	7	0.2	?	?
Money	6	8	0.2	?	?
Power	8	5	0.25	?	?
Status	7	9	0.2	?	?
Sum of Restricted weights (Looks and Power)	?		Sum of restricted shares	?	?
Sum of Unrestricted weights (Athleticism, Money, Status)	?		Sum of unrestricted shares	?	?
Jake's SMV (Sum of all his Shares)	?				
Biff's SMV (Sum of all his Shares)	?				

What can we say about Stephanie's preferences now? Which guy must she choose to realize this (look at the sum of unrestricted shares)?

OCCUPATIONAL VALUE AND SOCIAL BENEFITS

○ The role that one partner engages in to provide value to another can be estimated in dollars by locating the value of the role in the open market. This "occupational value" uses the SMV of the individual as a proxy for their level of earnings.

○ Since there are only 24 hours in a day, there is an upper limit to the amount of time a person can spend satisfying such roles. This amount of time multiplied by the earnings per unit of time results in an "Endowment Value" which approximates the amount of value, in dollars, that one person gives to another over the life of the relationship.

○ Using MSFT Excel tools, a linear regression can be produced to estimate the Endowment Value based on SMV.

○ Social Benefits (SB) are intangible benefits that people receive at various SMVs (one reason why attractive people often get paid more, and/or have a "halo effect"). SB increase when SMV increases, but at a decreasing rate.

CHAPTER 8

OCCUPATIONAL **VALUE AND** SOCIAL BENEFITS

Putting a price on your head

From images/accounts of tribes who "pay" a number of goats in exchange for the right to marry the daughter (bride price), to families that pay a given amount to a suitor to marry the daughter (dowry), to the "wanted dead or alive" with a reward attached to it from the wild west, people have used various methods to calculate a tangible value of another human being for some time.

A more rational and modern determination comes from life insurance companies that, by method of formulation, are able to determine the death benefit (the amount that beneficiaries are to be paid in the event of the death of the benefactor) of a person based on health statistics/life expectancy, income and other indemnification factors.

Valuations done on companies that have different business areas that autonomously generate income, and portfolios with different assets generating different levels of income, usually use the weighted average (which is an ongoing theme in this book) to determine the total portfolio value. That is

$$V(P) = \sum_{i=1}^{N} a_i w_i$$

Where:

$V(P)$ = *Value of a Portfolio that is a collection of smaller assets*

$$a_i = Value\ of\ ith\ asset\ in\ portfolio$$

$$w_i = weight\ of\ the\ ith\ asset\ in\ portfolio$$

$$\sum_{i=1}^{N} = sum\ of\ items\ i\ through\ N$$

And

$$w_i = \frac{a_i}{\sum_{i=1}^{N} a_i}$$

Using this same methodology, we will determine the social benefit dollar value of a relationship partner by the value of what they would provide in the open market, or

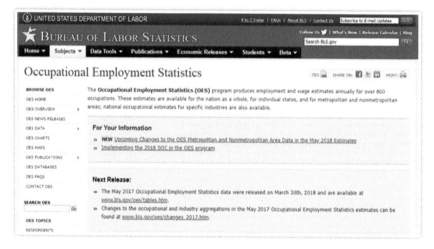

Figure 25.   Bureau of Labor Statistics Webpage

"Occupational Value". The Bureau of Labor Statistics (BLS) has data on the value of each occupation per their annual "Occupational Employment Statistics" (OES) [36a].

The tables used in this example are acquired from this federal website and the data is per May 2017:

Figure 26. Occupational Employment Statistics Data

I have hand-picked several different occupations that may represent the types of things people bring to table in a relationship based on traditional (think *Leave It to Beaver*) gender roles:

1. husband/male partner does handiwork/odd jobs/heavy lifting and provides income
2. the wife/female partner does housework and provides sexual intimacy and childcare
3. both male and female partners provide companionship and emotional intimacy

Below is a truncated table with extractions from the BLS' May 2017 OES statistics (I added all of the column headers A thru H):

TABLE 34.	Genders and OCCs						
A	**B**	**C**	**D**	**E**	**F**	**G**	**H**
Gender traditionally associated with OCC	AREA_NAME	OCC_TITLE	H_MEAN	H_PCT10	H_PCT25	H_PCT75	H_PCT90
F/M	Los Angeles-Long Beach-Anaheim, CA	Counselors, All Other	22.02	13.87	16.95	26.48	30.94
M	Los Angeles-Long Beach-Anaheim, CA	Landscaping and Groundskeeping Workers	15.59	10.78	11.77	17.80	24.20
F	Los Angeles-Long Beach-Anaheim, CA	Childcare Workers	13.26	10.47	11.08	14.57	17.71

A. Column A: I added this column. M = Male and F= Female. These are what gender are traditionally associated with the occupation in column C

B. Column B: Is the region and state of what the stats represent

C. Column C: The occupational title

D. Column D: The hourly mean (average) income paid to this occupation. This is also can be interpreted as the 50th percentile if the data is normally distributed (50 percent of the population makes less than or equal to this amount)

E. Column E through H: The hourly $10^{th}, 25^{th}, 75^{th}$, and 90th percentiles hourly income (10,25,75 and 90 percent of the population makes less than or equal to the amount)

We will continue with using the percentiles divided by 10 to indicate rank on a Min/Max scale (i.e. 10th percentile = 1, 25th percentile = 2.5, Mean = 50th percentile = 5, 75th percentile = 7.5 and 90th percentile = 9).

Based on the information above, if the SMVs of a husband and wife are 7.5 and 5 respectively, and they both spent equal amounts of their available time doing the duties traditionally associated with them, what is their hourly value?

Per the above extracted table and gender role assumptions laid out here, a husband would be expected to assume the roles of landscaping/groundskeeping and counseling, the hourly values of which, in the 75th percentile, are 17.80 and 26.48, respectively. If he spends 50% of his time on each, we have a weighted average hourly value of (50%) x (17.80) + (50%) x (26.48) = $22.14.

With the same logic, a wife would be expected to assume the roles of child care workers (13.26) and counseling (22.02), and her weighted average hourly value (50%) x (13.26) + (50%) x (22.02) = $17.64.

These are "quick n' dirty" conceptual values, and of course does not show the whole picture, because the husband, while overall is a 7.5 out of 10, may really be good at landscaping (like a 9 at landscaping) and just a little better than average at counseling (like a 6) the average of which gives him the value of 7.5. This is easy to deduce, because we're only dealing with two variables but when the number of variables (roles) increases, trying to determine averages, whether they be simple or otherwise, becomes more tedious than what is necessary for this book.

Also, there's the case of the wife who has a greater occupational value than the husband based on roles alone (and as we'll see, the occupational value of sex comes at a much higher hourly value that almost any paid wage). To keep things simple, the husband's occupational value will either be the weighted average value of his roles (if more than the wife's), or his occupational value can be backed out using the wife's lambda because the underlying assumption is that if a man has a woman in his "employ" he is generating the value to "pay" a return to capital. As a result, his value represents the ability to pay.

But in simplicity, we have:

$$V(Occ) = \sum_{i=1}^{N} o_i\, w_i$$

Where:

$V(Occ) = Occupational\ Value$

$o_i = Value\ of\ ith\ occupation\ per\ unit\ of\ time\ (hour,\ month,\ day,\ etc.)$

$w_i = \%\ of\ time\ spent\ in\ the\ ith\ occupation\ in\ the\ stated\ interval\ (hour,\ month,\ day,\ etc.)$

$$\sum_{i=1}^{N} = sum\ of\ items\ i\ through\ N$$

Estimating Values on a 10 Scale

In the upcoming examples, and for simplicity, I will evaluate a minimum of two duties and no more than four. The data given by the BLS applied to my framework here have given the values in such a manner:

TABLE 35. BLS Value Scale

BLS Value	Percentile	Max/Min Scale Value
H_PCT10	10	1.0
H_PCT25	25	2.5
H_MEAN	50	5.0
H_PCT75	75	7.5
H_PCT90	90	9.0

Suppose we wanted to estimate the value of someone in between one of those ranges? It could be averaged, which would be good if it were equidistant between the two scores. For example, if we wanted to find the value of a 1.75 (which is equidistant between 1 and 2.5), we could average the hourly wages of the 25th and 10th percentiles. Another way to do it is to plot the range of values using excel and use the regression function to get the formula for the line that is closest to all the points. Say we wanted to estimate the value of a counselor in the Los Angeles area on a Min/Max scale? Using our above example, we have:

TABLE 36. Genders and OCCs (Truncated)							
A	B	C	D	E	F	G	H
Gender traditionally associated with OCC	AREA_ NAME	OCC_TITLE	H_ MEAN	H_ PCT10	H_ PCT25	H_ PCT75	H_ PCT90
F/M	Los Angeles-Long Beach-Anaheim, CA	Counselors, All Other	22.02	13.87	16.95	26.48	30.94

This data can be truncated and rearranged into a table that orders the 10-scale value and the hourly wages. It's reasonable to assume that the hourly wage depends upon the percentile it falls in, as we see a clear positive relationship between percentile and hourly wage. Therefore, the hourly wage is the dependent variable and the 10-scale value (which is directly mapped from the percentiles) is the independent variable.

TABLE 37. Hourly Wage Scale		
Percentile	10-Scale Value (x var.)	Hourly Wage (y var.)
10	1.0	13.87
25	2.5	16.95
50	5.0	22.02
75	7.5	26.48
90	9.0	30.94

A real quick and dirty estimation is to use the MSFT Excel data analysis Tool Pak or any regression software to give you a formula that estimates the relationship between the 10 Scale values and the Hourly Wage. Here is an example using the data above:

First, choose "Data Analysis" from the data tab in MSFT Excel:

Second, choose "Regression" from the drop-down menu

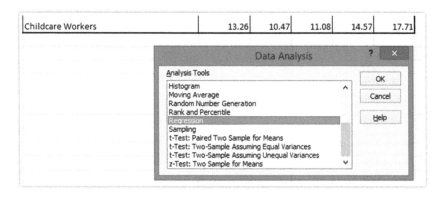

Third, select the hourly wage range for the Y inputs and the 10 Scale variable for the X inputs (use the variables from the table above) your confidence level should automatically be at 95%:

After this step, click "OK". Your output data should appear in another sheet tab. Here are the results highlighted with the pertinent data:

SUMMARY OUTPUT

Regression Statistics	
Multiple R	0.997534
R Square	0.995075
Adjusted R Square	0.993433
Standard Error	0.560841
Observations	5

ANOVA

	df	SS	MS	F	gnificance F
Regression	1	190.6367	190.6367	606.0758	0.000147
Residual	3	0.943628	0.314543		
Total	4	191.5803			

	Coefficient	andard Err	t Stat	P-value	Lower 95%	Upper 95%	ower 95.0%	pper 95.0%
Intercept	11.70312	0.489508	23.90794	0.00016	10.14529	13.26096	10.14529	13.26096
X Variable 1	2.069775	0.084074	24.61861	0.000147	1.802216	2.337335	1.802216	2.337335

The "R Square" value, the "coefficient of determination", is the percentage of variance in the dependent variable that comes from the independent variable. In terms of what we're measuring, this says "99% of the variation in hourly wage can be explained by your rank on a scale of 1 to 10". One counter to what I've done here could be: "Well, he doesn't have a large enough sample size". But my rebuttal is that the data compiled by the BLS to calculate percentiles already include a large enough sample size to justify a further analysis (meta-analysis) of the summary data.

The "Intercept" is the value of hourly wage when the rank on the Min/Max scale is 0. In other words, the absolute "bottom of the barrel" counselors make $11.70 per hour.

The "X Variable 1" is the value that y incrementally changes with when x changes. So, when a person's rank rises by 1 on the Min/Max scale of 1 to 10, their hourly income *in that occupation* increases by $2.07.

Combining the Intercept and X Variable 1 gives us the regression equation:

$$y = \$2.07x + \$11.70; \text{ or}$$

$$V(occ) = \$2.07 \times (SMV) + \$11.70$$

This relationship can answer the following question: "If in 2017 you were a counselor in the greater Los Angeles area with an SMV of 3.5 on a 10 scale, what is your average hourly wage?

$$V(occ) = V(Counselor) = \$2.07 \times (3.5) + \$11.70 = \$18.95$$

To consider multiple profession/roles, we simply take the weighted average of the income based on time spent in each profession/role and then estimate the relationship of the 10-scale rating to the weighted average of the incomes from all of the professions. Suppose you have the following information from the BLS regarding Annie's Roles:

TABLE 38. Genders and OCCs (Truncated)

AREA_NAME	OCC_TITLE	H_MEAN	H_PCT10	H_PCT25	H_PCT75	H_PCT90
Los Angeles-Long Beach-Anaheim, CA	Laundry and Dry-Cleaning Workers	12.50	10.29	10.60	13.79	15.88
Los Angeles-Long Beach-Anaheim, CA	Counselors, All Other	22.02	13.87	16.95	26.48	30.94
Los Angeles-Long Beach-Anaheim, CA	Cooks, Private Household	21.09	16.01	18.84	22.75	23.95
Los Angeles-Long Beach-Anaheim, CA	Childcare Workers	13.26	10.47	11.08	14.57	17.71

Annie is a 5 on the 10 scale and she spends her time equally between cleaning the clothes, counseling her husband, cooking, and taking care of the kids. What is the average value of the services that she produces at an hourly rate?

$$V(occ(Annie)) = (25\%)(12.50) + (25\%)(22.02) + (25\%)(21.09) + (25\%)(13.26) = \$17.23$$

KNOWLEDGE CHECK

- Jerry and Jan are a match made in heaven. Jerry is the breadwinner and Jan is a stay-at-home wife. Jan is a 2.5 on the 10 scale, has a lambda of 0.8, and spends 10 hours per day fulfilling "wifely duties" of cooking, laundry, and taking care of their son, Tyler. Jan spends 30% of her time taking care of

Tyler and the rest of her time is spent equally between cooking and laundry.

- Based on the data in Table 39, answer the following questions:
- What is Jan's occupational value?
- What is Jerry's SMV?
- If Jerry and Jan are a couple for 20 years, and Jan works every day, what is the total gross endowment value of Jan's role as a wife?
- If Jan was a 4.5 on a 10 scale, how would the above answers change? It involves Excel Regression work
- If Jerry and Jan are a couple for 20 years, what is the total value of Jan's role as a wife?

Time Endowment Issues

Since, in all practicality, one cannot sustainably work 24 hours around the clock, I will make certain base assumptions regarding time endowment—or the base maximum hours a human can sustainably work and still be "human". First, I'll take the 24 hours and deduct 8 hours for sleep and sleep-related activity. At minimum eating one meal per day, bathing once per day and defecating once per day. This should take about 2 hours minimum. This allows for 14 discretionary hours. In addition, figures thrown about quote marriages that are lifelong (end with the death of one of the partners) are on average 40 to 45 years and marriages that end in divorce are an average of 8 to 10 years and dating relationships an average of 3 years.

Therefore, the maximum number of hours that has a contributing role for the purposes of this book is:

1. Lifelong partnership/marital relationship: 45 years x 365 days/year x 14 hours/day = **229,950**

2. Cohabitations/marital relationships that end due to breakup/divorce: 10 x 365 x 14 = **51,100**

3. Dating relationships: 3 x 365 x 14 = **15,330** (dating relationships).

The assumptions can be tweaked to meet the specific situation but the above calculations will be applied to assumptions of a male breadwinner with a cohabitating female child care giver. These are rough estimates.

The principle of social benefits

The purpose of ascertaining the occupational value is to find out whether or not a person at a certain SMV is paid the value of the benefits they bestow. Or more importantly to find out if that person is "worth it". If you hire a cook, and the cook provides $30 in value, you don't want to pay more or less than $30. If you pay less, the quality of the food is likely to decline because the cook can find better wages elsewhere. If you pay more, you could possibly find a cook of a higher caliber to cook the meals (but who knows, the current cook might step up to the task).

Social benefits, in the context of this work, are those items which are given to another for exchange of their personal occupational value. When a man buys a woman dinner, with the intention of dating her, he is investing his time and money for the future possibility of sex and companionship and anything else that may come from his relation to the woman. When a woman "gives it up" she is doing so because she has assessed that there is a benefit that the man she "gives it up to" can return to her—be it through safety and security, status, sexual gratification, etc.

The value of social benefits should be roughly equal to the occupational value, adjusted for time (the endowment value). For example, if a man and a woman are dating for 3 years and spend about 33% of that time together, we can measure the total occupational value as of 1 year's time. We do this by taking the hourly or annual rate (the annual rate of each occupation can also be found on the BLS site in the same fashion as I determined the hourly) and multiplying it by the time spent to get the value of that time. This is the endowment value. The rates, as shown above, are weighted by time spent.

Social Benefits = (Endowment Time) × (Annual Occupational Value)

Let's suppose that out of a year, 200 days are spent with someone who gives us value 10 hours a day at a rate of $10 in value per hour. The level of total social benefits is calculated as

Social Benefits = (20 days) × (10 hours/day) × ($10) = $20,000

What this means is that in a year, you should not spend more than $20,000 (in cash or value) on the person in question. The higher the SMV of the person, in theory, the higher the market value of the occupational services. Common sense tells us that a man taking a supermodel out on a date is likely to spend more money than if he took out an "ugly Betty". Therefore, from this assertion, we can draw a connection between SMV and Social Benefits. Here is a table that shows the relationship between scaled percentiles (SMV) and Average Hourly Occupational Value (Social Benefits):

TABLE 39. SMV and Average Hourly Occupational Value

SMV	Laundry and Dry-Cleaning Workers	Counselors, All Other	Cooks, Private Household	Childcare Workers	Maids and Housekeeping Cleaners	"Escort" Services (range from $80 to $250) [32b]	Average (Assuming Equal Time Spent)
1	10.29	13.87	16.01	10.47	10.34	50.00	18.50
2	10.56	15.84	17.72	10.88	10.72	82.45	24.70
3	11.24	17.91	18.65	11.73	11.61	134.14	34.21
4	11.92	19.98	19.58	12.58	12.50	185.83	43.73
5	12.5	22.02	21.09	13.26	13.12	237.50	53.25
6	13.28	24.12	21.44	14.28	14.28	289.21	62.77
7	13.96	26.19	22.37	15.13	15.17	340.90	72.29
8	14.64	28.26	23.30	15.98	16.06	392.59	81.81
9	15.88	30.94	23.95	17.71	17.81	500.00	101.05

This is a rough assumption of what would be the traditional duties of a stay-at-home wife and mother if they were outsourced, from left to right: cleaning clothes, providing emotional support (counseling), cooking, taking care of children, cleaning the house, and providing sex. If we assume that she spent an equal amount of time performing these duties (weighted 1/6 each), the average hourly rate profile appears as such:

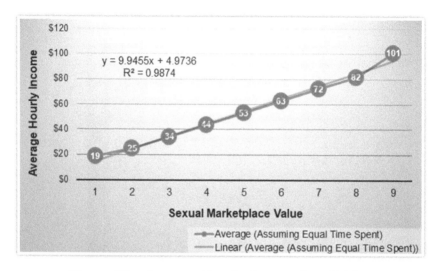

Figure 27.   Average Hourly Occupational Value

The trendline of best fit with respect to the different options Excel has is a linear one with the equation (rounded to two decimal places):

Hourly Social Benefits (SB) = (9.95)SMV + 4.97

KNOWLEDGE CHECK

- Based on the above equation, answer the following question:
- If Molly spends her time equally between each of the occupations above, and her SMV is a 6.25, how much should Hal expect to pay if he's taking her out to dinner for 2 hours?

Law of diminishing social benefits and the "Adjustable 7" Theory

In the last section, we determined an occupational value based on the roles fulfilled. That was a "bottoms-up" approach that rests on the notion that the financial value that a person adds is equivalent to the sum of the weighted average of the price one could pay on the open market for those services, weighted by the amount of time spent performing each service/role. After using actual data, we saw a positive linear relationship between SMV and SB. In this section, the theory that I am putting forth is that most natural phenomena regarding a person's satisfaction with something tends to increase at a decreasing rate.

In economics, the "law of diminishing returns" refers to a smaller proportional increase in incremental output as the amount of a single input is incrementally increased, holding all else constant. "Output" can be viewed as what one expects to get out of a process and, likewise, input is what was "put in" to get the output.

An example of this is diminishing utility. Utility is something that makes you happy/satisfies you. Suppose you were hungry and hadn't eaten all day—would one slice of pizza make you happy? Of course. A second slice might make you feel better and then a third or fourth slice of pizza would probably fill you. But if I give you 5, 6 or 7 slices, they would make you nauseous or vomit, or sick:

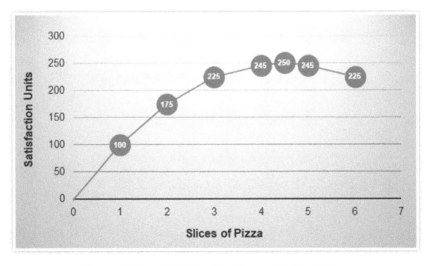

Figure 28. Satisfaction from Eating Pizza

The point here is that more is not necessarily better past a certain point. The higher you go past the optimum, the less satisfying it is to go higher. A simple summary of this behavior is to use a function like $\sqrt{x}$. If you let $y = f(\sqrt{x})$ and the x's are your inputs and the y's are your outputs, you'll have a situation where y increases at a slower rate incrementally than x:

TABLE 40. Diminishing Returns Example		
x (inputs)	y (output) = $f(\sqrt{x})$	$\dfrac{\Delta y}{\Delta x}$
0	0.00	n/a
1	1.00	1.00
2	1.41	0.41
3	1.73	0.32
4	2.00	0.27
5	2.24	0.24
6	2.45	0.21
7	2.65	0.20
8	2.83	0.18
9	3.00	0.17
10	3.16	0.16
11	3.32	0.16
12	3.46	0.14
13	3.61	0.15
14	3.74	0.13
15	3.87	0.13
16	4.00	0.13
17	4.12	0.12
18	4.24	0.12
19	4.36	0.12
20	4.47	0.11

As you can see, as x changes by 1, y changes by smaller and smaller increments. The last column is a profile of the incremental change of y with respect to x. As we increase the inputs, the incremental changes get smaller and smaller approaching 0. This is confirmation that putting more of x in will yield, in the "real world" no change in y at a certain point. Here is a graphic illustration of the above table:

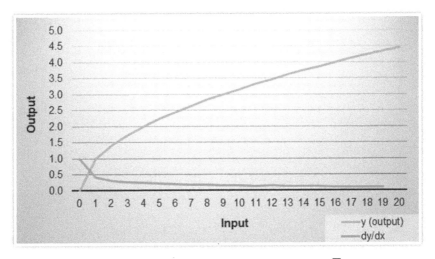

Figure 29. Decreasing Returns: $y = \sqrt{x}$

Translating from the dollar value of the occupation, the outputs (what a person gets as a result of SMV) are "social benefits" (SB) are things like perks, adulation, attention, free dinners out, favors performed for a woman in order to court her interest. This is because the man trades his occupational value to purchase social benefits for the female of his choosing. The inputs are the woman's SMV. Social benefits increase for a woman as her Sexual Marketplace Value increases, but it does so at a decreasing rate [appendix note 12]. Therefore we can make the following statement about Social Benefits (SB):

$$SB = f(SMV)$$

That Social Benefits depend upon Sexual Marketplace Value, if we apply the rationale $SB = \sqrt{SMV}$ we get the following:

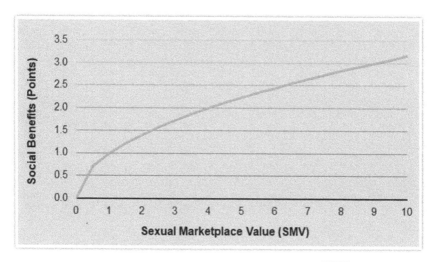

Figure 30.   Social Benefits Points: $\sqrt{SMV}$

In practical terms, it's helpful to view it in terms of dollars spent. Suppose that a man would spend $100 to go out on a date with a woman who has a minimum SMV of 0.5. This is his particular "adornment" profile:

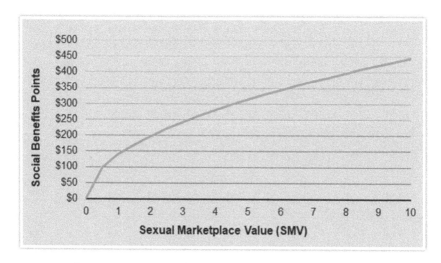

Figure 31.   Social Benefits Based on $100 Spent

Here is the table of values that would result from such a preference ("Social Benefits Points" and "Social Benefits Dollars" rounded to two digits):

TABLE 41. Social Benefits Points					
t	A	$B = \sqrt{A}$	$C = (B_{t+1} - B_t)/B_t$	$D = D_{t-1} \times (1 + C_t)$	$E = (D_t - D_{t-1})$
Index	SMV	Social Benefits Points	SB % Chg.	Social Benefits Dollars	Marginal Dollars Spent
1	0	0	n/a	n/a	n/a
2	0.5	0.71	n/a	100	n/a
3	1.0	1.00	41%	140.85	$40.85
4	1.5	1.22	22%	171.84	$30.99
5	2.0	1.41	16%	198.60	$26.76
6	2.5	1.58	12%	222.54	$23.94
7	3.0	1.73	9%	243.67	$21.13
8	3.5	1.87	8%	263.39	$19.72
9	4.0	2.00	7%	281.70	$18.31
10	4.5	2.12	6%	298.60	$16.90
11	5.0	2.24	6%	315.50	$16.90
12	5.5	2.35	5%	330.99	$15.49
13	6.0	2.45	4%	345.07	$14.08
14	6.5	2.55	4%	359.15	$14.08
15	7.0	2.65	4%	373.23	$14.08
16	7.5	2.74	3%	385.91	$12.68
17	8.0	2.83	3%	398.59	$12.68
18	8.5	2.92	3%	411.27	$12.68
19	9.0	3.00	3%	422.54	$11.27
20	9.5	3.08	3%	433.81	$11.27
21	10	3.16	3%	445.08	$11.27

As you can see from the above chart, the largest increases in social benefits come from incremental increases in lower SMVs (below 5) value. At higher SMVs, the percent change in SB tapers off gradually rendering SMVs from 6 to 7, 7.57.5 to 8.5, 9 to 10 having the same marginal incremental costs. This could be the case that the guy is indifferent between those SMVs and, in this case, if he's in the market for a 6, he might as well go for a 7. This is a good reason why guys should shoot as high as they can go and then work backwards, rather than accepting the "bare minimum".

As you can see that the amount being spent (SB) rises as you go up in SMV (you can expect to spend 3 times as much on a 9 than a 1), but the decreasing return to SB in marginal dollars spent decreases:

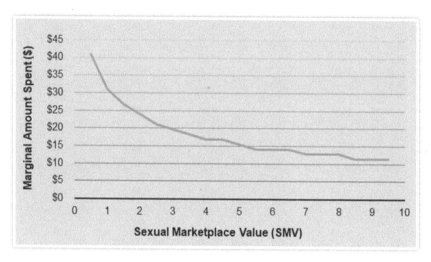

Figure 32. Marginal Dollars Spent

A mere point increase of 2 depending on where a man is on the SMV curve changes his life. If a man is dating a 5 to get a girl that's a 7 would require much more out of pocket resources marginally than a man who already has a 7 and wants to date a 9. Therefore, most men, rather than risk excessive costs, don't often "monkey branch". For all intents and purposes, there's no difference between a 9 and a 10. That's why higher status men, like George Clooney, Leonardo DiCaprio and their ilk, can change higher SMV women with little cost on their part—because they're already playing in the "big leagues". A swap from a 7 to 9 costs them little. Meanwhile, it costs a rank-and-file man much more to leave his precious Petunia for an Agnes—hence the "cheaper to keep her" sayings of the blue-collar man—lamenting in his social and sexual predicament.

KNOWLEDGE CHECK

- If Lustin' Larry would spend 175.00 to go out on a date with a woman whose SMV he considers to be 0.5, fill in the following table, then answer the questions:

TABLE 42.	Social Benefits Points				
t	A	$B = \sqrt{A}$	$C = (B_{t+1} - B_t)/B_t$	$D = D_{t-1} \times (1 + C_t)$	$E = (D_t - D_{t+1})$
Index	SMV	Social Benefits Points	SB % Chg.	Social Benefits Dollars	Marginal Dollars Spent
1	0.0	0	n/a	n/a	n/a
2	0.5	0.71	n/a	?	n/a
3	1.0	1.00	41%	?	?
4	1.5	1.22	22%	?	?
5	2.0	1.41	16%	?	?
6	2.5	1.58	12%	?	?
7	3.0	1.73	9%	?	?
8	3.5	1.87	8%	?	?
9	4.0	2.00	7%	?	?
10	4.5	2.12	6%	?	?
11	5.0	2.24	6%	?	?
12	5.5	2.35	5%	?	?
13	6.0	2.45	4%	?	?
14	6.5	2.55	4%	?	?
15	7.0	2.65	4%	?	?
16	7.5	2.74	3%	?	?
17	8.0	2.83	3%	?	?
18	8.5	2.92	3%	?	?
19	9.0	3.00	3%	?	?
20	9.5	3.08	3%	?	?
21	10.0	3.16	3%	?	?

- How much would Lustin' Larry spend on a date with women he considered to be a 4.5, 6.5 and 8?
- How much would Lustin' Larry spend on a date with women he considered to be a 5, 7 and 8.5?
- If Larry's current girlfried is a 6, and he had the opportunity to go out with at woman who is a 7, how much extra would a date cost him?
- If Larry's current girlfriend is a 7 and he has an opportunity to go out with at woman he considers an 8, how much extra would it cost him?
- Based on the previous answers (Larry trading up from a 6 to a 7 or a 7 to an 8), in which situation is it riskier to trade up ("cheaper to keep her")?

SUPPLY AND DEMAND

CHAPTER SUMMARY

○ In accordance with diminishing Social Benefits (SB) the "Adjustable 7 Theory" states that there is more demand for women who are 7's on the Max/Min scale than other SMVs. Since the demand for men mimicks demand for luxury goods, the "Inflection 7 Theory" states that demand for men increases faster as he approaches 7, but then begins to diminish, however always increasing.

○ Sexual supply for men and women are similar—population wise, most people are average, with less amounts of very high or very low value people.

○ Since there are multiple equilibria, it is never static, and thus "settling down" is more a concept than reality.

CHAPTER 9

SUPPLY AND
DEMAND

THE **ADJUSTABLE 7 THEORY**" is the theory that the optimal sexual marketplace value for a woman is 7 to maximize her Social Benefits. This is because of social ideas of what is physically attractive have already been achieved at it's baseline (i.e. the canvas of bone structure, facial features, etc.). With a little makeup, hairdo, or sexy outfit, a woman who is "7" in her pajamas and collegiate sweater can easily appear as a value higher than 7 when fitted. Getting a 7, in an essence, becomes the "goldilocks" zone. Also, men weary on competition can fly low with a 7. She's cute, definitely a "head turner" but doesn't attract so much attention that he'll get tested in front of her. Based on this theory, here is my proposed demand structure for women in the Sexual Marketplace:

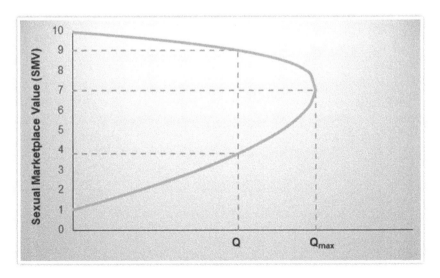

Figure 33. Female Demand Curve

The logic for this backwards bending demand curve originates in the decreasing return to social benefits. As you can see, the quantity demanded (Q) for women with an SMV of 9 and 3.8 are about the same.

When SMV changes, the quantity of that type of female demanded changes. This causes movement along the female demand curve. For example, at points at A1 and A2, demand for women of SMVs lower than 9 and higher than 3.8 increase as they approach point B, and Q approaches Qmax:

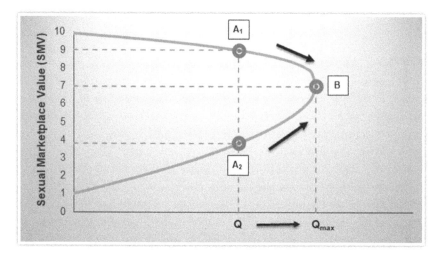

Figure 34. Female Demand Curve (Comparison)

Then there are items that cause overall demand to increase or decrease quantity demanded at every level. This kind of item is outside of SMV changes that cause the demand to shift at all levels. For example, increases in public opinion of women, such as media messages promoting women, or an increase in the male population can cause demand to increase at all levels. We'd end up with something like this:

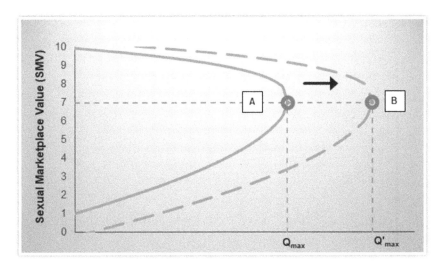

Figure 35. Demand Curve Shift: Q'_{max}

As A approaches B, Q_{max} approaches Q'_{max}, and at every SMV, there is more demand.

Inflection 7 Theory

Analogous to the "Adjustable 7" Theory for women is the Inflection 7 theory for men. It's based on the premise that when a man's SMV increases his quantity demanded increases at an increasing rate; but after an SMV of 7, this demand increases at a slower rate than SMV values below 7.

This premise is counterintuitive to Alfred Marshal's simple supply and demand model. In the simple model, the higher (lower) the price, the lower (higher) the quantity demanded. Demand for men has a quality akin to demand for luxury or "Veblen" goods—where past a certain breakpoint price, the higher the price, the higher the demand.

Veblen goods (Inflection 7)

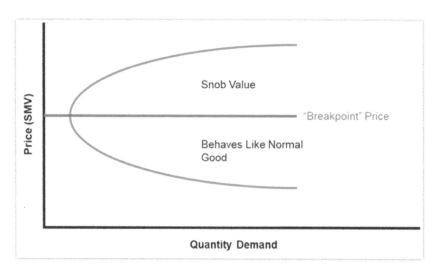

Figure 36.   Veblen Good Demand Curve

The breakpoint price is illustrated by the blue line above. Below the blue line, the lower the price the higher the quantity demanded. This can be viewed as the desire for "orbiters", who will undervalue themselves and provide value without desired value in return for hopes of a future payoff. The orbiters supply "provider value", or the value that comes with a man who is willing to provide tangible goods and services like money, menial services (fix her car, computer, do plumbing work etc.), and referrals (status may be high enough to refer, but because she's not physically attracted to him).

Above the breakpoint price are more desired men who provide "genetic value" and/or provider value. They are attractive enough for the women to consider them for mating, and if they provide more value, then that takes them up to a higher level. Contriving the inflection 7 demand curve, which has two upward slopes:

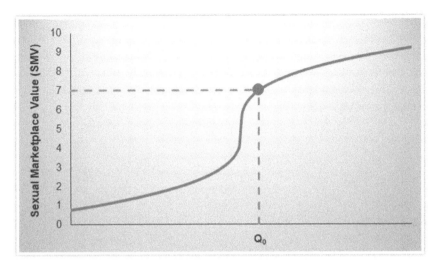

Figure 37. Male Demand Curve

The first upward slope increases at an increasing rate for SMV values below 7—the higher the SMV, the more he is demanded. At just below 7, a woman can receive the maximum value (minimized "asshole" qualities). But at 7 and above, the hypergamy has to tone down, because there are not that many more men available with SMVs in the upper echelons. Because of this, we expect the "Chad(s)" and "Stacy(s)" of the world, who are 9s and 10s to be dating each other.

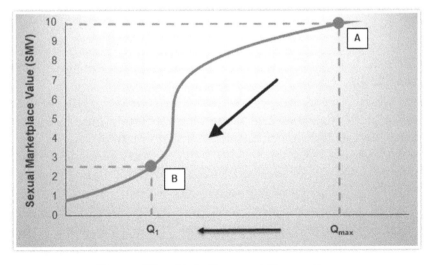

Figure 38. Male Demand Curve: Q_{max}

As SMV decreases, quantity of men demanded decreases and causes movement along the curve, as point A goes to point B, Q_{max} goes to Q_1. If there is a situation outside of SMV that influences demand, just like in the demand for women, the demand curve for men will shift. For example, take a negative media or social ad that demonizes men. It will have this effect:

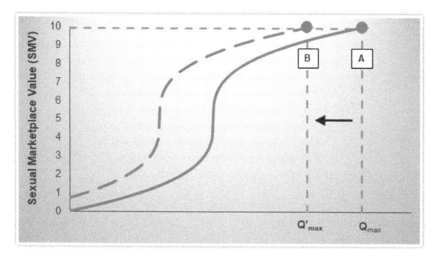

Figure 39.   Male Demand Curve: Q'_{max}

A negative media promotion causes the overall level of demand for men to decrease causing point A to shift back to point B and Q_{max} to Q'_{max}.

The Chad(s) have no biological qualms about "dipping down" to bang a 5 or 6 on a drunk night out. This answers the age-old adage: "Why do men cheat?" Backed by the Coolidge Effect, and in the spirit of Samuel L. Jackson: "Muthafucka, because they can!"

When Chad (8) bangs Jane (5) it may give her a false sense of inflation because men and women have different base biological drives. By her biological standards, the man who is an 8 fulfills most of her criteria and is a catch—so if he shows interest towards her, she internally bids her own price up. When all actuality he has no intention of fulfilling her biological imperative, only his own.

This experience, from the woman's point of view, is colloquially called—with a nod to stock trading— "pump and dump". This experience this may cause them to view the higher value men as assholes and apply it to all men and hence "all men are dogs".

Supply of the sexes

The Sexual Supply curve applies to both males and females because the population distribution of men and women at various SMVs are assumed to be normal. That is, if you go to any location with 30 people or more, you are likely to see that most people are average (have an SMV of 5 on a 10 scale), and on either extreme, gorgeous people (like having an 8 on a 10 scale), and ugly people (having a 2 on a 10 scale) occupying relatively smaller chunk of the distribution (in the "tails"). Since SMV is on the "Y" axis, it is analogous to an "inverted" Probability Density Function (PDF):

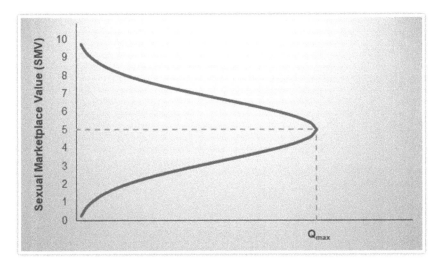

Figure 40. Sexual Supply Curve

Since the quantity of supply in any given market is unknown, we will either make assumptions about the number of people in the market arbitrarily, or will use ordinal subscripts (i.e. $Q_2 > Q_1$) to suggest the magnitude of quantity demanded. This distribution of SMV is what is available to people in the Sexual Marketplace. Movement along the supply curve is SMV specific, and we will primarily be dealing with a static Sexual Supply Curve in this volume, however when we deal with location sexual economics in later volumes, we'll discuss the shifting of this curve.

Sexual Market Dynamic Equilibria

The interaction between the demand and supply for females and males constitute how "dynamic" the market is. For example, consider the female demand curve and its interaction with the Sexual Supply Curve:

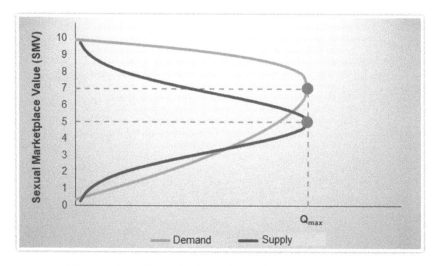

Figure 41. Female Supply and Demand Curves

As you can see the maximum quantity of females demanded at SMV =7, is not equal the maximum quantity supplied at SMV =5. This keeps the market "dynamic" in the sense that it's never at "rest".

Equilibrium in the Sexual Marketplace

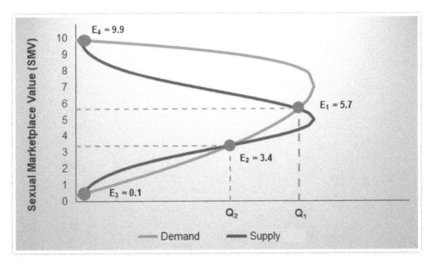

Figure 42. Female Supply and Demand Curve Equilibria

There are four equilibria in the market for females. Two at the "tails" of the Sexual Supply Curve (SSC) and two in the "middle". The equilibria at the tails are self-explanatory: at very high and low SMVs, the quantity demanded and supplied are few. Women at the super high-end are "too much trouble" and women at the super low-end are "not sought after" (he ain't checkin' for ya' sis).

In the middle, there are some interesting things going on. As we re-enter the practical discussion of where most people are. At about 5.7 and 3.4 the market supply and demand are met. Therefore, it may be the case that more long-term pairings happen at these two points. Keep in mind that the resulting value of the man will be reflected in the market's hypergamy factor (we know his value will be higher than 5.7 and 3.4, but we don't know how much higher).

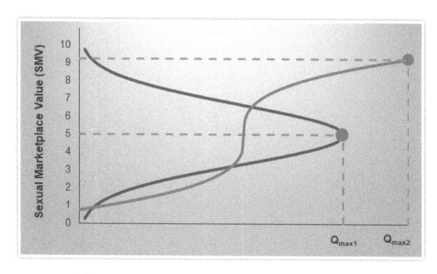

Figure 43. Male Supply and Demand Curves

As in the market for females, the maximum quantities supplied and demanded, represented by Qmax1 and Qmax2 respectively, don't intersect—but here to a greater degree. There will always be a higher demand than supply for men SMV = 8 and above.

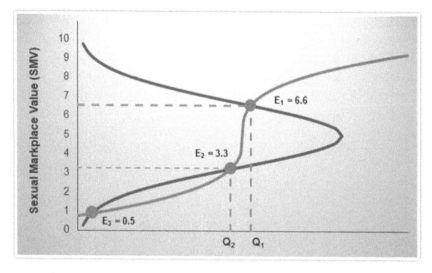

Figure 44. Male Supply and Demand Curve Equilibria

The male demand curve and supply curve share three equilibria. One in the lower tail of the supply curve, and two at quantities Q1 and Q2. This shows the lower equilibrium at SMV = 3.3 at Q2 and SMV = 6.6 at Q1 almost seem to correspond to the lower/higher equilibriums of females at 3.4 and 5.7 respectively. According to the hypergamy theory, we would expect levels of hypergamy to decrease (hypergamy factor approaches 1) at lower values of SMV, making the men and women rather equally "yoked". The male SMV of 6.6 is almost 1 SMV point higher than the equilibrium female SMV of 5.7. At 5.7, there is expected to be hypergamy, and the hypergamy rises (hypergamy factor approaches 0) as SMV approaches 7. Therefore, it may also be the case that Men at a level of 6.6 and women at a level of 5.7 might optimally pair off.

CHAPTER SUMMARY

○ As time marches forward, all humans tend to depreciate. Thus, the way humans live their life in the way of vices affects how fast the depreciation will occur. The more vices a person has, the higher their "Effective Age" and the lower their SMV.

○ Using what is known about a person's vices, their SMV can be projected into the future, and the effects of vices compound over time, eroding SMV.

○ By comparing our forecast of a person's future value versus a market appraisal, a determination can be made whether their value has declined too fast. If this is the case, an exit strategy that takes into consideration the costs of exiting can be employed.

CHAPTER 10

EXIT
STRATEGIES

Depreciation and Value Erosion

Depreciation is an economic/financial term that parallels the scientific concepts of entropy, atrophy and oxidation as it pertains to breakdown of systems over time. With entropy, galaxies break apart. With atrophy, the muscles start to waste away and bones become brittle. With oxidation, that favorite metal thingamajig begins to rust.

Like the rest of nature, humans tend to break down over time and it's generally accepted that as we age, gravity begins to make things that were once firm, loose. Tits begin to sag, and nut sacs begin to droop—jowls begin to emerge, and wrinkles and frown lines begin to form. Men become women and women become men. In men, hair loss, testosterone and lean muscle decline, the once deep voices become shrilly. In women, estrogen declines and once soft voices become raspier and deep—not as much hair loss as men but hair where there once was no hair—especially on the face—emerge. In both men and women, reaction times get slower, balance trickier, and weight gain, partially a result of slowing metabolisms becoming more commonplace.

Whole industries have emerged to "combat" the phenomena of aging which, in reality, is more a testament to salvaging SMV. The fitness industry and healthcare industry (alongside cosmetic healthcare) with the different diets, fasts, and medical procedures to make firm what is loose and to lift what is falling are gaining traction. I would argue that the price juxtaposed with the financial value of these procedures can be determined by who the procedure is meant to attract.

A reasonable person can understand the general decline age brings. However, there are some things that can cause a more rapid decline by their use (i.e., drugs, alcohol, smoking, sugary and refined processed foods etc.) and/or cause a more rapid decline by neglect (i.e., not getting enough sleep, not taking proper dental care, hair care, ignoring a structural problem (like a shoulder impingement) until it balloons, etc.). The reasonable person needs to be aware of signs of excessive decline so that he/she can make an informed decision on how to respond if the declines in physical value along with other factors (money stock, character traits outside of looks etc.) result in a net decline that may get worse with time.

In the next volume, I will address age-based sexual marketplaces but for now we will discuss the common sense how to "forecast" SMV to get a good E[SMV] and, based on market factors (usually lambda), how to determine if it is still worth sticking with that person.

For example, at the age of 23, Smokin' Hot Sally was getting trashed on the weekends with cocaine and alcohol where Home Body Holly spent her Saturday nights getting prepared for bible study on Sunday. Hal the Hunter, if looking for a good time will pick Sally but, if looking for a woman to raise his children, will choose Holly. Hal knows down the road if Sally gets a medical condition as a result of her choices it will adversely affect him and/or he could be held liable. When it comes to a long-term choice, Hal would likely choose Holly.

Wired Willy likes to spend his Thursday nights sniffing methamphetamine and watching *bukkake* online, while Studious Stephen is such a book worm that he has a different prescription in each eye. Maidenly Madison, when looking for an exciting night, may take Wired Willy but knows that if she gets pregnant, it's likely that Studious Steve will take care of the monsters she is going to squirt out.

Time Decay and the Natural Depreciation Rate (NDR)

There are many ways to express the decay of something over time. The decay of radioactive isotopes often takes on an exponential decay pattern, decaying rapidly initially and then slower and slower as time goes on:

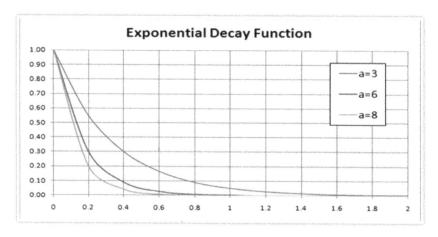

Figure 45. Exponential Decay

Exponential "decay" of a human can be modeled after an accident where someone is debilitated rather rapidly and then slowly deteriorates. The Christopher Reeve's horse accident that left him a quadriplegic that lead to other deleterious problems up until his death is an example of this.

If the pattern is concave, it slowly decays initially and then rapidly declines towards the end of its "life" like so:

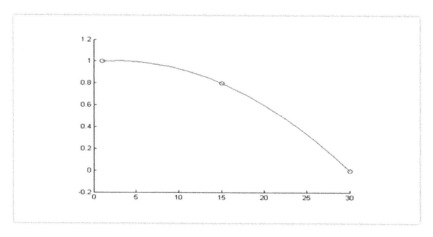

Figure 46. Concave Decay

The concave pattern would be a choice pattern to mimic someone who "ages off of a cliff" due to substance abuse—maybe aging slowly and normally initially until the habits wreak havoc on the organ systems and things take a downward turn for the worse.

But, for the purposes of this book, we'll use a linear (straight line) pattern like this:

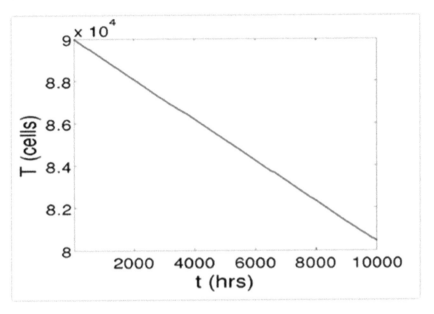

Figure 47. Straight-Line Decay

This keeps the math simple and straightforward. For our analysis, the linear pattern will be a straight-lined pattern consistent with normal wear and tear and factors that "speed up" depreciation will simply result in a steeper slope and will be averaged across the entire lifespan.

The formula by which this depreciation rate will be applied to an SMV to determine its future level is:

$$\delta_t = \textit{effective avg depreciation rate} =$$

$$= \frac{EAge_t}{Age_t} * \left(\frac{1}{LE}\right) | \textit{ where } EAge_t \geq Age_t$$

Where

LE = Life Expectancy (in years)

Age_t = Age at time t

$EAge_t$ = Effective Age at time t

NDR = Natural Annual Depreciation Rate = 1/LE

The NDR represents the "base level" of depreciation, which is natural aging and decline without any extraneous circumstances. The Effective Age is the age calculated that is the adjusted biological age due to having vices that shorten their lifespan.

For example, suppose a scientific study says that smoking a pack of cigarettes per day for 10 years or more will take an average of 10% off of a person's lifespan and Smokehouse Sam has smoked a pack per day since he was 23 and is now 33 years old. What is his effective age?

First the formula for effective age is

$$\text{Effective Age}_t \ (EAge_t) = Age_t \ (1 + v_i)$$

Where

$$v_i = \% \text{ of lifespan decreased by vice (life style factor}_i)$$

Therefore, Sam's Effective Age is

$$EAge_t = 33(1 + 10\%) = 36.3$$

Sam, because he is a smoker is effectively 36.3 years old.

If his life expectancy is 80 years, what it is his average annual depreciation rate?

$$\delta_t = effective \ avg \ depreciation \ rate = \frac{EAge_t}{Age_t} * \frac{1}{LE} =$$

$$= \frac{36.3}{33} * \frac{1}{80} = 0.01375 \ or \ 1.38\%$$

Sam depreciates at an average rate of 1.38% per year.

The Effective Age is the key to calculating depreciation, because it is where the effects of lifestyle factors (vices) are contained. Imagine Sam had three vices: smoking, drinking, and cocaine use, and they each decrease the total lifespan by 10%,12% and 14% respectively. What is Sam's new Effective age?

The effect of multiple vices/Lifestyle Factors on Effective Age are as such:

$$EAge_t = Age_t \prod_{t=1}^{n} LSF_t$$

$$where\ LSF_t = (1 + v_t)$$

$$and = v_t = |v_t|$$

Therefore,

$$(EAge_t) = Age_t\ (1 + v_1) \times (1 + v_2) \times (1 + v_3) =$$

$$= 33(1.10) \times (1.12) \times (1.14) = 46.35$$

Sam's effective age is 46.35. The gamma, δ_t is geometric, in the sense that Sam "compounds" his problems by having a negative lifestyle factor year after year.

If he drinks or does drugs one year, his health does not "reset" (not considering healing regimens) and start again fresh the next year. Each year is affected by the year before it, hence the compounding effect of the lifestyle factors.

KNOWLEDGE CHECK

- Mary likes Marlboro Reds and Jack Daniels on summer nights. She is 35 years old. The health ministry says that life expectancies are decreased by 11% and 13% for smoking and drinking, respectively. Also, the female life expectancy is 82 years.
- What is Mary's depreciation rate if she had no vices (her NDR)? Round to three decimal places and express as a percent. What is Mary's Effective Age?

Forecasting SMV

Earlier in the book, we discussed the concept of the "Expected Sexual Marketplace Value" or E[SMV] which was the weighted average SMV based on various attributes in the form of:

$$E[SMV_j] = \sum_{i}^{n} w_i * i$$

This $E[SMV]$ was estimating SMV for a specific *point in time* based on attributes i and their relative importance to the observer of w. Since $E[SMV]$ is an estimation and a best guess of SMV, it becomes the mean value, μ.

This concept can also be applied to observations of lifestyle habits and, subsequently, SMV *over time*. Yielding the following condition:

$$E[SMV_{t+k}] = f(SMV_t)$$

Which means that SMV in a future period is a function of the SMV in the current period. Using the effective annual depreciation rate, we get:

$$E[SMV_{t+k}] = SMV_t(1 - \delta_t)$$

This means that of the person we are observing, we start with a known or estimated SMV (for now we'll assume that it's known and based on market data) and use the gamma to forecast the SMV into the next time period. A future time period can be forecasted starting with the new expected value of SMV as such:

$$E[SMV_{t+(k+1)}] = E[SMV_{t+k}] \times (1 - \delta_{t+k})$$

Notice that there are two $E[SMV]$ notations. This is because we're assuming that we're doing our forecasting on subsequent periods from time t (our current time). In reality, people get into relationships based on what they know (the bad habits and vices are expected remain the same— Sam only smokes in addition to his natural rate of decline) however, gamma can change. If, in the first period, Sam's only vice is smoking and in the second period $(t + k)$ he decides to add another vice, then

$$\delta_t \neq \delta_{t+k}$$

And we'd face a **moral hazard**, which we will discuss later. However, the math would be the continuous compounding of these negative behaviors which would take on the form of:

$$E[SMV_{t+(k+1)}] = (SMV_t)*(1-\delta_t)*(1-\delta_{t+2})*(1-\delta_{t+3})* \ldots (1-\delta_{t+k})$$

However, in a person's choice to date Sam, it is reasonable to assume that his current actions will continue for some time and, thus, the assumption gamma will not change:

$$\delta_t = \delta_{t+k} = \delta$$

That implies that

$$E[SMV_{t+k}] = (SMV_t)^* (1 - \delta)^k$$

We can estimate the SMV in any future time period using the initial SMV, gamma, and the number of time periods that pass as represented by k—which may or may not be terminal. It is when k = n that we have forecasted Sam's SMV through the end of the relationship.

Based on Statistical Theory, when N, or the number of observations, needs to be at least 30 to have statistical significance. For practicality's sake, we can assume SMV to be observed daily (social interactions and events and/or day to day health, weight, age, etc.) and, therefore, at a minimum 30 days or 1 month or 1/12 of a year. The assumption here is that a coupling must have at least 30 days together before an inference about SMV must be made. As a result, we are expecting δ_t to be a monthly figure in this example rather than an annual one in the discussion of δ_t and Effective Age. Assume the following:

TABLE 43. Smoking and Life Expectancy

Smoking can reduce life expectancy by about 18 years on a 30-year-old person (medical news today article)		
A	Life Expectancy (LE)	83
B = (1/A)	Natural Depreciation Rate (NDR)	0.012
C = (B/12)	**Monthly NDR**	**0.001**
D	Age	30
E	Decrease in total life expectancy (18 years reduced/30 years age) summarized from article	60%
F = (D x E)	Additions to Age as a result of smoking	18
G = (D+F)	Effective Age	48
H = [(G/D) x B]	Effective Annual Depreciation Rate (Gamma)	0.019
I = (H/12)	**Monthly Gamma**	**0.0016**
J	**Market Lambda Assumption**	**0.8**

The table above is self-explanatory based on our theory of depreciation. Instead of the compounding (breaking the 60% down into monthly amounts divided by 18 and based on the 18th root) I simply add F to the Age (D) to get Effective Age. The calculations and the other full tables can be found in the appendix. Based on this, we'll apply this to our theoretical story of "Smokehouse Sam".

If Smokehouse Sam is a 7 today through the first month, in a three-year relationship and is valued based on estimations of monthly NDR and gamma above, we have the following:

TABLE 44. SMV and Smoking (Truncated)			
A	**B**	**C**	**D**
t (months)	Sam's SMV (NDR, no smoking)	Sam's SMV (1 pack per day Gamma)	Sam's SMV (1 pack per day, quits at end of 17th month)
1	7.00	7.00	7.00
6	6.96	6.94	6.94
9	6.94	6.91	6.91
12	6.92	6.88	6.88
15	6.90	6.84	6.84
18	6.88	6.81	6.82
21	6.86	6.78	6.79
24	6.84	6.75	6.77
27	6.82	6.71	6.75
30	6.80	6.68	6.73
33	6.78	6.65	6.71
36	6.76	6.62	6.69

Per his one-pack-per-day habit, Sam started as a 7 but declined to a 6.62 at the end of 36 months or 3 years [appendix note 13]. What the person dating or in a relationship with Sam has to decide is whether his SMV as a result of his bad habits still holds weight in the market. To test this, Sam would have to go into the open market to get an assessment. Using the actual value models and a group/market opinion of Sam, we can assess his current valuation as opposed his habits. Here's a hypothetical (opinion of 5 women in a bar):

TABLE 45. Observed SMV

Woman (observer)	A SMV of Observer	B = (A/Σ (A1:A5)) Opinion Weight	C Woman's Opinion of Guy	D = C x B Rating Shares
1	8	26%	6.5	1.7
2	7	23%	6.7	1.5
3	6	19%	7.2	1.4
4	6	19%	7.2	1.4
5	4	13%	8	1.0
SMV (Σ(D1:D5))	7.0			

Based on the above assessment, to people in the open market, Sam's smoking habit didn't erode his as much as the estimates, as he came in at a premium (7-6.62) of 0.38 SMV points. There are many other "practical" items to consider. As the old saying goes "you never know someone until you live with them". In essence, the forecast may be more accurate since the women at the bar don't have information on Sam's habit (more on information further down in the text). It would be safe to say his true value would lie between the estimate and the assessment.

The other columns above contain information regarding Sam if he never smoked (B), if he smokes one pack per day (C), and if he smokes one pack per day but then quits smoking at the 18th month (D). The table is abridged to show extended time periods and the effect of these habits/non-habits:

TABLE 46. SMV and Smoking Habit (Truncated)

A t (months)	B Sam's SMV (NDR, no smoking)	C Sam's SMV (1 pack per day Gamma)	D Sam's SMV (1 pack per day, quits at end of 17th month)
1	7.00	7.00	7.00
12	6.92	6.88	6.88
18	6.88	6.81	6.82
24	6.84	6.75	6.77
36	6.76	6.62	6.69
54	6.64	6.43	6.57
72	6.52	6.24	6.46

If Sam chooses to quit smoking, the effect is captured in column D. As a result, all of Sam's SMVs decline at the monthly NDR instead of the monthly gamma.

Determining when your Significant Other's (S/O) SMV has declined too rapidly

There's an anonymous saying that women get married hoping that a man will change and men get married hoping that a woman won't change. The unifying truth in those statements is that the man who is willing to change a little and the woman who is willing to stay the same a little can meet in the middle—and, if they do, then they may less likely bid each other adieu.

When men and women get married/enter Long Term Relationships (LTR), they are banking that their relative SMVs stay the same and weather the "inflation" of the market. The assumption is that when a woman gets in an LTR, the "change" she expects is that her S/O's resources incrementally increase (provider model) and his physicality to decline relatively slower than the rest of the people in their age cohort (protector). When a man gets in an LTR, hoping that the woman won't change, it's the same principle—he's hoping that her SMV declines incrementally slower than their cohort (especially for physicality's sake).

The act of a person declining slower than the rest of their age cohort is like being in two separate moving vehicles both going in reverse—with one moving faster than the other. While an outside observer can see that the cars are both moving backwards, the people in either car will get the impression that one is moving forward faster than the other (the car that moves backwards slower appears to move forward faster by the person in the other car).

Some people can win the dating game by attrition. I recall a story whereby a man had an interest in a childless female who did not return his interest. He reported approximately 7 to 8 years later she was 50lbs heavier and with one kid and a divorce. She had been stressed out due to the conditions of the child and put through the emotional ringer, sleeping roughly 4 to 5 hours per night. He, on the other hand, had gotten leaner and started taking better care of himself. He also obtained a financial windfall. When he crossed her path 7 to 8 years later, the woman told the man that she had "widened her horizons" and was interested in dating him.

If the man in my previous example is still interested in dating the woman who turned him down 7 to 8 years prior, he has won by attrition. All the man would have to do is preserve his value—and slow its decline relative to hers. Her physicality declined at a faster rate because of all of the physical and emotional stressors she endured. It is a time-based scenario as opposed to location-based scenarios (that would have a male/female go from a less favorable market to a more favorable one) which address place, but not time.

Entropy is the concept that systems tend to break down over time and, in the universe, entropy is the prime example of why galaxies and stars change and break down. Humans are also subject to the breakdown/wear and tear of physical and molecular systems in the body. This is one reason that couples immortalize themselves in wedding pictures—knowing that one day, if they're lucky, they'll look back at themselves when they were hot—while sitting in a rocking chair.

As a result, when interested in a LTR, we instinctively pick a partner at a point in time whose composition and habits will result in a less deteriorated person at a later point in time. For example, if you're 60 years old and you look and have the health of a 50-year-old, then for all intents and purposes (I love that phrase—because it sounds like "intensive purposes" when said fast), you are 50 and if all of your peers are 60, your SMV is higher in that cohort.

Therefore, the gamma assists us in the self-serving goal to predict where our S/O is headed to ascertain whether their SMV is significantly less than the average person we could obtain in the open market.

To the first point, take the example of Smokehouse Sam. He's in a relationship with Generous Jenny and they're in the 20th month of a 36th month relationship, and his SMV is confirmed by the market, so his SMV = ESMV = 7.00. At this particular time, the market lambda is 0.8. Jenny has the following relative SMV:

$$\lambda SMV_M = SMV_F$$

$$0.8(7.00) = SMV_F = 5.60$$

Jenny's SMV, relative to Sam's is 5.60. She's been off of the market and only sees herself in terms of her relationship. Now let's say she goes out with the girls for the evening and four guys hit on her and we have the following data about them:

TABLE 47. Market Value of Female Based on Interested Men

A	B	C	D = (B x C)	E = B/ (Σ (B1:B4))	F = (D x E)
Guy	SMV	Market Lambda	Translated Female SMV	Weight	Shares
1	8.5	0.8	6.8	0.27	1.84
2	8.0	0.8	6.4	0.26	1.66
3	7.5	0.8	6.0	0.24	1.44
4	7.0	0.8	5.6	0.23	1.29

Woman's SMV (Σ (B1:B4))	6.23

Now Jenny has a dilemma—because the market says she's a 6.23, but *relative* to Sam, she's a 5.60. The hanging question for Jenny becomes: "Does the value differential between who she's with and who she can be with in the market warrant a termination of relationship?"

Most of the guys who hit on her are fairly higher in SMV than Sam. Jenny might consider various time-related factors like her age because the longer she waits the faster she'll decline. Or cost factors, such as "How will my Social Benefits change if I terminate this relationship?" For now, let's look at the facts. Here's her relative increase in valuation in percentage terms:

$$\frac{New\ Value - Old\ Value}{Old\ Value} = \%Chg\ In\ Value$$

$$\frac{6.23 - 5.60}{5.60} = \%Chg\ In\ Value = 11.25\%$$

Jenny's "stock" increased by 11.25%, so we have to determine whether or not that is a significant amount. One way to do this is to back out what Sam's value would be if Jenny was able to derive the same value from him:

$$\frac{Jenny's\ New\ Market\ Value}{\lambda} = Sam's\ lambda\ equivalent\ value$$

$$\frac{6.23}{0.8} = 7.79$$

In order for Jenny to derive a 6.23 from Sam, he would have to be a 7.79. Seeing as this only a 36-month arrangement, Jenny may likely break up with Sam. Likewise, if Sam were to go into the market and get a valuation of higher than 7.00, then it's possible that Sam may break up with Jenny. For them to stay together after Jenny's re-evaluation, it would be good if Sam could get marked again to market and get a valuation of 7.79 or higher. While it's not likely to occur in the market where Sam met Jenny, it is possible in other markets where Sam is viewed as a higher SMV.

Picking an Exit Strategy

At times, no, often, especially in the post-modern era, relationships find their end when either person gets "fed up" with the other or marriages split on "irreconcilable differences". Another term for a marriage that splits with an irreconcilable difference is called a "no fault" divorce. Where nobody is to blame per se—the relationship "ran its course" and no longer serves one of the participants.

While there is data that can show that the rise in women's incomes correlate with the rise in divorce, I will not address it here—but common sense tells us that when a man is a breadwinner in a marriage, a woman has more of an incentive to stay because she's economically dependent on that man for survival. These were the times of old—the "greatest generation" era and so on—the *Leave It to Beaver* folks.

When women began earning alongside and even in competition with men, it effectively decreased their relative importance to Money and/or Status (w_M/w_S) and increased the level of Money (M) and/or Status (S) that a man has to earn to be attractive previously through the total effect of Money and/or Status ($w_M \times M$ and/or $w_S \times S$). Thus, women with higher ambitions would choose an M with a proportionally higher score on the decile scale than their own. The growth rates of women's income versus men's will be addressed in the *"Racial Hypergamy"* section.

The end result is a "markdown" of those men who have in the past had a strong "M", even if other elements were lacking and if they were a "one-trick pony", only being a viable mate on making a moderate income, they would be phased out. The M being lower than expected can be one way a woman in a marriage could become "irritated" and want out. Look no further than statistics that 70% of divorces are initiated by women [35] and that people making less than $25K annually can decrease their divorce risk by 30% by earning more than $50K per year [36].

In this post-modern era—people are being "marked to market" on a constant basis. Items like social media sites, granting likes and comments, dating sites when somebody swipes right or blows virtual kisses and so-on are a reminder of the approval/disapproval of a given market almost instantaneously.

In the past, communication was not as instantaneous and people often had to travel miles or go into town to meet someone who wasn't their cousin. Maybe go to the local square dance—a good old fashioned "hoedown" (I love that phrase).

In a previous chapter, the link was drawn between ranking on a Min/Max scale and a dollar figure based on how much it would cost to obtain value of the benefits one brings to the relationship in the open market and how much time the person would be doing the various "duties" or elements in the relationship to establish the total dollar figure. The maximum time of which is the time "endowment" (people can't spend 100% of their time practically doing things—they need to eat, sleep, shit, etc.).

Here's a rough example of what Jenny's valuation would look like with respect to Sam's (assuming his decline with vice of smoking included). Since "like attracts like" or a person is a reflection of the person they are intimate with, therefore, it is a safe assumption to say that, at any given time, one partner's value is a function of the other partner's value. Hence, lambda. We'll label Jenny as "Female B" and, as previously done, Jenny's lambda will be a 0.8 and translating Jenny's values based on Sam smoking one pack per day we have:

TABLE 48. Jenny's Endowment Value

t (month)	Laundry	Counselors	Cooks	Childcare Workers	Maids	Escort Services	Average (Assuming Equal Time Spent)	Monthly Endowment Value
1	13.01	23.29	21.07	13.94	13.92	268.53	58.96	$8,844
12	12.94	23.09	20.98	13.86	13.84	263.37	58.01	$8,701
18	12.91	22.98	20.93	13.81	13.79	260.78	57.53	$8,629
24	12.87	22.88	20.88	13.77	13.75	258.20	57.06	$8,558
36	12.80	22.65	20.78	13.68	13.65	252.51	56.01	$8,401
54	12.70	22.34	20.64	13.55	13.51	244.76	54.58	$8,187
72	12.60	22.05	20.51	13.43	13.39	237.52	53.25	$7,987

TABLE 49. Jenny's SMV

t (months)	Jenny (Female B)'s SMV
1	5.60
12	5.50
18	5.45
24	5.40
36	5.29
54	5.14
72	5.00

Remember the hourly value is determined by SMV and that the SMV is then entered into the trendline estimation between the different percentiles and hourly pay levels. To summarize, from the end of the first month to the end of the 36th month, Jenny loses about $443 in value:

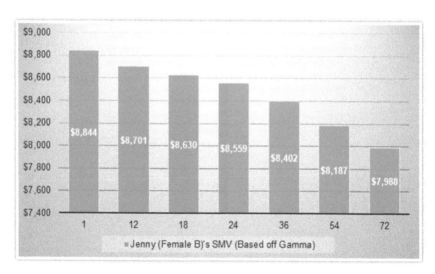

Figure 48. Endowment Value in Given Month

For Sam, one hanging question is, "Can I do better?" Or, in other words, could Sam choose someone else that loses less than $443 in endowment value over three years? "Better" would be someone who declines at a slower rate than Jenny. All else equal, Sam generally would not be expected to get another woman who provides better value than Jenny, but not for the reason you might expect. However, we see that if he changes his actions or his market, his SMV can improve (decline slower) and, thus, the caliber of women he attracts will improve.

Recalling Table 44, we have Sam's profile in three scenarios: One where he doesn't smoke, smokes one pack per day, and quitting at the beginning of the 18th month.

TABLE 50. SMV and Smoking			
A	B	C	D
t (months)	Sam's SMV (NDR, no smoking)	Sam's SMV (1 pack per day Gamma)	Sam's SMV (1 pack per day, quits at end of 17th month)
1	7.00	7.00	7.00
12	6.92	6.88	6.88
18	6.88	6.81	6.82
24	6.84	6.75	6.77
36	6.76	6.62	6.69
54	6.64	6.43	6.57
72	6.52	6.24	6.46

Notice the difference in Sam's decline between continuing to smoke one pack per day versus stopping at the beginning of the 18th month. What happens is that his "gamma" in the 18th month becomes the NDR as his decline is determined naturally rather than accelerated by a vice. Here is a table regarding women Sam would attract given his habits:

TABLE 51.   Example Attraction Table

t (months)	Hypothetical Female A (Based off NDR)	Jenny (Female B)'s SMV (Based off Gamma)	Hypothetical Female C (Based off improved 18th month health)	Hypothetical Female D (NDR applied backward to C)
1	5.60	5.60	n/a	5.55
12	5.54	5.50	n/a	5.49
18	5.51	5.45	5.45	5.45
24	5.47	5.40	5.42	5.42
36	5.41	5.29	5.35	5.35
54	5.31	5.14	5.26	5.26
72	5.21	5.00	5.16	5.16

Above is a table that represents the different women who are/would be in a three-year relationship with Sam at different levels of Sam's SMV as determined by a 0.8 lambda. Female A represents the type of woman that Sam would have attracted had he initially had no vices. Female B (Jenny) is the woman that he attracted with his vices, and Female C is a hypothetical woman that Sam can attract after changing his ways in the 18th month through the gamma effect. Finally, Female D is a "backward" estimate of Female C using the NDR. This gives us an idea of how Female C would have appeared like to Sam had he met her before the 18th month (when he decided to change his health for the better).

The important thing to note is that D (which is a backward estimate of C) started off with a lower SMV than B before the 18th month. In theory, this means that the bad boy/girl, initially living a "fast" life, attract people in that way of life but then, as time passes and attitudes about life change, people whom they were not aware of initially (i.e. the slightly chubby yoga woman, the nerdy network engineer man) may catch their eye as they learn from mistakes. Life circumstances that cause emotional pain (Jenny getting run through with non-committal "bad boys"), physical pain (all-star asshole jock has a life-altering injury that humbles him), or other types of things serve to debilitate the human and make them more aware of their mortality.

For this reason, Female D initially would have been "less attractive" than Female B but, as time passes, Female B's health declines fast.

Female C (who is the "future" version of Female D after 18 months) preserves her value and wins by attrition. Sam may only notice her after his decision to change his life, but she was "there all along".

The appraisal (gamma effect)

If Sam engages in factors that lower his gamma (in this case, reverting to the NDR), he, by default, raises his SMV and, in turn, can attract a higher value mate. Some may argue that the *search costs*, or the cost of acquiring information about whom or where this other woman is, would diminish the value of switching and thus it would be more beneficial for Sam to stay put—another "cheaper to keep her" hypothetical. For now, let's assume that all Sam needs to do is to go out on the town once and he'll bump into the woman that would observe his new, higher value. Sam's significant other(s/o) must also be *aware* that other women of a higher SMV than her own notice and find him attractive. This marking to market may motivate his s/o to increase her own value (engage in healthier actions) and to treat Sam better. This is like getting a raise at your current job by showing them an offer letter from another job willing to pay you more. If Sam is appraised as an 8 but gets treated by his s/o as a 6, he's motivated to exit the relationship. The appraisal can backfire if the information regarding Sam's SMV is negative.

Lambda effect

On the other hand, an increase in SMV may not be a result of Sam changing his ways, but perhaps changing times and/or locations make *who he already is* more valuable. We deal with location economics in the next volume, but for now lambda is a sufficient "catch-all" variable that includes the market's locational effects and the changing attitudes and perceptions in that market.

Recall that, from the Oxford Study (speed dating experiment mentioned earlier), an abundance/scarcity of available male partners resulted in increasingly picky/lax women [34]. With this in mind, consider an unusual but not far-fetched dystopian example: After the 18th month, war has caused 20% of the male population to be decimated in the country that Sam lives. As a result, women become less picky—increasing the hypergamy factor.

TABLE 52. The Lambda Effect

t (months)	Sam's SMV (1 pack per day Gamma)	Jenny (Female B)'s SMV (Based off Gamma)	Jenny's Lambda Estimate	Hypothetical Female C (Based off improved 18th month health)	Female C's Lambda Estimate
1	7.00	5.60	0.8000	n/a	(n/a)
12	6.88	5.50	0.8000	n/a	(n/a)
18	6.81	5.45	0.8000	5.45	0.8005
24	6.75	5.40	0.8000	5.42	0.8034
36	6.62	5.29	0.8000	5.35	0.8092
54	6.43	5.14	0.8000	5.26	0.8181
72	6.24	5.00	0.8013	5.16	0.8269

Female C is relevant in the 18th month—after the catastrophe. I extended the decimal places on the lambda estimates to show the differences begin at that point when Sam's perceived value increases. In this example, we are merely "backing out" the lambda. The higher lambda for Female C in the 18th month signals that Sam can acquire a higher SMV female per the change in social perceptions. Since I have kept the relative values of the women the same, for the simplicity of math, the Endowment differentials proposed earlier are the same.

Deciding to Exit a Relationship

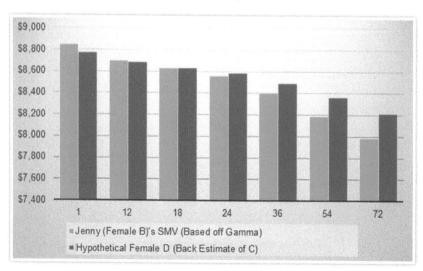

Figure 49. Endowment Value in Given Month

Earlier, we showed a table of Female B's endowment value in a given month (EOM). Here it is compared to Female D's combined profile (Female C back estimated). In the 18th month, B and D's values are set equal to benchmark the change.

The same slower rate of decline that stops D from "wearing out" as fast as B also causes D's value to initially be lower before the 18th month, when she was unnoticeable to Sam. If the *going concern* between B and C continued into the 72nd month, we can see how D's EOM value surpasses B's.

TABLE 53. Endowment Differential

A	B	C = CUM(B)	D	E = CUM(D)	F = (D-B)	G = (E-C)
t (months)	Jenny (Female B's) SMV (Based off Gamma)	Female B (Cumulative Benefits (CB))	Hypothetical Female D (Back estimate of C) (CB)	Female D (CB) (EOM Value)	Endowment Differential	Cumulative Differential (CD)
1	$8,844	$8,844	$8,772	$8,772	-$71.39	-$71.39
12	$8,701	$105,287	$8,687	$104,702	-$14.28	-$585.38
18	$8,629	$157,252	$8,629	$156,610	$0.00	-$642.49
24	$8,558	$208,761	$8,587	$208,247	$28.55	-$513.99
36	$8,401	$310,436	$8,487	$310,679	$85.66	$242.72
54	$8,187	$459,708	$8,358	$462,264	$171.33	$2,555.67
72	$7,987	$605,154	$8,215	$611,407	$228.44	$6,253.55

Using monthly EOM values, I constructed a "Cumulative Benefits (CB)" column for both B and D that gives the full picture of accumulated value over time. The "Cumulative Differential (CD)" column shows how much more value D would have added over B *over time*. Notice that from months 1 through 24, the CD is negative. This means that D *would have* offered less value over time up to that point. But after the 24th month, D offers substantially more value in the long run:

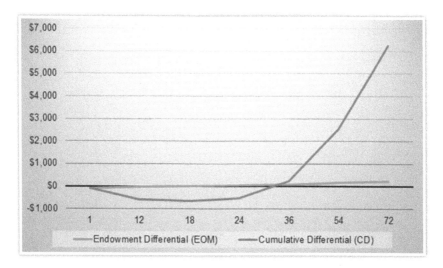

Figure 50.   Endowment Differential

While it is true that B (Jenny) offers more value than C, the *going concern* value is what we are after. The "going concern" value is the time value for the relevant period in consideration—in this case, after the 18th month mark, which is the time that Female C becomes a relevant option in the analysis. The use of Female D to back estimate Female C's value was for effect. After month 18, choosing C becomes a viable alternative to B, and this will be a factor in Sam choosing to exit a relationship with B.

Costs of Exit

There are two types of costs that must be accounted for—the explicit or stated costs (i.e. the actual cost of court fees, alimony and/or child support, police reports, movers etc.) and the opportunity cost, which is the next best available option to a person:

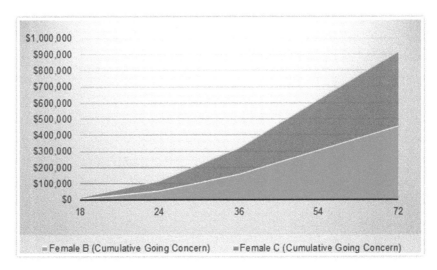

Figure 51. Cumulative Going Concern Value

The above graph shows the value that C adds over B starting from month 18; it continues out to the 72nd month for effect.

According to Nolo.com [35], the average divorce in America costs about $15,500 ($12,800 of that being attorney's fees). The average divorce takes about 18 months, so the annual average is

$$\frac{12}{18} * \$15{,}500 = \$10{,}333 = annualized\ cost\ of\ divorce\ (ACD)$$

We'll assume the above $10,333 is the explicit exit cost for simplicity. We'll apply this cost as a "balloon payment" with the minimum relationship length of 3 years (36 months). Using the cumulative benefits as being the opportunity cost for foregoing one relationship over the other and the explicit divorce cost referenced above, we get the following summary table:

TABLE 54. Analysis of Relationship Exit Costs

Scenario	Benefit	Opportunity Cost	Explicit Divorce/ Separation Cost	Total Costs	Net Benefit (Benefit-Cost)
Sam has no improvement in SMV (either through health or different market) stays with Female B	$310,436.83 (Jenny's 36th month cumulative benefits)	$0	$10,333	$10,333	$300,104
Sam experiences an improvement in the 18th month, but passes up Female D to stay with B	$310,436.83	$154,069.08 (difference in D's 36th and 18th month cumulative benefits)	$10,333	$164,402	$146,035
Sam experiences an improvement in the 18th month, but leaves B to be with D and then stays with D for 36 months (relationship with D ends in month 54)	$157,252.96 (benefits from B in first 18 months) + $314,283.86 (benefits from D from 18th to 54th months) = $471,536.82	$153,183.87 (the benefits he would have accrued if he stayed with B another 18 months)	10,333 * 2 = 20,666 (multiplied by 2 because he'll experience 2 "breakups")	$173,850	$297,687

Ironically, the "cheaper to keep her" logic falls into place as Sam maximizes his net benefit from staying put. However, if there are other factors (i.e. the "happiness" or level of utility Sam derives from being with D) the worst thing that could happen to Sam is *know* that D exists but doesn't factor her into his analysis, possibly because of his history with B and the benefits that he had accumulated thus far have made him biased towards B. One might inquire "What about all of the benefits that B brought him initially? Shouldn't that count for something?" Economically, the answer is "no".

Sunk Costs

I had a finance professor, who during one of his lectures, used the example of a relationship between a man and a woman whereby they had spent many happy years together and now one of them had begun to feel dissatisfaction and the relationship was on the rocks. He then asked the class about the prospective course that the couple should take. In attempting to answer, students asked questions regarding whether or not other people were vested in their union, their time together and other factors and many made the determination that since they have been together for so long, they should stay together. Finally, a student made the point that it didn't matter how long they were together, the only thing that mattered was if they were on the same page going forward. The professor said to the student: "You, my friend, have a perfect understanding of sunk costs." and went on to explain to the class that being unaware of sunk costs is one major reason managers run a company into the ground at the expense of stockholders. When managers are too personally vested in a project, they continue with it even if it is consistently losing money--hoping that the situation will turn around. When in reality, it's time to cut the loss as soon as possible to avoid future losses—the money already spent is "sunk".

With regards to an intimate relationship, the same is also true. Things said and done (good and bad) in the past are gone forever and are no longer of going concern. While they may be factors in the emotional state of the human, they are not relevant in the analysis on whether to continue. This may be a major factor people stay in relationships that are toxic—because they are holding on to memories of the "good times" hoping they will return—instead of facing the reality that is in front of them.

If separating didn't cost anything, Sam would be operating solely on a benefits perspective. If he had to look down the road to compare the value that B and D would bring for another 18 months at the 18-month mark months, B (his original s/o) yields $153,184 versus D's yield of $154,069 in cumulative benefits, making D a better option.

This "leave one for another" is a motif in human literary works and appears to be more condoned in women than in men. It is not uncommon for humans to sympathize more with a woman whose husband has left her for another than vice versa. In the case of the former, said husband was a "dog", a "no good piece of shit", a "son of a bitch" (this statement, while meant to disparage the man, is actually an insult to the man's mother, so it would be a woman attacking another woman's standing) or a "bastard" (again, an attack on the man's mother and status in society since this implies lower status through being unmarried and having a pregnancy—a "love child").

There is also language to refer to a woman for whom the man left as a "homewrecker". But in the case where the woman has left the man, the prevalent term is "gold digger" if there's wealth involved, a few utterances of the word "bitch" possibly even a "whore" here and there, but nothing with as much vitriol as the insults towards the man. Even, in the case of women leaving the man, a justification of how the man didn't measure up to standards as the cause is valid reason for her to leave him for something better.

INFORMATION PROBLEMS

CHAPTER 11

INFORMATION PROBLEMS

O NE OF THE MOST difficult parts of making a decision comes with having the information necessary to do so. Minimization of risk is tantamount to avoiding blowback in any decision. Two major stumbling blocks to decision making are *adverse selection* (the risk of making an uninformed decision before the fact) and *moral hazard* (the risk that once the decision is made, the outcome is altered beyond one's control).

With adverse selection, whole industries have popped up to become the middlemen/women between a buyer and a seller to give the buyer pertinent information. Angie's List is one example of an intermediary that vets certain handymen (and women, but mostly men doing the odd jobs—not going to go into the details of how this like a "replacement husband" but, I digress) for criminal backgrounds so that a buyer, usually a woman, can feel safe that the person she hires for an odd job is less likely to be "low quality" or commit a crime with her as the victim.

This does not necessarily mean that people who have made mistakes in the past will repeat them in the future, but the *best guess* that any rational person has of the future is the average of past events (hence our dialogue throughout this whole book about expected value, etc.), and most people would rather not take the risk of hiring an ex-con to install a security system—I'm just sayin'.

There's also the risk that a vetted person can render themselves untrustworthy if they have been a career criminal that has never been caught and, therefore, are still in the running—and if this person is hired via Angie's List and subsequently commits his/her (but likely to be a "him") first crime and/or is caught their first time with an Angie's List customer, a moral hazard has occurred.

Moral hazards are easy to see because they involve a discrepancy between the incentives between the agent (someone acting on behalf of the principal) and the principal (the person who hires the agent). Take the 90-day provisional hire period in a lot of jobs. This 90-day period is to see how the employee (agent) works out for the manager (principal) and/or to see if the employee is a good fit for the organization. Or the warranty on a particular piece of electronic equipment, whereby it has two years to malfunction before it is no longer the responsibility of the company that sold it.

The issue is that these "solutions" (the 90-day provisional hire period, and the equipment warranty) are only band-aids—temporary fixes. There is no guarantee that the behavior exhibited, or service/satisfaction obtained over the mitigated period will continue ad infinitum. An employee may be on their best behavior for the first 90 days—coming in to work early and staying late—dressed to the nines with a suit, tie and shoes that look like they were spit-shined in ROTC. Then on the 91st day, they come in wearing jeans frayed at the ankles and Margaritaville boat shoes. Or the electronics that you purchased mysteriously breaks down after on the 731st day of ownership.

There is no complete insulation from risk. The more insulation, the higher the cost, until it outweighs the benefit. It might almost seem that items are constructed to hold out just past the warranty period or a little after for good measure. The only thing that can be done is acknowledge the risk, be aware, and make the best decisions with the information given—and this involves who we date and/or who we are married to/in LTRs with.

Adverse Selection ("The Lemons Problem")

The "Market for Lemons" also referred to as "The Lemons Problem" is a term used to describe that phenomena that absent information, the average person buying a used car is going to end up with a "lemon" (back then, imagined as a big yellow car that doesn't work, so it just sits, hence "lemon"), or a "clunker".

It plays on the fact that before information was widely known—before the advent of companies like Carfax—people went on gut instinct when buying used cars. Lucky people have a mechanic with them, either for hire or by acquaintance (or the person purchasing would be a mechanic) and the mechanic would be able to tell if the car was faulty or not.

Having a mechanic at one's disposal, whether by employ or acquaintance, raises the price of the car by the value of this relationship (diagnosis/analysis of car problems) and, therefore, the information alone should, in theory, be the value of the mechanic's time/expertise plus the costs avoided from buying a lemon. But without such information/expertise, the average person is liable to purchase a lemon because their assessment of how much they pay for a used car takes into consideration that they could be purchasing a lemon. Thus, the money they offer to the dealership is less than necessary to buy a quality car and then the dealer naturally sells them a lemon. Like a self-fulfilling citrus prophesy.

Why it's easier for men to attract lower quality women (looks are not the only thing that matter)

The "Lemons Problem" can be applied to the sexual marketplace. Just like it's a shit ton easier to close a sale when you have a referral as opposed to "cold calling" (trying to sell a product to a complete stranger). It's easier to get a date when your reputation precedes you.

A male with a given market value (SMV_M) is looking optimally for a female with a value ($SMV_F = \lambda SMV_M$) that's relatively "equally yoked" (trying to get λ as close to 1 as possible). Let's say this is happening in a bar in a town that the male is visiting. The issue is that if the male has no connections or networks in that area, he's meeting females "cold" and depending on objective assertions about his market value (i.e. Looks, Money) will determine the female he'll attract. The network/connections piece (i.e. Status) will be missing and this will generally lower the man's value slightly. When this happens, the value of the woman he'll attract will also have a lower value.

Also, there's the case that, also with the women, only objective assertions can be made with certainty about their values. But for the sake of fun, let's assume that the man is buying (trading his SMV for the SMV of the woman) in a market where he's unfamiliar. Since he doesn't really know the women there, each individual woman will be less heterogenous to him. Thus, his only option is to subconsciously "average" the values of lower and higher value women.

What ends up happening is that he gives out "average" quality energy/vibes. This average energy won't attract the higher value women, but it will attract every female with an energy level lower than the guy puts out, which will tend to be a lower value woman.

Suppose there is a bar with two different women; with the same level of attractiveness, but there is information about their value that can't be ascertained by their looks alone (i.e. level of conscientiousness, virtuosity, and age). The women themselves both know their true value (i.e. how many sexual partners they've had (virtuosity) or whether or not they'd kick you while you're down (conscientiousness)) –one has a higher value than the other but the guy doesn't know which one is which.

$ESMV_{Fi}$ = *The ith female's sexual market value*
(i.e. Female 1, i = 1; Female 2, i = 2 and so on)

We also know from our previous theory

$$E[SMV_{t+k}] = f(SMV_t, \delta_t)$$

Such that

$$E[SMV_{t+k}] = (SMV_t)^* (1 - \delta_t)$$

Where δ_t is the effective rate of decline.

The fact is that various elements cannot be ascertained by looks alone. There remains a relative "risk" that the other important elements, such as virtuosity, age and conscientiousness would be sub-par and, therefore, δ would be a decline rate such that it includes that particular risk and the actual vices (the vices are the "negative" of the good habits, so if conscientiousness is lower than expected, that lower level is practically a conscientiousness "vice").

Let $ESMV_{F1}$ and $ESMV_{F2}$ know their own respective values of x_1 and x_2 but SMV_M, the guy trying to choose from one of them, does not. $ESMV_{F1}$ and $ESMV_{F2}$ are the only sellers in the market (only two women in the bar) and SMV_M is the only buyer (exchanging his value for theirs). In addition, $ESMV_{F1}$ and $ESMV_{F2}$ have vices of δ_1 and δ_2 (there's no need for a "t" or time indicator in the subscript because this is a single period model). *ESMV* of female 1 and 2 are based only on gamma and looks and, thus, gamma includes the risk of all non-looks items that cannot be objectively ascertained. Here's what we have:

$$ESMV_{F1} \times (1 - \delta_1) = x_1; \text{ (female 1's value is } x_1)$$

$$ESMV_{F2} \times (1 - \delta_2) = x_2; \text{ (female 2's value is } x_2)$$

where $x_1 > x_2$; (female 1 has a higher value than female 2);

and $\delta_1 < \delta_2$; (female 2 has more vices than female 1);

and $x_1 - x_2 = z \mid where\ z > 0$; (the difference in ESMV between females 1 and 2; female 1 is z units higher than female 2—so if female 2 is a 5, and z =1, then female 1 is a 6).

Since SMV_M doesn't know the values of x_1 and x_2, he is willing to pay the average price: $(x_1 + x_2)/2$

Because he's only willing to pay $(x_1 + x_2)/2$, the following prices he's offering in terms of

$$ESMV_{F1} \text{ and } ESMV_{F2}$$

Are

$$\frac{x_2 + x_2 + z}{2} = \frac{2x_2 + z}{2} = x_2 + \frac{z}{2}$$

and by the same logic

$$x_1 - \frac{z}{2}$$

Since

$$x_1 - \frac{z}{2} < x_1 \text{ and } x_2 + \frac{z}{2} > x_2 ;$$

SMV_M will always "attract" SMV_{F2} (lower quality) because he's willing to pay above her price. He doesn't pay enough to attract SMV_{F1}.

Knowledge Check

Henry meets two girls in a coffee shop, and on just looks alone, he estimates that they both have an SMV of 7.5. What he does not know is that girl one has a δ of 5%, and girl two has a gamma of 8%. If Henry is willing to pay the "average" price for the two girls, which girl will he attract?

Moral Hazard ("Bait and Switch")

Moral hazard is the lack of incentive to reduce costs and/or guard against risk because one is exempt from it. This "exemption" or insulation of risk to the individual who wantonly takes more risk than necessary can come through the costliness it takes to replace said individual. This cost may be bolstered by contractual agreements, social and political inconveniences/bottlenecks or it could be that an investment in that individual has not paid off yet.

Like in our above example, when a person gets hired for a relatively safe government job that has a 90-day free-look period, and after getting the job, stays out of trouble for 90 days. As soon as the 90-day free-look period is up, they regress to bad behavior. The moral hazard for the employer is the costliness that comes with replacing a trained employee, especially if there are numerous barriers to entry (i.e. the person has a Top-Secret Clearance).

The same can happen in a relationship contract like marriage and common law arrangements, where termination of the marriage contract, past the annulment period (i.e. the "free look" one-year period where a marriage can be terminated without a divorce), is rather costly. To illustrate this, imagine we take the scenario of Jenny (Female B) from earlier and that she had the same gamma for smoking one pack of cigarettes per day. Let's also add to this scenario that Sam and Jenny will go 72 months (6 years) in a marriage/relationship. As of the 18th month, the cumulative befits that Jenny produces each month are listed below in the "Original Gamma" column:

TABLE 55. Jenny's Cumulative Endowment Values					
Month	Original Gamma	Gamma 2.5% Increase	Gamma 5% Increase	Gamma 7.5% Increase	Gamma 10% Increase
18	$8,629	$8,629	$8,629	$8,629	$8,629
36	$161,813	$161,799	$161,746	$161,694	$161,641
54	$311,085	$310,938	$310,737	$310,537	$310,338
72	$456,531	$456,164	$455,727	$455,290	$454,853

In addition to the additional gamma, four more scenarios that show the net effect on cumulative benefits when the gamma is increased incrementally. These scenarios would occur as a result of additional vices, like a worsening diet, weight gain, more negative outlook on life, nagging, and a host of behaviors that one can imagine cause deleterious effects on an LTR. Any unexpected increase in gamma that occurs after the annulment period (only 12 months) presents a moral hazard to Sam.

CHAPTER 12

RACE-BASED SMV—OK CUPID'S "CURIOUS CASE"

I added this section as a sample of the type of research I intend subsequent volumes to expand into—which is applications of the concepts to real-world data. In addition, this section will not be riddled with sources that allude to every single example that I state here. I will make some assertions which may seem like common sense to most people, but to people who often like to point out exceptions to the rule to nullify the rule—these assertions may not hold water. I am not primarily concerned with being exact on each point but being in the ballpark of general understanding. For now, I am assuming the reader will take some of my claims as "common sense", especially if they are at least 36 years old and grew up in "mainstream" United States. Let's begin.

One day, while sitting in the waiting room for a dental appointment, I overheard a "conversation" between a female receptionist and female patient some might consider offensive. The patient was waiting on her husband to pick her up.

A little background here—I am of West African and Black-American ethnic background. The receptionist, "Maria", was "black" according to various American definitions of "blackness", but being from the Dominican Republic, according to the U.S. Census, her ethnicity is "Hispanic/Latino". The patient, "Cecile" was "black" like the Dominican receptionist was "black", but she was from Jamaica. Maria had just recently gotten engaged and the conversation went like this:

Cecile: Wow! Look at that ring! I take it you're about to be married?

Maria: Yea, we've been together for a couple years and he popped the question.

Cecile: So, the guy—he's... what is he?

Maria: Huh?

Cecile: Is your fiancé—is he American? Where is he from?

Maria: Oh, he's from Puerto Rico—it's kind of a loaded question since Puerto Rico is almost like a state.

Cecile: Whew! Child, I'm happy for you. At first, I thought you were going to say that your husband-to-be was black, you know—a Black American.

Maria: I guess I would be "blacker" than him, but he's not African American, if that's what you're asking.

Cecile: Yeah, ya afee (you have to) get you a man that's not one of *them.*

Shortly after this exchange, a man, who appeared to be East Indian (South Asian) entered the office with a little curly-haired *dougla* boy by his side. Cecile introduced her husband to Maria and her family and explained that they were all Jamaican—that's the "island pride" of their family— and went on to yap a little bit about how people of Caribbean heritage should stick together blasé blasé.

Without attempting to delve too deep into the concepts of race, culture, nationality, ethnicity and heritage, I was a little taken aback by the appearance that black women of any ethnicity can get away with openly discussing their racial/ethnic preference in men, while nonblack women and men are "dinged" for doing the same thing. I imagined if the roles were reversed, and I were talking to my Dominican buddy about why I'm glad his wife wasn't African American in the presence of an African American woman, that I would be called everything but a child of God—but I digress. Like Run DMC said: "It's like that, and that's the way it is."

Look no further than the science behind the *Bateman Principle* to confirm that. To survive, the female must choose the male most likely to guarantee the survival of her offspring—which encompasses resource provision and genetic health. If you care to reference some of the tribal behaviors of humans, you can review the "Evolutionary Biology Refresher" in this book, which talks about how humans survived in foraging groups. And, while the references in this book may not provide an in-depth coverage of social interactions and tribalism, I urge you to research this topic for yourself.

I would wager that most people know that humans have tribal tendencies and are able to survive together knowing who is with them and who is against them (i.e., who is in their tribe and who isn't). Before the advent of mechanical technology like planes and boats that sped up human migration patterns across vast distances, the earliest humans for the longest times existed in phenotypically homogenous (i.e., similar outward genetic features, like skin color, hair texture/color, eye color etc.) tribes for the majority of their existence.

Getting straight to the point, wealth wise, the dominant phenotype in the US is ethnically Northern European — "white" for all intents and purposes. This is the reason why Eurocentric features, are considered attractive in mainstream American society.

Now back to the data, consider the following four statements that the Speed Dating study (referenced earlier) made:

- "Women [place] greater emphasis on earning potential, considering such attributes as ambition, intelligence and social status [35b]."

- "[Female mate selection] reflects women's desire to find men who can provide resources to aid in the upbringing of their offspring [35b]."

- "Women strongly discriminate on the basis of race. They are 14 percentage points more likely to accept a partner of their own race. Given [the fact that they are likely to accept a person of their own race 38% of the time], this is a large effect [35c]."

- "Women exhibit strong preferences for partners of their own race, while men do not [35a]."

Addressing the first bullet point, I'll assume that the women in the study infer a positive correlation between earnings, intelligence, ambition and social status. The second point creates a bridge between the biological reasoning and the outward preference. Combining the first two points, a reasonable person can logically infer that traits such as earning potential, intelligence, ambition and social status can positively impact the "upbringing of offspring", which is another way to say "enhance survival".

The only tangible item in the attributes mentioned above, earnings, can be measured. Below is a graph, constructed from BLS data, that show men's annual average weekly earnings (the yearly figure is arrived at by a simple average of the quarterly figures), from 2008 to 2012 [32]:

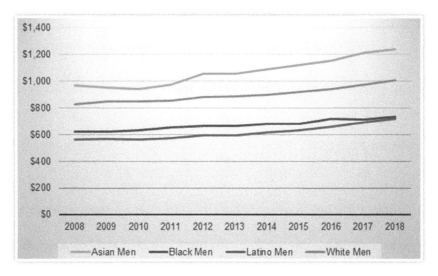

Figure 52. Men's Average Weekly Earnings by Race, Ages 16 and Older

The data shows that Asian men have out-earned other races of men on average since 2008. Asian men have consistently earned about $200 more weekly than White men. Latino and Black men earned $400 and $200 dollars less weekly than Asian and White men respectively. Notably, Latino men have caught up with Black men, really making ground since 2017, though Black male earnings are slightly higher.

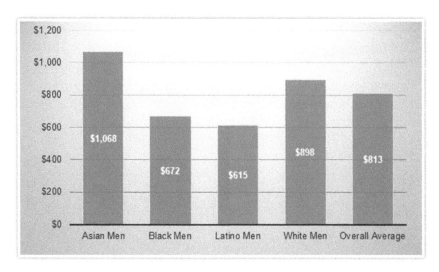

Figure 53. Men's 10-Year Average Weekly Earnings by Race, 16 and Older

Above is a graph of the 2008-2018 10-year average earnings of each race individually and the four races themselves collectively. Asians and Whites earn above average earnings and Blacks and Latinos below average earnings. How much above or below?

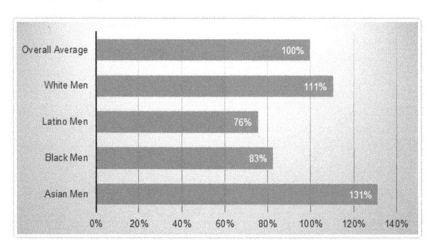

Figure 54. "High-Low" of 10-Year Earnings Average

Average earnings being 100%, Asians and Whites earned 31 and 11 percent above average respectively, and Blacks and Latinos earned 17% and 24% below average respectively, of the four races.

Really looks like a "race" 😋. Regardless, the ability to acquire resources, that can be tangibly used to "help in the upbringing of offspring", are in the order of: Asian, White, Black and Hispanic. Based on the Speed Dating study, one can logically conclude that women's selections in men would be backed up by sexual marketplace data indicating that women prefer men in the order of Asian, White, Black and Hispanic.

The last two bullet points from the Speed Dating study above summarize that women, in general, lean more towards dating men of their own race, versus men of other races. If earnings dictated women's preferences, this logic would conflict for all races accept Asians. While there is evidence that suggest Asian women marry interracially at higher rates, and that Black women have lower marriage rates than other races of women, I am not going to delve into that research in this book. I will, however, juxtapose sexual marketplace data against the earnings data above to see if Speed Dating study's claims hold water.

The Coveted yet Controversial OK Cupid Study [37]

The dating site "OK Cupid" conducted research to determine if people using their app had a racial preference. They used reply rates (if you were to reply to a message, this indicates willingness to communicate and, thus, expresses interest) as a proxy for desirability. Before I go on to summarize what was found, there are a couple of caveats: one, I did not have access to the raw data. The article, or what I was able to save from the article, indicates that the average replies by ethnic group were weighted. I am going to make the assumption it was weighted by the number of users in each racial category.

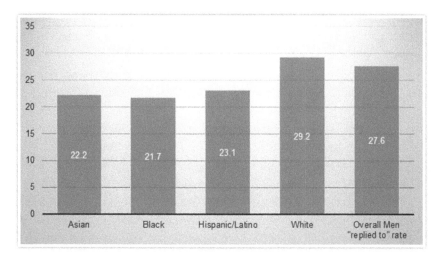

Figure 55. "Replied To" Rates by Race/Ethnicity

The above graph shows the likelihood of reply when 100 messages are sent out (this is my commonsense interpretation of their data). Men, overall, were replied to 27.6 percent of the time. This would represent our overall average, as we also did for earnings above. However, unlike above, we see that White men are the only men to be replied to above average—everyone else was replied to less than average.

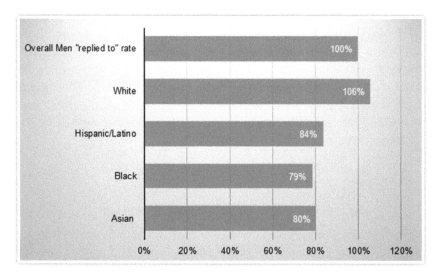

Figure 56. High Low of "Replied To" Rates by Race/Ethnicity

Average reply rates at 100%, White men were replied to 6% above average, followed by Latino, Asian, and Black men who were replied to 16%, 20%, and 21% below average. If we compare female preferences for race and potential earnings data, we have the following ordinal ranking, which I entitle "Attributive Desirability":

TABLE 56. Attributive Desirability

Rank	Dating Preference	Earning Potential
1	White	Asian
2	Hispanic/Latino	White
3	Asian	Black
4	Black	Latino

In a nutshell, Whites and Latinos are preferred above their earnings ranks, and Blacks and Asians are preferred below their earning ranks. The 3000-pound gorilla in the room that everyone knows and nobody talks about is first, the dual mating strategy of women and, second, women's tendency to prefer different types of men, ethnically, comes with the ruling class in a given culture—whose faces are predominant in media and marketing (people of European descent in America but also in the world) which comes as a looks/status hybrid.

Latinos: The Perfect Cohort

The perfect place to start an analysis on race, ethnicity and status is with Latinos, because "Latinos" are not a particular race but a, I daresay, "socio-linguistic-geographical" ethnic group. What most Latinos have in common is that they geographically originate from Latin America (including, but not limited to, countries of the Caribbean, Central and South America, and Mexico), usually adhere to Roman Catholicism and speak a Latin language (Spanish, French, and Portuguese). While the proper definition of "Latino" includes Brazilians and Haitians, I will focus on the Spanish-speaking population and will use the term "Latino" interchangeably with "Hispanic".

Latinos are multi-racial, but in popular media are most represented by *mestizos* (Native American and European admixture) and *criollos* (full-blooded or near full-blooded European admixture). Popular culture regarding Latinos often bring the mind of people like Sophia Vergara, Selma Hayek, Antonio Banderas, Desi Arnaz, and much later, Zoe Saldana and Christian Milian (the last two mentions representing "Afro-Latinas").

According to the 2017 Census figures [39], the largest Hispanic group in the U.S. by number of people are of Mexican descent, comprising 36,668,018 people. This is 62.3% of the entire U.S. Hispanic population. The second largest are of Puerto Rican descent which, in contrast, made up 5,588,664 people at 9.5% of the total Hispanic population. The gap between first (Mexican) and second (Puerto Rican) largest Hispanic ancestral groups is about 6 times—for every Puerto Rican in the US, there are about 6 Mexicans.

While Mexico has a larger admixture of *mestizo* and *criollo*, with a minute Afro-Mexican population, Puerto Ricans and other Spanish-speaking Caribbean countries have much heavier admixtures of African blood and these traits can also be seen in their music and culture (i.e. Santeria—which is a mix between Catholicism and African religions that many liken to Vodun). The pie charts below show the change in the racial makeup of Hispanics in 2010 and 2017:

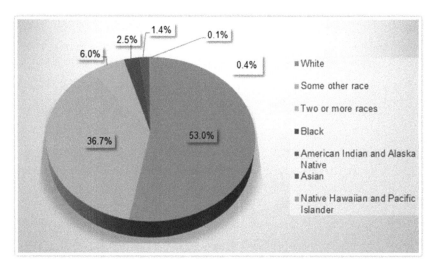

Figure 57. 2010 Hispanic Racial Distribution

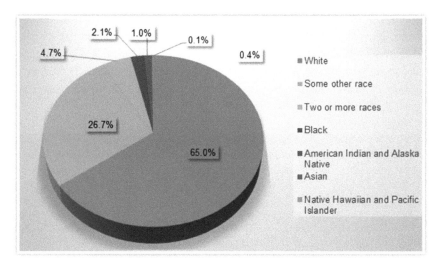

Figure 58. 2017 Hispanic Racial Distribution

The movement of the largest chunks of the pie—an increase of Hispanics identifying as White and a decrease in the ones who identify as "some other race" are shown here. However, I want to draw attention to the "two or more races" and the Native American categories for the point I am revving up to make regarding race and status. Here is a more precise summary of the data illustrated in the graphs above:

TABLE 57. Hispanic Racial Distribution				
	2010		**2017**	
Race	Population	Distribution %	Population	Distribution %
White	26,735,713	53.0%	38,222,255	65.0%
Some other race	18,503,103	36.7%	15,719,042	26.7%
Two or more races	3,042,592	6.0%	2,782,900	4.7%
Black	1,243,471	2.5%	1,263,898	2.1%
American Indian and Alaska Native	685,150	1.4%	581,116	1.0%
Asian	209,128	0.4%	215,482	0.4%
Native Hawaiian and Pacific Islander	58,437	0.1%	61,441	0.1%
Total	**50,477,594**	**100.0%**	**58,846,134**	**100.0%**

In our discussion above regarding the types of races Latinos identify with, we can see the following: an increase in the distribution of Hispanics who identify as White, a decrease in Hispanics who identify as "some other race", "two or more races", and American Indian and Alaska Native ("AIAN"). Here are the specific 7 year and average annual growth (decline) rates:

TABLE 58. Seven-year Annual Growth		
	2017-2010 Total Growth Rate	2017-2010 Avg Annual Growth Rate (compounded)
Race	Growth Rate	Avg Growth Rate
White	43.0%	5.2%
Some other race	-15.0%	-2.3%
Two or more races	-8.5%	-1.3%
Black	1.6%	0.2%
American Indian and Alaska Native	-15.2%	-2.3%
Asian	3.0%	0.4%
Native Hawaiian and Pacific Islander	5.1%	0.7%
Total	**16.6%**	**2.2%**

An element regarding the decrease in the Native American Hispanic population in the above table can be read as: "The Hispanic AIAN population has declined a total of 15.2% from 2010 to 2017 at an average decline of 2.3% per year." It can also be reasonably assumed that the average growth rates can be used to estimate up to another 7 years, within reason.

Here is my big leap before I make logic of the figures above: **there is no material phenotypic difference, in the USA, between a White person who is a brunette and a White person mixed with AIAN (Native American) ancestry, sociologically**. Anecdotally, I have met and heard of many people who, on the surface, are considered White, speaking about their Cherokee and Irish ancestry. I believe that in the US, the AIAN people have greatly assimilated into and are heavily mixed into the greater White population—and that most non-Latino people in the US identify with their skin color (phenotype) rather than their ancestry (genotype).

Because of the sociological assumptions I have made and the data above, one can reasonably assume that Hispanic mestizos and, by extension, *castizos* (One-fourth Native and three-fourths European ancestry) most likely identify as White in America. The decline of the "some other race", AIAN, and "two or more races" categories, and the growth of the "White" category may be an indication that sociologically Hispanics are identifying more as practically and phenotypically white (i.e., becoming more "American" -- to the degree that the definition of race is derived from concepts of nationality).

An extension of my assumption/hunch would be that the growth in the White category is driven by change in identification from mestizo/castizo. The total 7-year growth rate (43%) and average annual growth rate (5.2%) of the White Hispanic population eclipsed the sum of the total 7-year decline rates (-38.8%) and is close to the sum of the average annual decline rates (-5.9%) of the "some other race", AIAN, and "two or more races" categories.

As a result, I assert two commonsense reasons for this stand out. Either Hispanics are changing how they identify racially, or White Hispanics are having babies with each other and/or other people who identify as "White" at higher rates than the other Hispanic racial groups; and the babies are identifying as Hispanic and white when they reach the age of maturity. Since I doubt that white Hispanics are out-mating Hispanics of other races, identification is likely the culprit. What would be the motivation behind the change in identification? Societal status.

Attributive Desirability and Duality of Mating Strategy

In my earlier example, the Jamaican woman had a concept of what man was preferred based on ethno-cultural traits. Granted, while Jamaicans on average may have high percentage of Sub-Saharan African blood, in the United States, they may consider themselves a separate cultural and even linguistic group from Black Americans. In addition, in Jamaica, the wealthier tend to be of South Asian (East Indian) and Southern Chinese descent. Cecile's husband was a Jamaican of East Indian descent and she may associate that with higher status. East Indians, while frequently dark-skinned, often have hair texture and bone structure more comparable to Europeans than Sub Saharan Africans do—i.e., they're closer to White than Blacks (as to the degree "Blackness" is associated with Sub-Saharan "Africanness").

In the points regarding female mating strategies, the ability to raise children and provide resources were of tantamount importance, and yet we see a disparity in female preferences and earning potential. Again, since Asian males out-earn other males, this is indicative of a better ability to provide resources for offspring, and yet, they are not the most desired. This relative "Attributive Desirability" looks like this:

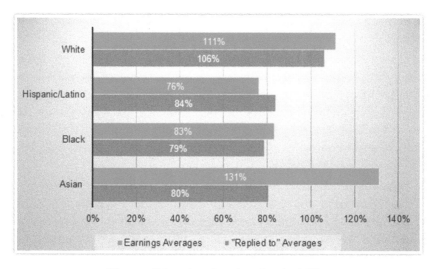

Figure 59. Attributive Desirability

We can see that the disparity between the earnings potential and being on females' list for desirable mates are the highest for Asian men. Latino men may be the sexiest, though, because they enjoy a desirability that is higher than their potential to earn. Every other race of man has higher earnings relative to the desire women have for him:

TABLE 59. Desirability Differential (Replied Rate - Earnings)	
Man's Race	**High-Low Differential**
Asian	-51%
Black	-4%
Hispanic/Latino	8%
White	-5%
Overall Average	**-13%**

On average across the four races of men, men earn 13% more than their replied to rate, the outliers are Asians earning a whopping 51% more and Hispanics earning 8% less than their replied to rate—with Whites and Blacks together about the same earning 5 and 4 percent more than their replied to rate. A logical conclusion that can arise from the data proposed is that how much a man earns is of much less importance to her than his phenotypical race—and, by extension, his looks and status. As it applies to the theories proposed in this book, the combined *relative importance weights* for women in the U.S.A for looks and status are higher than the *relative importance weight* for money (as a flow, as determined by earnings, and as a stock (to the degree that assets are based on earnings). Consider the following:

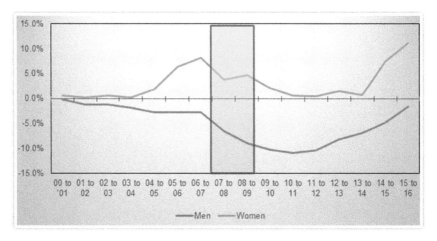

Figure 60. Median Income Growth Since Year 2000

The above chart shows the growth (decline) in men's and women's incomes since the year 2000 [39]. The growth in men's incomes have consistently been below the zero mark since the year 2000—and took a huge big dip during the 2008/2009 recession (as indicated by the highlighted box) and bottoming out between 2010 to 2011, and have climbed, but have not yet made it to 2000 levels. Women's incomes, by contrast, have grown since 2000, having a pre-recession top at 8.1% as compared to 2000 in 2006 to 2007 and, like the growth in men's incomes, bottomed out between 2010 and 2011 at 0.5% growth—but they always continued to grow since 2000.

Since women's incomes have grown higher relative to men's, it can follow that the value of a man for resource provision is diminished. With regards to phenotypic race preference, it stems from social acceptance. Tying together the above data, women in general don't need men to provide resources for them, but likely consider Latino men "sexiest". Although Asian men may be considered "most financially stable", in a world where women's incomes are growing faster compared to men, a la Juan Luis Guerra, *"no vale la pena"*.

APPENDIX

APPENDIX ITEMS

Appendix Note 1

Geometric Averaging

The relevance of compounding

When we say things have "compounded" we generally mean that whatever comes next is relevant to what has happened in the past. In the case of compound interest, the word "compound" means that interest in the future is being earned on top of previously earned interest. This can be applied to relational data in a time series. The geometric average of a variable X_i is

$$GEOMEAN_x = X_1^{\left(\frac{1}{n}\right)} + X_2^{\left(\frac{1}{n}\right)} + X_3^{\left(\frac{1}{n}\right)} + \cdots X_n^{\left(\frac{1}{n}\right)}$$

$$GEOMEAN = \prod_{t=1}^{n} X_t^{\frac{1}{n}}$$

Where "Geomean" is the Geometric Average and:

n = total number of periods in of observed data

t = a specific observation at a point in time

Rebasing (Indexing)

Rebasing is the act of take sequential data in a series relative to a common starting point and relate each item in that series so that it becomes the growth (decline) in relation to the initial point. It is important because when comparing diand it's growth in relation to the initial data point (usually with it being = 100):

$$Index_t = 100 * \frac{X_t}{X_0}$$

Where

X_0 = initial data value

X_t = value at time

Appendix Note 2

a. Female Fertility over time [Original Wallace & Kelsey (2010) NGF% Remaining Chart]

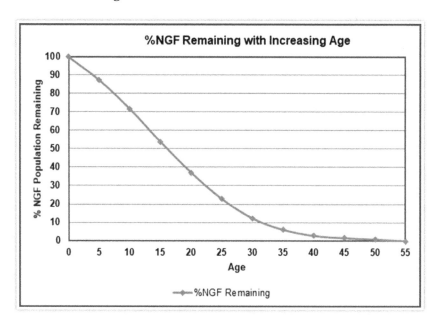

Besides reproductive hormones, the human ovarian reserve can be used to estimate the level of fertility of females from birth to menopause. The human ovary normally contains a specific number of non-growing follicles (NGF) whose population declines with age from conception to menopause. This decline can be used to model female fertility. In this case, a chart of % NGF population remaining versus age is reconstructed by its extracting numerical data and deriving the corresponding function. The data exhibits a non-linear quadratic model in which the percentage population of NGF remaining declines from age 0 to 55 years. According to Wallace & Kelsey (2010), menopause is reached at the age of 49.6 years. The chart was obtained from a study conducted by Wallace & Kelsey (2010) who attempted to model the age-related population of NGF from conception to menopause. The data was extracted into a table by overlaying the chart on gridlines and using a ruler to read the coordinates as shown in Figure 1 below. The resulting data and the indexes are summarized in Table 1.

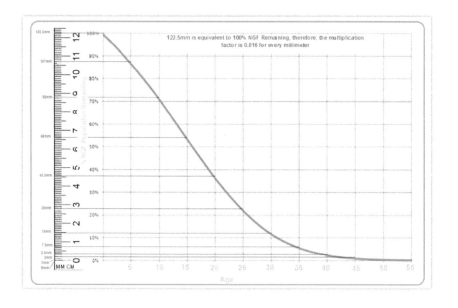

Using a metric ruler, the following logic was used to obtain the multiplication factor:

$$122.5\ mm = 100\%\ NGF\ Remaining$$

$$\frac{122.5\ mm}{122.5} = \frac{100\%\ NGF\ Remaining}{122.5}$$

$$1mm \approx 0.816\%\ NGF\ Remaining$$

TABLE A1.	Relational Values Table		
	A	B = (A x 0.816); rounded to nearest whole number (Adjustment factor: 1mm = 0.816)	Pegged to original data points in research paper for accuracy
Age	Length (mm)	%NGF Remaining (rounded)	%NGF Remaining (Wallace & Kelsey)
0	122.5	100	
5	107	87	
10	88	72	
15	66	54	
20	45.5	37	
25	28	23	
30	15	12	12
35	7.5	6	
40	3.5	3	3
45	2	2	
50	1	1	
55	0	0	

Demonstrating post-pubescent measurement (ability to bear young) and for comparison to other biological factors, we took the 15 to 55-year range datapoints on %NGF remaining to obtain a functional form for the data using Microsoft Excel data analytics trendline equation:

TABLE A2.	Age 15-55
Age	%NGF Remaining
15	54
20	37
25	23
30	12
35	6
40	3
45	2
50	1
55	0

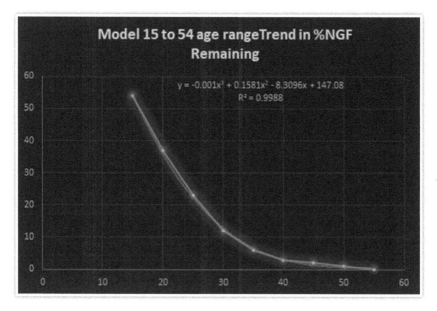

Figure A3.

Using the third-order trendline equation given above and translating it into variables pertinent to our discussion we get:

$\%NGF\ remaining = -0.001Age^3 + 0.1581Age^3 + 8.309Age^3 + 147.08$

Using the %NGF remaing equation above and estimating for the in-between years we get:

Age	%NGF remaining	Ranking (based on trendline modeling)	*Rebased to Age 18 = 10 for Age Ranking
TABLE A3. Calculating the %NGF			
15	55	10	n/a
16	51	9.27	n/a
17	47	8.55	n/a
18	43	7.82	9.99
19	39	7.09	9.06
20	36	6.55	8.37
21	33	6.00	7.66
22	30	5.45	6.96

23	27	4.91	6.27
24	25	4.55	5.81
25	23	4.18	5.34
26	20	3.64	4.65
27	18	3.27	4.18
28	16	2.91	3.72
29	15	2.73	3.49
30	13	2.36	3.01
31	12	2.18	2.78
32	10	1.82	2.33
33	9	1.64	2.10
34	8	1.45	1.85
35	7	1.27	1.62
36	6	1.09	1.39
37	5	0.91	1.16
38	5	0.91	1.16
39	4	0.73	0.93
40	4	0.73	0.93
41	3	0.55	0.70
42	3	0.55	0.70
43	3	0.55	0.70
44	2	0.36	0.46
45	2	0.36	0.46
46	2	0.36	0.46
47	2	0.36	0.46
48	2	0.36	0.46
49	2	0.36	0.46
50	2	0.36	0.46
51	2	0.36	0.46
52	2	0.36	0.46
53	2	0.36	0.46
54	2	0.36	0.46
55	2	0.36	0.46

*The far-right column will be used for the Age ranking discussion that occurs later in the book.

Then I geometrically averaged the above data into select 10-year intervals for purposes of discussion and comparison, resulting in the following data table (which is the source for **Figure 16 and 17**):

TABLE A4. Rebased %NGF		
Age	%NGF Remaining	Rebased %NGF Remaining
15-24	37	100.0
25-34	14	37.8
35-44	4	10.8
45-54	2	5.4

Appendix Note 3

Free Testosterone (Based on Vermeleun and Simon studies)

Age	Total Testosterone (ng/dL)	Free Testosterone (ng/dL)	SHBG (nmol/L)
25-34	617	12.3	35.5
35-44	668	10.3	40.1
45-54	606	9.1	44.6
55-64	562	8.3	45.5
65-74	524	6.9	48.7
75-84	471	6.0	51.0
85-100	376	5.4	65.9

Figure A4.   A. Vermeleun (1996)

Age	Mean Total Testosterone (ng/dL)	Median Total Testosterone (ng/dL)	5th %	95th %
<25	692	697	408	956
25-29	669	637	388	1005
30-34	621	597	348	975
35-39	597	567	329	945
40-44	597	597	319	936
45-49	546	527	329	846
50-54	544	518	289	936
55-59	552	547	319	866

Figure A5. D. Simon (1996)

The data was transferred to the following data table(s):

TABLE A5. A. Vermeleun 1996		
Age Range	**Total Testosterone (ng/dL)**	**Free Testosterone (ng/dL)**
25-34	617	12.3
35-44	668	10.3
45-54	606	9.1
55-64	562	8.3
65-74	524	6.9
75-84	471	6
85-100	376	5.4

Table A6. D. Simon 1996	
Age Range	**Mean Testosterone**
<25	692
25-29	669
30-34	621
35-39	597
40-44	597
45-49	546
50-54	544
55-59	552

To since Simon's ranges are in 5 year increments and Vermeleun's (and for comparison purposes) are in 10 year increments, I geometrically averaged Simon's 5 year ranges to arrive at ten year ranges:

TABLE A7. Age Range Bridge: D. Simon 1996	
Age Range (5-year periods averaged to 10-year periods)	Mean Testosterone (Geomean)
25-34	645
35-44	597
45-54	545

Since free testosterone is a function of total testosterone, and Vermelun's study on free testosterone only went back as far as the 25 to 34 year range, I used the relationship between free and total testosterone to estimate what free testosterone would be at less that 25 years to use as a proxy for the 15 to 24 year range:

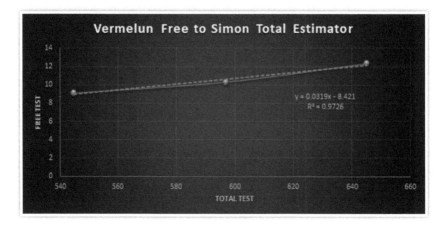

Figure A6.

As a result, the formula was used to determine Vermelun's free testosterone from 15 to 24 by using Simon's less that 25 years old with the following formula:

$$Vermelun\ free\ test = -0.0319 * (Simon's\ total\ test) - 8.421$$

Therefore

$$Vermelun\ free\ test_{15\ to\ 24\ years} =$$

$$= -0.0319 * (Simon's\ total\ test_{<25\ years}) - 8.421$$

And

$$Vermelun\ free\ test_{15\ to\ 24\ years} = -0.0319 * (692) - 8.421 = 13.7$$

Combining the estimation for Vermeleun's free test for 15 to 24 years with the averaged and stated Simon values in 10 year increments we get the following table (which is the source for **Figure 18 and 19**):

Age Range	Simon Total Test	Vermeleun Free Test	Researcher Source	Notes
TABLE A8. Summary of Calculated Vermeleun's Free Test				
15-24 (< 25)	692	13.7	D. Simon 1996	Vermeleun Free test estimated using Simon Mean under 25 Total Test level
25-34	645	12.3	A. Vermeleun (1996)	
35-44	597	10.3	A. Vermeleun (1996)	
44-54	545	9.1	A. Vermeleun (1996)	

Appendix Note 4

Median Income

Census table "P08ar" was pulled from this site: https://www.census.gov/topics/income-poverty/income/guidance/cps-historic-footnotes.html

The source data used came from the tables labeled: "**15 TO 24 YEARS**", "**25 TO 34 YEARS** ", "**35 TO 44 YEARS** ", and "**45 TO 54 YEARS**".

First, the data was reorganized by rearranging the source data from descending to ascending year order. Next, the data was broken into cohorts assuming the individual in question is age 15 in 1977, I used data from the table "15 to 24 Years" and data years 1977 to 1986. Then assuming in 1987, the 15-year-old would be 25, I used the second age band "25 to 44 Years" and data years from 1987 to 1996. Repeating this logic, I obtained all of the datapoints "following" the hypothetical 15-year-old in 1977 until his 54th birthday in 2016. Here is an example of the first two age bands:

TABLE A9				
		15 TO 24 YEARS		
			Male	
Age of random person during sample/survey who appears annually throughout life	Age and year	Number with income (thous.)	Median income	
			Current dollars	2016 dollars
15	1977	16,595	3,237	11,682
16	1978	17,161	3,652	12,334
17	1979	17,436	4,256	13,129
18	1980	16,971	4,597	12,753
19	1981	16,775	3,072	7,787
20	1982	15,996	4,427	10,583
21	1983	15,868	4,284	9,821
22	1984	15,571	4,709	10,365
23	1985	15,403	4,995	10,629
24	1986	14,998	5,283	11,049

TABLE A9

Age of random person during sample/survey who appears annually throughout life	Age and year	25 TO 34 YEARS		
		Male		
		Number with income (thous.)	Median income	
			Current dollars	2016 dollars
25	1987	20,783	19,927	40,288
26	1988	20,912	20,782	40,552
27	1989	20,998	21,367	39,947
28	1990	20,856	21,393	38,116
29	1991	20,523	21,595	37,125
30	1992	20,578	21,497	36,060
31	1993	20,178	21,927	35,877
32	1994	19,976	22,606	36,231
33	1995	19,617	23,609	36,949
34	1996	19,354	25,179	38,384

The age bands above were organized into the following table, which was the source for men's median income:

TABLE A10. Men's Income

Age Range	Year	Expected Age	2016 Dollars	2016 dollars 10-year Geometric Averages	2016 dollars 10 yr averages (use Geomean for time series)
15 to 24	1977	15	$11,682.00	n/a	n/a
	1978	16	$12,334.00	n/a	n/a
	1979	17	$13,129.00	n/a	n/a
	1980	18	$12,753.00	n/a	n/a
	1981	19	$7,787.00	n/a	n/a
	1982	20	$10,583.00	n/a	n/a
	1983	21	$ 9,821.00	n/a	n/a

	1984	22	$10,365.00	n/a	n/a
	1985	23	$10,629.00	n/a	n/a
	1986	24	$11,049.00	$10,904.32	100.00
25 to 34	1987	25	$40,288.00	n/a	n/a
	1988	26	$40,552.00	n/a	n/a
	1989	27	$39,947.00	n/a	n/a
	1990	28	$38,116.00	n/a	n/a
	1991	29	$37,125.00	n/a	n/a
	1992	30	$36,060.00	n/a	n/a
	1993	31	$35,877.00	n/a	n/a
	1994	32	$36,231.00	n/a	n/a
	1995	33	$36,949.00	n/a	n/a
	1996	34	$38,384.00	$37,915.09	347.71
35 to 44	1997	35	$49,019.00	n/a	n/a
	1998	36	$51,789.00	n/a	n/a
	1999	37	$52,468.00	n/a	n/a
	2000	38	$52,872.00	n/a	n/a
	2001	39	$51,975.00	n/a	n/a
	2002	40	$50,570.00	n/a	n/a
	2003	41	$51,148.00	n/a	n/a
	2004	42	$51,504.00	n/a	n/a
	2005	43	$50,345.00	n/a	n/a
	2006	44	$50,756.00	$51,233.30	469.84
45 to 54	2007	45	$53,074.00	n/a	n/a
	2008	46	$50,766.00	n/a	n/a
	2009	47	$50,039.00	n/a	n/a
	2010	48	$50,031.00	n/a	n/a
	2011	49	$49,023.00	n/a	n/a
	2012	50	$48,574.00	n/a	n/a
	2013	51	$49,768.00	n/a	n/a
	2014	52	$51,009.00	n/a	n/a
	2015	53	$51,712.00	n/a	n/a
	2016	54	$51,476.00	$50,531.24	463.41

Appendix Note 5

Looks Calculations

Looks Ranking $(L) = SMV_L = W_{TA}(L_{TA}) + W_{WRM}(WRM)$

(where W_q are the relative importance of sub-attributes)

The "New" Golden Ration calculates Face Length Percent (FLP) as

$$FLP = Face\ Length\ Percent = \frac{Distance\ from\ eyes\ to\ mouth}{Distance\ from\ hairline\ to\ chin}$$

The calculation for FLP is based off optimizing the Thurstonian attractiveness T(A) formula below:

$$T(A) = -51(FLP)^2 + 37(FLP) - 6$$

Let "FLP" = "L"

$$T_A = -51L^2 + 37L - 6$$

To find optimum (the height of the curve has the highest SMV), set the derivative equal to zero:

$$\frac{dT_A}{dL} = -102L + 37$$

And

$$0 = -102L + 37$$

Therefore, solving for L, we get $L \approx 0.36$

And per our theory, this maximal L will be equivalent to the maximal SMV, 9.99

The following table based on the rationale in the paper was constructed:

$T(A) = Thurstonian\ Attractiveness\ Measure;$
$maximized\ at\ [FLP, T(A)] = (0.36, 0.71)$

Therefore, the optimal FLP is 36%. Based off this, the optimal T(A) is 0.71, and we can construct the following table:

TABLE A11. FLP vs. Looks Ranking

Face Length Percent (FLP)	T(A)	Percentile	Looks Ranking (L_{TA})
0.1	-2.81	0%	0.00
0.12	-2.29	8%	0.77
0.14	-1.82	15%	1.54
0.16	-1.39	23%	2.31
0.18	-0.99	31%	3.07
0.2	-0.64	38%	3.84
0.22	-0.33	46%	4.61
0.24	-0.06	54%	5.38
0.26	0.17	61%	6.15
0.28	0.36	69%	6.92
0.3	0.51	77%	7.68
0.32	0.62	85%	8.45
0.34	0.68	92%	9.22
0.36	**0.71**	**100%**	**9.99**
0.38	0.70	92%	9.22
0.4	0.64	85%	8.45
0.42	0.54	77%	7.68
0.44	0.41	69%	6.92
0.46	0.23	61%	6.15
0.48	0.01	54%	5.38
0.5	-0.25	46%	4.61
0.52	-0.55	38%	3.84
0.54	-0.89	31%	3.07
0.56	-1.27	23%	2.31
0.58	-1.70	15%	1.54
0.6	-2.16	8%	0.77
0.62	-2.66	0%	0.00

Appendix Note 6

Men's Waist to Hip Ratio (WHR)

Using a proxy WHR of 0.88 to be an L_{WHR} of 9.99, and a WHR of 1.1 to be an L_{WHR} of 0.5 Excel was used to plot the relationship and show the trend:

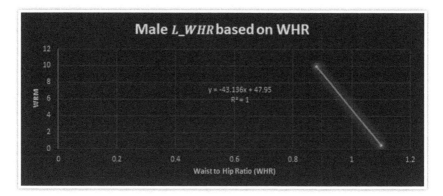

Figure A7.

The resulting equation is:

$$L_{WHR} = -43.136(WHR) + 47.95$$

Transforming it to find arbitrary WHRMs, it was rewritten:

$$\frac{L_{WHR} - 47.95}{-43.136} = WHR$$

$$WHR = 1.11 - 0.023L_{WHR}$$

Where y = L_{WHR} and x = WHR. Based on this regression line, the following table was constructed:

TABLE A12.	Values of L based on WHR
WHR	L_{WHR} **(looks based on WHR)**
1.10	0.5
1.09	1.0
1.08	1.5
1.06	2.0
1.05	2.5
1.04	3.0
1.03	3.5
1.02	4.0
1.01	4.5
1.00	5.0
0.98	5.5
0.97	6.0
0.96	6.5
0.95	7.0
0.94	7.5
0.93	8.0
0.91	8.5
0.90	9.0
0.89	9.5
0.88	9.99

Appendix Note 7

Athleticism Calculations

$$Athleticism\ Rank\ (A) = -4.458lnBF\% + 17.239$$

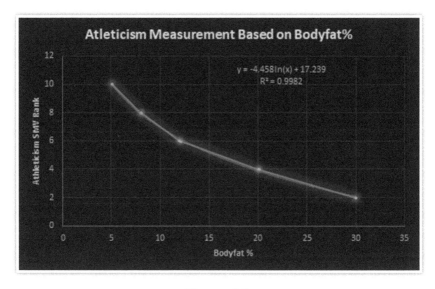

Figure A8.

$$\frac{A - 17.239}{-4.458} = lnBF\%$$

$$lnBF\% = 3.867 - 0.0224A$$

$$BF\% = e^{3.867 - 0.0224\ Athleticism\ Rank}(A)$$

Using the relationship to construct an arbitrary table of Bodyfat% Values:

TABLE A13.   Rating based on Body Fat Percent

BF%	AR
42.7	0.5
38.2	1.0
34.2	1.5
30.5	2.0
27.3	2.5
24.4	3.0
21.8	3.5
19.5	4.0
17.4	4.5
15.6	5.0
13.9	5.5
12.5	6.0
11.1	6.5
10.0	7.0
8.9	7.5
8.0	8.0
7.1	8.5
6.4	9.0
5.7	9.5
5.1	9.99

Appendix Note 8

Money, Power, Status, and Virtuousness Calculations (scalar linear rating)

If we assume that the rating of an attribute (Money, Status, etc.) is based upon a measurable variable (Amount of money in bank, level of income, etc.), and that the relationship between the ranking and the variable is linear, we can assume that ratings lie on a line that is dependent upon the variable, and thus, we can use the traditional linear approach

$$y = mx + b; \ where \ m = \frac{\Delta y}{\Delta x}$$

$$y = (\frac{\Delta y}{\Delta x})x + b$$

Since the slope of the line will concern the most extreme points of x and y, we can write:

$$\Delta y = y_{max} - y_{min}$$

$$\Delta x = x_{max} - x_{min}$$

And thus:

$$y = \frac{(y_{max} - y_{min})}{(x_{max} - x_{min})}x + b$$

Since we want to only measure the effects interms of x and y, we rewrite b as:

$$b = y_{max} - x_{max} \cdot \frac{(y_{max} - y_{min})}{(x_{max} - x_{min})}$$

And then substitute back in to get

$$y = \frac{(y_{max} - y_{min})}{(x_{max} - x_{min})}x + y_{max} - x_{max} \cdot \frac{(y_{max} - y_{min})}{(x_{max} - x_{min})}$$

Combining like terms we get

$$y = y_{max} + (x - x_{max}) \cdot \frac{(y_{max} - y_{min})}{(x_{max} - x_{min})}$$

And then renaming to fit our model:

Scalar Attribute Rating (SAR) =

$$= Rating_{max} + (Xvar - Var_{max}) \cdot \frac{(Rating_{max} - Rating_{min})}{(Var_{max} - Var_{min})}$$

Where

$Rating_{Max}$ = *highest rating on the scale (i.e. 1 to 10) for population*

$Rating_{Min}$ = *lowest rating of attribute*

Var_{Max} = *highest real world variable amount*

Var_{Min} = *lowest real world variable amount*

$Xvar$ = *variable amount in question*

The above equation can be manipulated algebraically to yield the following forms:

$$Var_{Min} = Var_{Max} - \frac{(Rating_{Max} - Rating_{Min})}{(SAR - Rating_{Max})}(Xvar - Var_{Max})$$

$$Var_{Max} = Xvar * \frac{(Rating_{Max} - Rating_{Min})}{(SAR - Rating_{Min})} + Var_{Min} * \frac{(SAR - Rating_{Max})}{(SAR - Rating_{Min})}$$

$$Xvar = Var_{Max} + \frac{(SAR - Rating_{Max})}{(Rating_{Max} - Rating_{Min})} * (Var_{Max} - Var_{Min})$$

For Virtuousness, there is a modified linear rating based on a piecewise analysis of different linear points based on the assumption that there are three points of interest (low, medium and high) that affect the rating:

If $Xvar \leq Var_{Mid}$:

Piecewise Rating $= \frac{(Rating_{Max} - Rating_{Mid})}{(Var_{mid} - Var_{min})}(Xvar - Var_{mid}) + Rating_{Max}$

If $Xvar > Var_{Mid}$:

Piecewise Rating $= \frac{(Rating_{Min} - Rating_{Max})}{(Var_{max} - Var_{mid})}(Xvar - Var_{max}) + Rating_{Min}$

Appendix Note 9

Weight Calculations

Guidelines for Body Mass Index (BMI) and disease risk summarized here [**cite source**]:

TABLE A14.	BMI [cite source here]			
From	**To**	**Disease Risk**	**Classification**	**Notes**
below	18.50	Increased	Underweight	Throw out
18.6	21.90	Low	Acceptable	
22.0	24.99	Very Low	Acceptable	
25.0	29.99	Increased	Overweight	
30.0	34.99	High	Obese	
35.0	39.99	Very High	Obesity I	
40.0	greater	Extremely High	Obesity II	Throw out

First discarding the extreme values and assigning arbitrary scalar ratings for the acceptable range BMIs:

TABLE A15.	BMI Between 18.6 and 24.99	
Item	**BMI Acceptable Range**	**SMVs Related to Acceptable Range (Arbitrary)**
From	24.99	5.00
To	18.6	9.99
Differential	-6.39	4.99
slope (SMV diff)/(BMI diff)	-0.78	

Using the above arbitrary points and plotting it to get the trendline formula ("BWR" = Body Weight Ranking):

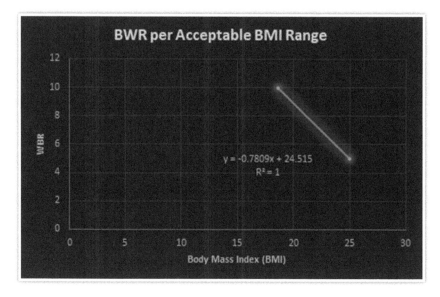

Figure A9.

BMI to SMV conversion:

If "acceptable weight" (18.6 ≤ BMI ≤ 24.99), then:

$$BWR = -0.7809(BMI_{F,acceptable}) + 24.515$$

Manipulate above formula to derive a few arbitrary values for BMI based on SMV:

$$\frac{BWR - 24.515}{-0.7809} = BMI_{acceptable}$$

$$BMI_{acceptable} = 31.39 - 1.28BWR$$

Then constructing at table of these values:

TABLE A16.   BWR based on acceptable BMI

BMI	BWR
24.99	5.0
24.35	5.5
23.71	6.0
23.07	6.5
22.43	7.0
21.79	7.5
21.15	8.0
20.51	8.5
19.87	9.0
18.60	9.99

Then repeating the same process with the overweight and obese BMIs:

TABLE A17.   BMI Between 25 and 39.99

Item	BMI Overweight and Obese Range	SMVs Related to Overweight and Obese (Arbitrary)
From	39.99	0.5
To	25	4.99
Differential	-14.99	4.49
slope (SMV diff)/(BMI diff)	-0.30	

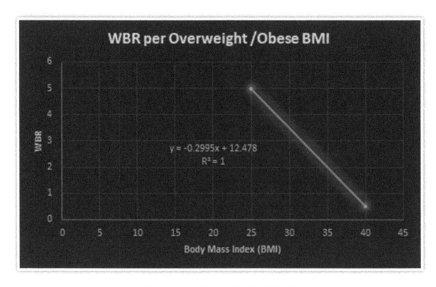

Figure A10.   BMI [30c]

BMI to SMV conversion

If "overweight/obese" ($25 \leq$ BMI ≤ 39.99) then:

$$BWR = -0.2995(BMI_{overweight/obese}) + 12.478$$

$$\frac{BWR - 12.478}{-0.2995} = BMI_{overweight/obese}$$

$$BMI_{overweight/obese} = 41.66 - 3.33BWR$$

TABLE A18.	BWR Based on Overweight/Obese BMI		
BMI	**BWR**	**BMI**	**BWR**
39.99	0.5	31.67	3.0
38.33	1.0	30.01	3.5
36.67	1.5	28.34	4.0
35.00	2.0	26.68	4.5
33.34	2.5	25.00	4.99

The two BWR tables were pieced together to form Table 16 in the manuscript.

Women's Waist to Hip Ratio (BSR)

Using a proxy WHR of 0.7 to be a "Body Shape Ranking" (BSR) of 9.99, and a WHR of 1.0 to be an BSR of 0.5 Excel was used to plot the relationship and show the following trend:

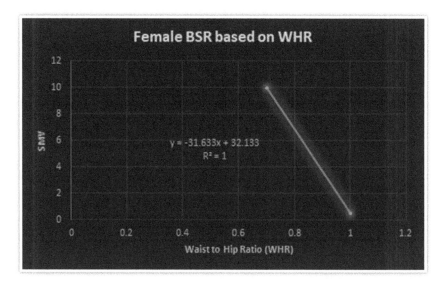

Figure A11.

WHR to BSR conversion:

$$BSR = -31.633(WHR) + 32.14$$

$$\frac{BSR - 32.133}{-31.633} = WHR$$

$$WHR = 1.02 - 0.032BSR$$

The above formula was used to construct Table 18 in the manuscript.

Appendix Note 10

Hypergamy Factor

1. Mean Overall Lambda: The average of "Lambda (based on contrived theory)" values in the D column from D10 to D100, using the formula "=ROUND (AVERAGE (D10:D100),3)"

2. Increment of Determination: an arbitrary increment based on the "Basic Assumptions" used to add to male SMV after the SMV of 1; for the purposes of making it slightly higher and rise faster than the female SMV. This increment can be changed depending on research, but for now, this is an assumed increment of 0.15 (female SMV increases by 0.1)

3. Mean Overall Smoothed Lambda: The average of "Piecewise Trendline Lambda (mean estimates given SMV)" values in the E column. The values in the E column were calculated by using Excel to graph the values in the D column (based off of assumptions of the "Increment of Determination") and using the "trendline" function, derive a functional form by which values from the A column ("X value Index (SMV F)") can be plugged into to model the behavior of the values in D column.

TABLE A19. Hypergamy Factor Data	
Mean Overall Lambda	0.799
Increment of Determination	0.15
Mean Overall Smoothed Lambda	0.799
Mean Smoothed 1 to 7	0.75
Mean Smoothed 7.1 to 10	0.89

TABLE A20						
(t)	A	B = B (t-1) + 0.10	C = C (t-1) + 0.15	D = (B/C)	E = ROUND (-0.073 * LN(A) + 0.9851,3)	F = IF (ROUND (B/E,1) > 10,10,ROUND (B/E,1))
Row Line (t)	X value Index (SMV F)	Female SMV	Male SMV	Lambda (based on contrived theory)	Piecewise Trendline Lambda (mean estimates given SMV)	Male SMV based on Piecewise Lambdas
10	1	1	1	1	0.985	1
11	2	1.1	1.15	0.96	0.935	1.2
12	3	1.2	1.3	0.92	0.905	1.3
13	4	1.3	1.45	0.9	0.884	1.5
14	5	1.4	1.6	0.88	0.868	1.6
15	6	1.5	1.75	0.86	0.854	1.8
16	7	1.6	1.9	0.84	0.843	1.9
17	8	1.7	2.05	0.83	0.833	2
18	9	1.8	2.2	0.82	0.825	2.2
19	10	1.9	2.35	0.81	0.817	2.3
20	11	2	2.5	0.8	0.81	2.5
21	12	2.1	2.65	0.79	0.804	2.6
22	13	2.2	2.8	0.79	0.798	2.8
23	14	2.3	2.95	0.78	0.792	2.9
24	15	2.4	3.1	0.77	0.787	3
25	16	2.5	3.25	0.77	0.783	3.2
26	17	2.6	3.4	0.76	0.778	3.3
27	18	2.7	3.55	0.76	0.774	3.5
28	19	2.8	3.7	0.76	0.77	3.6
29	20	2.9	3.85	0.75	0.766	3.8
30	21	3	4	0.75	0.763	3.9
31	22	3.1	4.15	0.75	0.759	4.1
32	23	3.2	4.3	0.74	0.756	4.2
33	24	3.3	4.45	0.74	0.753	4.4
34	25	3.4	4.6	0.74	0.75	4.5

TABLE A20

(t)	A	B = B (t-1) + 0.10	C = C (t-1) + 0.15	D = (B/C)	E = ROUND (-0.073 * LN(A) + 0.9851,3)	F = IF (ROUND (B/E,1) > 10,10,ROUND (B/E,1))
Row Line (t)	X value Index (SMV F)	Female SMV	Male SMV	Lambda (based on contrived theory)	Piecewise Trendline Lambda (mean estimates given SMV)	Male SMV based on Piecewise Lambdas
35	26	3.5	4.75	0.74	0.747	4.7
36	27	3.6	4.9	0.73	0.745	4.8
37	28	3.7	5.05	0.73	0.742	5
38	29	3.8	5.2	0.73	0.739	5.1
39	30	3.9	5.35	0.73	0.737	5.3
40	31	4	5.5	0.73	0.734	5.4
41	32	4.1	5.65	0.73	0.732	5.6
42	33	4.2	5.8	0.72	0.73	5.8
43	34	4.3	5.95	0.72	0.728	5.9
44	35	4.4	6.1	0.72	0.726	6.1
45	36	4.5	6.25	0.72	0.724	6.2
46	37	4.6	6.4	0.72	0.722	6.4
47	38	4.7	6.55	0.72	0.72	6.5
48	39	4.8	6.7	0.72	0.718	6.7
49	40	4.9	6.85	0.72	0.716	6.8
50	41	5	7	0.71	0.714	7
51	42	5.1	7.15	0.71	0.712	7.2
52	43	5.2	7.3	0.71	0.711	7.3
53	44	5.3	7.45	0.71	0.709	7.5
54	45	5.4	7.6	0.71	0.707	7.6
55	46	5.5	7.75	0.71	0.706	7.8
56	47	5.6	7.9	0.71	0.704	8
57	48	5.7	8.05	0.71	0.703	8.1
58	49	5.8	8.2	0.71	0.701	8.3
59	50	5.9	8.35	0.71	0.7	8.4

TABLE A20

(t)	A	B = B (t-1) + 0.10	C = C (t-1) + 0.15	D = (B/C)	E = ROUND (-0.073 * LN(A) + 0.9851,3)	F = IF (ROUND (B/E,1) > 10,10,ROUND (B/E,1))
Row Line (t)	X value Index (SMV F)	Female SMV	Male SMV	Lambda (based on contrived theory)	Piecewise Trendline Lambda (mean estimates given SMV)	Male SMV based on Piecewise Lambdas
60	51	6	8.5	0.71	0.698	8.6
61	52	6.1	8.65	0.71	0.697	8.8
62	53	6.2	8.8	0.7	0.695	8.9
63	54	6.3	8.95	0.7	0.694	9.1
64	55	6.4	9.1	0.7	0.693	9.2
65	56	6.5	9.25	0.7	0.691	9.4
66	57	6.6	9.4	0.7	0.69	9.6
67	58	6.7	9.55	0.7	0.689	9.7
68	59	6.8	9.7	0.7	0.687	9.9
69	60	6.9	9.85	0.7	0.686	10
70	**61**	**7**	**10**	0.7	0.685	10
71	**62**	**7.1**	**9.85**	0.72	0.696	10
72	63	7.2	9.7	0.74	0.75	9.6
73	64	7.3	9.55	0.76	0.782	9.3
74	65	7.4	9.4	0.79	0.804	9.2
75	66	7.5	9.25	0.81	0.822	9.1
76	67	7.6	9.1	0.84	0.836	9.1
77	68	7.7	8.95	0.86	0.848	9.1
78	69	7.8	8.8	0.89	0.858	9.1
79	70	7.9	8.65	0.91	0.868	9.1
80	**71**	**8**	**9**	0.89	0.876	9.1
81	72	8.1	9.1	0.89	0.883	9.2
82	73	8.2	9.2	0.89	0.89	9.2
83	74	8.3	9.3	0.89	0.896	9.3
84	75	8.4	9.4	0.89	0.902	9.3

TABLE A20

(t)	A	B = B (t-1) + 0.10	C = C (t-1) + 0.15	D = (B/C)	E = ROUND (-0.073 * LN(A) + 0.9851,3)	F = IF (ROUND (B/E,1) > 10,10,ROUND (B/E,1))
Row Line (t)	X value Index (SMV F)	Female SMV	Male SMV	Lambda (based on contrived theory)	Piecewise Trendline Lambda (mean estimates given SMV)	Male SMV based on Piecewise Lambdas
85	76	8.5	9.5	0.89	0.907	9.4
86	77	8.6	9.6	0.9	0.912	9.4
87	78	8.7	9.7	0.9	0.917	9.5
88	79	8.8	9.8	0.9	0.922	9.5
89	80	8.9	9.9	0.9	0.926	9.6
90	81	9	10	0.9	0.93	9.7
91	82	9.1	10	0.91	0.934	9.7
92	83	9.2	10	0.92	0.937	9.8
93	84	9.3	10	0.93	0.941	9.9
94	85	9.4	10	0.94	0.944	10
95	86	9.5	10	0.95	0.947	10
96	87	9.6	10	0.96	0.95	10
97	88	9.7	10	0.97	0.953	10
98	89	9.8	10	0.98	0.956	10
99	90	9.9	10	0.99	0.959	10
100	91	10	10	1	0.961	10

Basic Assumptions

1. Everybody has value: there is no such thing as an absolute "0", as everybody has something to offer. Values can approach 0, but in the text, 1, 0.1, or 0.5 may be used as arbitrary low values. Calculations will essentially used to prove logical basis for movement up or down a decile scale

2. There are no perfect "10s": this is an extension of #1 above. Since perfection is only a concept, things can always be improved, and therefore everybody also has something that

detracts from them. In reality, the maximum value on the decile scale is 9.99, but 10 will also be used at times to again prove the logical basis from movement up or down the scale

3. Hypergamy is virtually non-existent at the lowest and highest ends of the scale ($\lambda=1$): this is the assumption that people at the very "top" and very "bottom" or forced to be together. The people on the bottom are because they don't have options, the people on the top (more specifically the women) because they maximize the SMV of their partners

4. Hypergamy behavior is based off of the Bateman principle and follows the assumptions of 1 thru 3 above:

Based on the Bateman Principle, we have the following:

$$\lambda(E[SMV_M]) = E[SMV_F]$$

And the condition that $0 < \lambda \leq 1$

And since we expect actual values to equal expected values, we have

$$\lambda SMV_M = SMV_F$$

where

SMV_M *is the Sexual Marketplace Value*

SMV_F *is the female Sexual Marketplace Value*

λ *is the hypergamy factor*

The behavior of λ is assumed to be such:

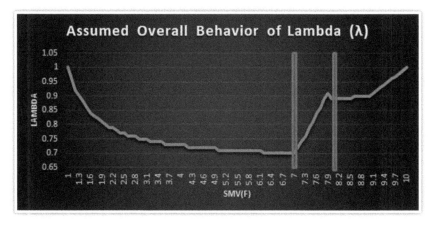

Figure A12

The two orange bars above are where hypogamy starts to change. My assumptions here are:

- **$1 \leq SMV_F \leq 7$:** the hypergamy factor decreases (**Hypergamy increases**) at an increasing rate because at very low SMV, women would tend to link up with men around their own SMV, and as a result are "forced" to be non-hypergamous at the low end as a result, the least attractive females and the least attractive males end up together. As the SMV increases, Hypergamy increases faster, maxing out at 7, since the 7 seems to be the most sought after SMV (per the adjustable 7 theory). The lambda estimate for SMVs in this range is:

$$\lambda_{SMV=1\ to\ 7} = -0.073 \ln (IND_{SMV_{F,(1\ to\ 7)}}) + 0.9851;$$

where 1 corresponds to an index value of 1 and 7 corresponds to an index value of 61.

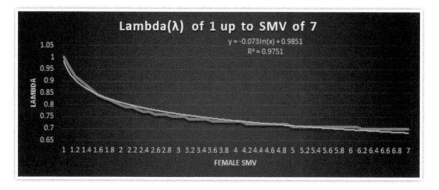

Figure A13

- **$7.1 \leq SMV_F \leq 7.9$:** the hypergamy factor begins to **increase fast** (Hypergamy decreases) at this point, women realize that there are not many points higher they can go. They don't have much to choose below them, and because guys greater than 7 have a better pool available to them, the pickings for women begin to get slim (ever heard the "Where are the good men?" statements?).
- **$8 \leq SMV_F \leq 9$:** From an SMV of 8 to 10 the hypergamy factor **increases** slower

- **9.1 ≤ *SMV_F* ≤ 10 (9.99):** all SMV_M = 10 because they can't go any higher. The hypergamy factor **increases** ever so slowly as it comes to a trickle and stops at SMV_F = 10. As values approach 10, a "forced" Hypergamy exists. A 10 in theory is actually 9.99999999 in reality since perfection is only a concept.

- **7.1≤ *SMV_F* ≤ 10 (9.99):** all of the increases are averaged to yield Lambda estimates in this range of

$$\lambda_{SMV=7.1\,to\,10} = 0.0779 \ln\left(IND_{SMV_{F,(7.1\,to\,10)}}\right) + 0.6964$$

where 7.1 corresponds to an index value of 1 and 10 corresponds to an index value of 30

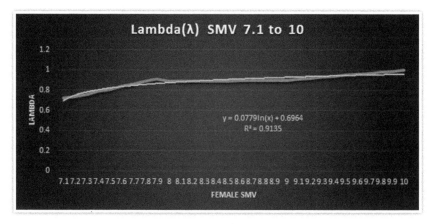

Figure A14

TABLE A21.	Corresponding *SMV_M* Range to *SMV_F* Range		
SMV_F Range	λ Estimate	Average λ	Corresponding *SMV_M* Range
1 to 7	$-0.073 \ln\left(IND_{SMV_{F,(1\,to\,7)}}\right) + 0.9851$	0.75	1 to 10
7.1 to 10	$0.0779 ln\left(IND_{SMV_{F,(7.1\,to\,10)}}\right) + 0.6964$	0.89	9.1 to 10

Appendix Note 11

Actual Value Models

All actual value models are calculated using the theoretical basis of

$$\lambda SMV_M = SMV_F$$

where

$$\lambda SMV_M = SMV_{F*}$$

The "F*" is the "market" female, or the hypothetical female that occurs when all of the females in a given group/market are amalgamated together—acting as one mind. This market "borg" female's value is derived from the values of the females that comprise "her":

$$w_{SMV_{F,j}} = \frac{SMV_{F,j}}{\sum_{j=1}^{n} SMV_{F,j}}$$

For example, in a group of 3 females (j = 1,2,3) and their SMV's are 5, 6, and 7 respectively, we have:

$$\sum_{j=1}^{3} SMV_{F,j} = \sum_{j=1}^{3} SMV_{F,j} =$$

$$\sum_{j=1}^{3} SMV_{F,j} = SMV_{F,1} + SMV_{F,2} + SMV_{F,3} = 5 + 6 + 7 = 18$$

For example, the weight of female 1 is

$$w_{SMV_{F,1}} = \frac{5}{18}$$

And like wise for 2 and 3, the weights are 6/18 and 7/18 respectively. These weights are used to weight the opinions of the rankings of a given male of SMV_M. But their personalized rankings will be $SMV_{M,j}$ so that

$$SMV_M = \sum_{j=k}^{n} w_{SMV_{F,j}} SMV_{M,j}$$

If females 1, 2 and 3 each have the opinion that a given male's SMV is 4, 8 and 6 respectively, we have

$$SMV_M = \sum_{j=1}^{3} \left(\frac{5}{18}(4) + \frac{6}{18}(8) + \frac{7}{18}(6) \right) = 6.11$$

Whether or not a female in the group will date him depends upon the group's lambda in the environment that they operate. If the market lambda is 0.9, then only female 1 would date him since:

$$\lambda SMV_M = SMV_F$$

$$0.9(6.11) = 5.50$$

$$5.50 > 5$$

Since 5.50 > 5

The same valuation logic can be applied to male opinion of females, it's just that the lambda dictates the dating decision of the females in question.

Appendix Note 12

Reasoning for Social Benefits decreasing (diminishing) returns to SMV:

$$if\ f(SMV) = \sqrt{SMV}, then\ f'(SMV) = \frac{d}{dSMV}(SMV) = \frac{1}{2\sqrt{SMV}}$$

And you can see as SMV rises, $\sqrt{SMV}$ still increases, but in smaller and smaller increments—hence the diminishing return to SMV.

Appendix Note 13

Exit Strategies

Estimation of Future SMV

Note table 44, where an initial value for Sam's SMV is 7 in the first month with different health conditions related to smoking:

TABLE A22.	SMV and Smoking (Truncated)		
A	B	C	D
t (months)	Sam's SMV (NDR, no smoking)	Sam's SMV (1 pack per day Gamma)	Sam's SMV (1 pack per day, quits at beginning of 18th month) part 1
1	7.00	7.00	7.00
6	6.96	6.94	6.94
9	6.94	6.91	6.91
12	6.92	6.88	6.88
15	6.90	6.84	6.84
18	6.88	6.81	6.82
21	6.86	6.78	6.79
24	6.84	6.75	6.77
27	6.82	6.71	6.75
30	6.80	6.68	6.73
33	6.78	6.65	6.71
36	6.76	6.62	6.69

The formula that was derived that forecasts SMV based on a value decline factor (δ) is:

$$E[SMV_{t+k}] = (SMV_t)^* (1 - \delta)^k$$

Where t is the time period and k is the number of additional time periods. If we are in the 2nd time period/month, t = 2. If we want to forecast to the 5th time period, then (t + k) = 5, and therefore k = 3.

Also note in Table 43 where we obtain the decline/depreciation rates:

TABLE A23.	Smoking and Life Expectancy	
Smoking can reduce life expectancy by about 18 years on a 30-year-old person (medical news today article)		
A	Life Expectancy (LE)	83
B = (1/A)	Natural Depreciation Rate (NDR)	0.012
C = (B/12)	Monthly NDR	**0.001**
D	Age	30
E	Decrease in total life expectancy (18 years reduced/30 years age) summarized from article	60%
F = (D x E)	Additions to Age as a result of smoking	18
G = (D+F)	Effective Age	48
H = [(G/D) x B]	Effective Annual Depreciation Rate (Gamma)	0.019
I = (H/12)	Monthly Gamma	**0.0016**
J	Market Lambda Assumption	**0.8**

On this table we have the monthly, per period NDR and Gamma. Both the NDR and Gamma are depreciation/decline rates. Gamma is essentially the NDR amplified by the effects of the ratio of Effective Age to Age.

Combining this logic from the two above tables and the formula, if calculating Sam's value from month 1 to month 6 in Table 44 column C do the following:

$$E[SMV_{t+k}] = (SMV_t)\,(1 - \delta)^k$$

And filling in the parameters:

$$E[SMV_6] = 7 * (1 - 0.0016)^5$$

$$E[SMV_6] = 6.94$$

For values in table 44 column B, you would use the monthly NDR instead of monthly Gamma, for example calculating from month 6 to month 21 in column B:

$$E[SMV_{t+k}] = (SMV_t)\,(1 - NDR)^k$$

$$E[SMV_{21}] = (SMV_6)\,(1 - NDR)^{15}$$

$$E[SMV_{21}] = 6.96 * (1 - 0.001)^{15}$$

$$E[SMV_{21}] = 6.86$$

Finally, for table 44 column D, it is a combination of column B and C techniques. Up to month 17 the gamma is used and afterwards the NDR is used (because he smokes his last cigarette in month 17). For example, to calculate Sam's value in column D for month 9 to 33, we have:

$$E[SMV_{17}] = (SMV_9)\,(1 - \delta)^8$$

And

$$E[SMV_{33}] = E[SMV_{17}]\,(1 - NDR)^{16}$$

Substituting:

$$E[SMV_{33}] = (SMV_9)\,(1 - \delta)^8\,(1 - NDR)^{16}$$

Filling in terms:

$$E[SMV_{33}] = (6.91)\,(1 - 0.0016)^8\,(1 - 0.001)^{16}$$

$$E[SMV_{33}] = 6.7135 \approx 6.71$$

In Table 51, the values of the women in the first 3 columns are based off of Sam's different health/SMV profiles. are found by applying the lambda to Sam's Values above per the following formula:

$$\lambda SMV_M = SMV_F$$

Where M = Male (Sam) and F = Female (A, B, C as mentioned in the table). Rewriting to take the time series and expected value into account:

$$\lambda E[SMV_{Sam,t}] = E[SMV_{F,t}]$$

In the table below, λ = 0.8, so for any time = t, we have

$$0.8 * E[SMV_{Sam,t}] = E[SMV_{F,t}]$$

For example, below, Female B (Jenny) in the 12th month (t = 12) is calculated by taking Sam's expected value in Table 44 column C above we have: (6.88) and applying the 0.8:

$$0.8 * E[SMV_{Sam,12}] = E[SMV_{Jenny,12}] =$$

$$0.8 * 6.88 = E[SMV_{Jenny,12}]$$

$$5.50 = E[SMV_{Jenny,12}]$$

TABLE A24.	Example Attraction Table			
t (months)	Hypothetical Female A (Based off NDR)	Jenny (Female B)'s SMV (Based off Gamma)	Hypothetical Female C (Based off improved 18th month health)	Hypothetical Female D (NDR applied backward to C)
1	5.60	5.60	n/a	5.55
12	5.54	5.50	n/a	5.49
18	5.51	5.45	5.45	5.45
24	5.47	5.40	5.42	5.42
36	5.41	5.29	5.35	5.35
54	5.31	5.14	5.26	5.26
72	5.21	5.00	5.16	5.16

This works for Female C as well but recall that she doesn't "exist" before the 18th month because until then, Sam was still smoking a pack per day. She only becomes available to him on the 18th month., as a result in months 1 thru 17 there is "n/a" because the value isn't calculated.

The purpose of having Female D was to show that if C "existed" in months 1 thru 17, what her value would be. Remember that according to our theory, D wouldn't have been on Sam's radar because Female B, whose value is always higher than D's is available to Sam, and thus, makes her a better alternative to D.

To calculate D's value the following assumptions were made:

1. The standard relationship length is 36 months. Since C is available at the beginning of the 18th month, Female C's SMV from month 18 to month 54 are used.

2. In month 18, Female C's SMV is 5.45 and in month 54 her SMV is 5.26. Therefore, we need to find the gamma that when compounded over 36 months will make 5.45 decline to 5.26 like so:

$$5.45 * (1 - \delta)^{36} = 5.26$$

Rearranging we get

$$\left(\frac{5.26}{5.45}\right)^{\left(\frac{1}{36}\right)} = (1 - \delta)$$

$$1 - \left(\frac{5.26}{5.45}\right)^{\left(\frac{1}{36}\right)} = \delta$$

$$1 - \left(\frac{5.26}{5.45}\right)^{\left(\frac{1}{36}\right)} = \delta$$

$$0.0010 = \delta$$

This number should look familiar to you, because this "backed out" gamma is actually the NDR from Table 43 row C. The reason is since Sam stopped smoking; his 18th month decline has reverted back to a level of natural depreciation.

Since compounding brings us forward in time, we must use discounting to take us backward. Our discount factor is dependent on the number of time periods with relation to the SMV starting in the 18th month, so:

$$\left(\frac{1}{(1 - \delta)^{(k)}}\right) * 5.45 = E[SMV_{Female\ D, t-k}];\ where\ k \leq 17$$

The discount factor is the leftmost expression in brackets. Our value for k is the number of periods we want to go back to from the 18th month ($t = 18$). For example, the value of Female D in month 12. That would make $k = 6$:

$$\left(\frac{1}{(1-\delta)^{(6)}}\right) * 5.45 = E[SMV_{Female\ D,18-6}] =$$

$$\left(\frac{1}{(1-0.0010)^{(6)}}\right) * 5.45 = E[SMV_{Female\ D,12}] =$$

$$1.0060 * 5.45 = E[SMV_{Female\ D,12}] =$$

$$5.49 \approx E[SMV_{Female\ D,12}]$$

Please note that the excel formulas used to generate the table numbers were exact and shortened to two decimals, not actually rounded to two decimals. Therefore there will be small discrepancies.

The occupational role hourly values can be seen on the following table:

TABLE A25.	Jenny's Endowment Value							
t (month)	L	C	Cooks	CW	Maids	ES	Average (Assuming Equal Time Spent)	Monthly Endowment Value
1	13.01	23.29	21.07	13.94	13.92	268.53	58.96	$8,844
12	12.94	23.09	20.98	13.86	13.84	263.37	58.01	$8,701
18	12.91	22.98	20.93	13.81	13.79	260.78	57.53	$8,629
24	12.87	22.88	20.88	13.77	13.75	258.20	57.06	$8,558
36	12.80	22.65	20.78	13.68	13.65	252.51	56.01	$8,401
54	12.70	22.34	20.64	13.55	13.51	244.76	54.58	$8,187
72	12.60	22.05	20.51	13.43	13.39	237.52	53.25	$7,987

L = Laundry; C = Counselors; CW = Childcare Workers; ES = Escort Services

This table used the following formula and assumed equal time spent (1/6) to calculate the monthly endowment value above:

$$V(Launderers\ and\ Dry\ Cleaners) = \$0.68 * (SMV) + \$9.20$$

$$V(Counselors) = \$2.07 * (SMV) + \$11.70$$

$$V(Private\ Cooks) = \$0.93 * (SMV) + \$15.86$$

$$V(Childcare\ Workers) = \$0.85 * (SMV) + \$9.18$$

$$V(Maids\ and\ Housekeepers) = \$0.89 * (SMV) + 8.94$$

$$V(Escort\ Services) = \$51.69 * (SMV) - 20.93$$

Simply substituting in the SMV and averaging it will equal time spent (simple average) will give the values in Table 53 column B below:

TABLE A26. Jenny's Endowment Differential

A t (months)	B Jenny (Female B)'s SMV (Based off Gamma)	C = CUM(B) Female B (Cumulative Benefits (CB))	D Hypothetical Female D (Back estimate of C)	E = CUM(D) Female D (CB)	F = (D-B) Endowment Differential (EOM Value)	G = (E-C) Cumulative Differential (CD)
1	$8,844	$8,844	$8,772	$8,772	-$71.39	-$71.39
12	$8,701	$105,287	$8,687	$104,702	-$14.28	-$585.38
18	$8,629	$157,252	$8,629	$156,610	$0.00	-$642.49
24	$8,558	$208,761	$8,587	$208,247	$28.55	-$513.99
36	$8,401	$310,436	$8,487	$310,679	$85.66	$242.72
54	$8,187	$459,708	$8,358	$462,264	$171.33	$2,555.67
72	$7,987	$605,154	$8,215	$611,407	$228.44	$6,253.55

Moral Hazard

Month	Original Gamma	Gamma 2.5% Increase	Gamma 5% Increase	Gamma 7.5% Increase	Gamma 10% Increase
TABLE A27. Jenny's Cumulative Endowment Values					
18	$8,629	$8,629	$8,629	$8,629	$8,629
36	$161,813	$161,799	$161,746	$161,694	$161,641
54	$311,085	$310,938	$310,737	$310,537	$310,338
72	$456,531	$456,164	$455,727	$455,290	$454,853

The Endowment Value in a given time period (in this case, the month) t is found by getting the weighted average hourly value and multiplying it by the number of hours [see Picking and Exit Strategy to review] once the monthly EV is found, the cumulative monthly values are found by adding on the EV in each month prior to the month we want to estimate the cumulative value. In table 55, we start with Jenny's monthly value as of month 18. From Table 51, her SMV is 5.45. We assumed she would spend an equal amount of time in each of the six relationship roles (which is 1/6). As a result, we have the following calculation:

$Endowment\ Value_t$

$$= \left(\frac{1}{6}\right) x\ [\,V(Launderers\ and\ Dry\ Cleaners) + V(Counselors) +$$
$$+ V(Private\ Cooks) + V(Childcare\ Workers) +$$
$$+ V(Maids\ and\ Housekeepers) + V(Escort\ Services)]$$

Substituting the regression equations for each role we have

$Endowment\ Value_t$

$$= \left(\frac{1}{6}\right) x\ [(\$0.68 * (SMV) + \$9.20) + (\$2.07 * (SMV) + \$11.70) +$$
$$+ (\$0.93 * (SMV) + \$15.86) + (\$0.85 * (SMV) + \$9.18) +$$
$$+ (\$0.89 * (SMV) + 8.94) + (\$51.69 * (SMV) - 20.93)\,]$$

Since the Endowment Value in month 18 is a function of the SMV in month 18, we plug it in:

Endowment Value $_{18}$

$$= \left(\frac{1}{6}\right) \times [(\$0.68 * (5.45) + \$9.20) + (\$2.07 * (5.45) + \$11.70) +$$

$$+ (\$0.93 * (5.45) + \$15.86) + (\$0.85 * (5.45) + \$9.18) +$$

$$+ (\$0.89 * (5.45) + 8.94) + (\$51.69 * (5.45) - 20.93)] \approx \$8,629$$

To find the Cumulative Value ($CUM_{(t+k)}$) in any subsequent month the following formula can be used:

$$CUM_{(t+k)} = CUM_{(t)} + \sum_{k=1}^{N} EV_{(t+k)}$$

$$CUM_{(t)} = EV_{(t)}$$

$$Equivalently, CUM_{(1)} = EV_{(1)}$$

Where $EV_{(t)}$ is the Endowment Value from the initial month and since there are no others before it, it will naturally be equal to $CUM_{(t)}$. Afterwards, each additional month's EV will be added on. Therefore, to get the value in month 36, the EV's of every month subsequent to the 18th month (19 to 36) will end up summing to the cumulative value in month 36 (which is $161,813).

This is an abbreviated version done in MSFT Excel:

t (month)	Jenny (Female B)'s SMV (Based off Gamma)	Average Hourly Income (AHI) (Assuming Equal Time Spent)	Monthly Endowment Value (Assuming 5 hours per day/30-day months)	B's Cumulative Going Concern
TABLE A28. B's Cumulative Going Concern				
18	5.45	57.53	$8,629.99	$8,629.99
19	5.44	57.44	$8,615.71	$17,245.70
20	5.43	57.34	$8,601.43	$25,847.13
21	5.42	57.25	$8,587.16	$34,434.29
22	5.41	57.15	$8,572.88	$43,007.16
23	5.41	57.15	$8,572.88	$51,580.04
24	5.40	57.06	$8,558.60	$60,138.64
25	5.39	56.96	$8,544.32	$68,682.96
26	5.38	56.87	$8,530.05	$77,213.01
27	5.37	56.77	$8,515.77	$85,728.78
28	5.36	56.68	$8,501.49	$94,230.27
29	5.35	56.58	$8,487.21	$102,717.48
30	5.34	56.49	$8,472.94	$111,190.41
31	5.34	56.49	$8,472.94	$119,663.35
32	5.33	56.39	$8,458.66	$128,122.01
33	5.32	56.30	$8,444.38	$136,566.39
34	5.31	56.20	$8,430.10	$144,996.49
35	5.30	56.11	$8,415.83	$153,412.31
36	5.29	56.01	$8,401.55	$161,813.86

To get the Gamma increase columns in Table 55, we start with the same SMV in the 18th month and then assume we have a gamma that is higher by increments of 2.5% to project it forward. Thus:

$$Original\ Gamma_t * (1.025) = Gamma\ 2.5\%\ Increase$$

$$Original\ Gamma_t * (1.05) = Gamma\ 5\%\ Increase$$

$$Original\ Gamma_t * (1.075) = Gamma\ 7.5\%\ Increase$$

$$Original\ Gamma_t * (1.10) = Gamma\ 10\%\ Increase$$

Which translate into the following Gammas to apply to the value of 5.45 in month 18 to project them forward into subsequent months given the percent change scenarios:

Gamma 2.5% Increase: $0.001606 * (1.025) = 0.001647$

Gamma 5% Increase: $0.001606 * (1.05) = 0.001687$

Gamma 7.5% Increase: $0.001606 * (1.075) = 0.001723$

Gamma 10% Increase: $0.001606 * (1.10) = 0.00176$

WORKS CITED

1. CBS News. "Dating Study: Women Are Choosier Than Men." *CBS News*, CBS Interactive, 4 Sept. 2007, *www.cbsnews.com/news/ dating-study-women-are-choosier-than-men/*

2. Smithsonian Institution . "Homo Erectus." *The Smithsonian Institution's Human Origins Program*, 10 Jan. 2020, *http://humanorigins.si.edu/ evidence/human-fossils/species/homo-erectus*

3. *Hierarchy in the Forest: the Evolution of Egalitarian Behavior*, by Cristopher Boehm, Harvard University, 1999, p. 198. *ISBN 0-674-39031-8.*

4. Smithsonian Institution. "Homo Sapiens." *The Smithsonian Institution's Human Origins Program*, 27 July 2020, *https://humanorigins.si.edu/ evidence/human-fossils/species/homo-sapiens*

5. Urry, David, and Lisa Hendry. "How We Became Human." *Natural History Museum, https://www.nhm.ac.uk/discover/how-we-became-human.html*

6. Smithsonian Institution. "Brains." *The Smithsonian Institution's Human Origins Program*, 16 Jan. 2019, *http://humanorigins.si.edu/ human-characteristics/brains*

7. *People of the Earth: an Introduction to World Prehistory*, by Brian M. Fagan and Nadia Durrani, Routledge, 1989, pp. 169–181.

8. *Hadza Fieldsite in Tanzania,* by Alyssa Crittenden. Arts and Humanities Research Counsil: Culture of the Mind, *http://www.philosophy.dept.shef. ac.uk/culture&mind/people/crittendena/*

9. *Last of the Maasai*, by Mohamed Amin et al., Camerapix, 2004, pp. 53–54. *ISBN 1-874041-32-6*

10. *Equality for the Sexes in Human Evolution? Early Hominid Sexual Dimorphism and Implications for Mating Systems and Social Behavior* by Clark Spencer Larsen. *PNAS*, National Academy of Sciences, 5 Aug. 2003, *https://doi.org/10.1073/pnas.1633678100.*

11. Fox, Maggie. "Genetics Suggest Modern Female Came First." *ABC News*, ABC News Network, 7 Jan. 2006, *https://abcnews.go.com/Technology/ story?id=119799*

12. Bateman, A J. "Intra-Sexual Selection in Drosophila." *Heredity*, U.S. National Library of Medicine, 2 Dec. 1948, *https://www.ncbi.nlm.nih.gov/ pubmed/18103134*

13. Trivers, R L. "Parental Investment and Sexual Selection." *Sexual Selection and the Descent of Man: 1871-1971*, edited by Bernard Campbell, Aldine, 1972, pp. 136–179.

14. Donald, Dewsbury A. *Portraits of Pioneers on Psychology*, vol. 4, 2000, pp. 269–281.

15. Tlachi-López, José L., et al. "Copulation and Ejaculation in Male Rats under Sexual Satiety and the Coolidge Effect." *Physiology & Behavior*, vol. 106, no. 5, 29 Apr. 2012, pp. 620–630., doi:10.1016/j. physbeh.2012.04.020.

16. Martin , Joyce A, and Et al. "National Vital Statistics Reports. Births: Final Data for 2002." CDC, 17 Dec. 2003. *https://www.cdc.gov/nchs/data/ nvsr/nvsr52/nvsr52_10.pdf*

17. Information on men and women and siring children habits

    a.   Hitti, Miranda. *"How Many Men Become Fathers?"* WebMD, WebMD, 1 June 2006, *www.webmd.com/men/news/20060601/ how-many-men-become-fathers.*

    b.   *"New Study Examines Men Who Father Children With More Than One Woman."* Child Trends, 8 Oct. 2006, *www.childtrends.org/news-release/new-study-examines-men-who-father-children-with-more-than-one-woman.*

    c.   Carroll, Linda. *"1 In 5 US Moms Have Kids with Multiple Dads, Study Says."* NBC News, 1 Apr. 2011, *www.nbcnews.com/id/42364656/ns/ health-childrens_health/t/us-moms-have-kids-multiple-dads-study-says/#.X399x4uSmM9.*

    d.   Bureau, US Census. *"Age and Sex Composition in the United States: 2011."* The United States Census Bureau, 6 July 2011, *www.census. gov/data/tables/2011/demo/age-and-sex/2011-age-sex-composition. html.*

    e.   Guzzo, Karen Benjamin. *"New Partners, More Kids: Multiple-Partner Fertility in the United States."* The Annals of the American Academy of Political and Social Science, U.S. National Library of Medicine, July 2014, *www.ncbi.nlm.nih.gov/pmc/articles/PMC4182921/.*

18. "Markets." Merriam-Webster, Merriam-Webster, *www.merriam-webster. com/dictionary/markets.*

19. Indiana University. "What Men And Women Really Want In A Mate." ScienceDaily. ScienceDaily, 7 September 2007. *www.sciencedaily.com/ releases/2007/09/070903204845.htm*

20. Singer, Marie. "Pear Shape Is Healthier than Apple Shape - Human Body." Market Business News, 13 Sept. 2018, *https:// marketbusinessnews.com/pear-shape/187339/*

21. Wallace, Hamish B, and Thomas W Kelsey. "Human Ovarian Reserve from Conception to the Menopause." PloS One, Public Library of Science, 27 Jan. 2010, *https://www.ncbi.nlm.nih.gov/pmc/articles/ PMC2811725/*

22. "Testosterone, Aging, and the Mind." Harvard Health, Jan. 2008, *https://www.health.harvard.edu/newsletter_article/ Testosterone_aging_and_the_mind*

23. Free and Total Testosterone Estimate Source Data

    a. Vermeulen, A, et al. "AVERAGE TESTOSTERONE LEVELS BY AGE IN MEN ." Declining Androgens with Age: An Overview, by A Vermeulen, New York: Parthenon Publishing, 1996, pp. 3–14.

    b. Simon, D., Nahoul, et al. "NORMAL TESTOSTERONE LEVELS IN MEN (NON-DIABETIC)." Sex Hormones, Aging, Ethnicity and Insulin Sensitivity in Men: An Overview of the TELECOM Study, by A Vermeulen, New York: Parthenon Publishing, 1996, pp. 85–102.

24. Weber, Max, et al. Politics as a Vocation. New York: Free Press, 1946.

25. Median Income over time and Male Dating Preferences

    a. Bureau, US Census. *"CPS Historical Poverty Footnotes."* The United States Census Bureau, 28 Aug. 2020, *www.census.gov/topics/income-poverty/poverty/guidance/poverty-footnotes/cps-historic-footnotes. html*.

    b. Petter, Olivia. "Older men like older women but would still prefer relationships with younger ones, study finds." The Independent, Independent Digital News and Media, 3 Apr. 2018, *www. independent.co.uk/life-style/love-sex/men-women-dating-age-older-younger-preference-marriage-study-attraction-a8286016.html*.

26. McChesney, Jasper. "Why You Should Summarize Your Data with the Geometric Mean." Medium, Medium, 8 Oct. 2017, *medium.com/@ JLMC/understanding-three-simple-statistics-for-data-visualizations-2619dbb3677a*.

27. Regarding the "Golden Ratio"

    a. "Golden Ratio." Wikipedia, Wikimedia Foundation, 15 Sept. 2020, *https://en.wikipedia.org/wiki/Golden_ratio*

    b. Pallett, Pamela M, et al. "New 'Golden' Ratios for Facial Beauty." Vision Research, U.S. National Library of Medicine, 25 Jan. 2010, *www.ncbi.nlm.nih.gov/pmc/articles/PMC2814183/*

28. Waist to Hip Ratio:

    a. Watson, Stephanie. "What Is the Waist-to-Hip Ratio?" Edited by Daniel Bubnis, Healthline, 17 Sept. 2018, *www.healthline.com/ health/waist-to-hip-ratio*.

    b. Gruendl, Martin. "Beautiful Figure." Beautycheck - Beautiful Figure, *www.uni-regensburg.de/Fakultaeten/phil_Fak_II/Psychologie/Psy_II/ beautycheck/english/figur/figur.htm*.

    c. Clark, Micheal. *NASM Essentials of Personal Fitness Training*. Jones & Bartlett Learning, 2018.

29. "Body Fat Percentage Chart: Ideal Body Fat for Men and Women - Fitness Lab Testing. Assessments." Fitness Lab Testing. Assessments. Personalized Diet and Exercise Insights, Diet and Exercise Insights, 1 Aug. 2020, *www.fitnescity.com/blog/body-fat-percentage-chart*.

30. Power

    a. Shalvey, Kevin. "50 Cent Ramps His Own Stock on Twitter." The Guardian, Guardian News and Media, 11 Jan. 2011, *www.theguardian.com/business/2011/jan/11/50-cent-ramps-stock-on-twitter*.

    b. Baxter-Wright, Dusty. "The Number of Followers You Need to Be a 'Celebrity' Is Probably Lower than You Thought." Cosmopolitan, Cosmopolitan, 5 July 2019, *www.cosmopolitan.com/uk/worklife/a28302319/number-of-followers-celebrity/*.

31. Virtuousness

    a. Spanier, Graham B. Dyadic Adjustment Scale (DAS): User's Manual. MHS, 2001.

    b. Hillin, Taryn. "New Study Claims People Who've Had More Sexual Partners Report Unhappier Marriages." HuffPost, HuffPost, 7 Dec. 2017, *www.huffpost.com/entry/more-sexual-partners-unhappy-marriage_n_5698440*.

32. Occupational Wages

    a. "May 2017 National Occupational Employment and Wage Estimates." U.S. Bureau of Labor Statistics, U.S. Bureau of Labor Statistics, 30 Mar. 2018, *www.bls.gov/oes/2017/may/oes_nat.htm*.

    b. *Miller, Gordon. "What Is the Typical Price for a Prostitute's Services?" Quora, 1 June 2018, www.quora.com/What-is-the-typical-price-for-a-prostitutes-services.*

33. LaBier , Douglas. "Women Initiate Divorce Much More Than Men, Here's Why." Psychology Today, 28 Aug. 2015, *www.psychologytoday.com/us/blog/the-new-resilience/201508/women-initiate-divorce-much-more-men-heres-why*

34. Fisman, Raymond, et al. "Gender Differences in Mate Selection: Evidence from a Speed Dating Experiment." *The Quarterly Journal of Economics*, vol. 121, no. 2, 2006, pp. 673–697. JSTOR, *www.jstor.org/stable/25098803*.

35. Nolo. "How Much Will My Divorce Cost and How Long Will It Take?" Www.nolo.com, Nolo, 30 Dec. 2019, *www.nolo.com/legal-encyclopedia/ctp/cost-of-divorce.html*.

    a. page 689

    b. page 675

    c. page 688

36. US Census. *"Current Population Survey (CPS)."* The United States Census Bureau, 11 Sept. 2020, *www.census.gov/programs-surveys/cps.html.*

    a. *Series ID for the following men's categories:*

        i. *White: LEU0252883900*

        ii. *Black: LEU0252884800*

        iii. *Latino: LEU0252885700*

        iv. *Asian: LEU0254468500*

37. Rudder, Christian. "Your Looks and Your Inbox How Men and Women Perceive Attractiveness." OkCupid, Archive.Today, 17 Nov. 2009, *https://archive.is/ZJymw*

38. Colttaine, director. Gender Attraction Differential. Youtube.com, 12 Dec. 2015, *www.youtube.com/watch?v=7vqRbScCIPU&has_verified=1.*

39. Bureau, US Census. "Modified Race Data 2010." The United States Census Bureau, 6 Dec. 2016, *www.census.gov/data/datasets/2010/demo/popest/modified-race-data-2010.html.*

40. Penton-Voak, I. S., and Et al. "Menstrual Cycle Alters Face Preference." Nature, vol. 299, no. 6738, 1 June 1999, pp. 741–742. *https://www.nature.com/articles/21557*

41. Jones, and et al. "Effects of Menstrual Cycle Phase on Face Preferences." Archives of Sexual Behavior, Springer US, 1 Jan. 1990, *https://link.springer.com/article/10.1007/s10508-007-9268-y*

KNOWLEDGE CHECK
AND PROBLEM SET
ANSWER KEY

Chapter 5 Knowledge Checks:

If the distance between Jake's eyes and mouth is 4 inches and the distance between Jake's hairline and chin is 8 inches, what is his ranking based on facial appearance?

Answer:

FLP = 4/8 = 0.5

Looks Ranking = 4.61

If Jake has a WHR of 0.89, what is his L value based on WHR?

Answer:

Jake's L value based on his WHR is 9.5

Using what we learned about Jake from the last two knowledge checks, and Janet's preferences, what is Janet's overall opinion of Jake when it comes to his looks?

Hint: Use the following formula:

$$L = (w_{FLP}) * L_{FLP} + (w_{WHR}) * L_{WHR}$$

Answer:

$$L = (0.8) * 4.61 + (0.2)9.5 = 5.59$$

Chad has an SMV of 8 based on Athleticism. What is his bodyfat % (use table above)?

Answer:

Bodyfat Percent = 8%

If Chad goes keto and lowers his bodyfat by 11.25%, what will his new SMV be?

Answer:

$$Old\ Bodyfat\% * (Bodyfat\%\ change) = Reduction\ in\ Bodyfat\%$$

$$Old\ Bodyfat\% + Reduction\ in\ Bodyfat\% = New\ Bodyfat\%$$

$$8\% * (-11.25\%) = -0.9\%$$

$$8\% - 0.9\% = 7.1\%$$

Plugging into the table, we find that a BF% of 7.1% gives you an SMV of 8.5. When Chad goes keto to change his bodyfat%, his new SMV is 8.5.

Generous Jerry has $400,000 in the bank. The bank manager pitching Jerry on their CD offerings told him that the largest average daily balance is about $2,000,000, and their lowest is $13,000. What is Jerry's Money rating on a scale of 1 to 10?

Answer:

$$\frac{(10-1)}{(\$2,000,000 - \$13,000)}(\$400,000 - \$2,000,000) + 10 = Money\ Rating$$

$$2.75 = Jerry's\ Money\ Rating$$

Now let's take the case of John E. Bwai, who has $300,000 in his Ameribux bank account. The largest bank balance at Ameribux is $500,000. If John is considered a 6 on a scale of 0.5 to 10, what is the minimum bank balance at Ameribux?

Answer:

by manipulating the rating formula to solve for the minimum value, we have:

$$Var_{Min} = Var_{Max} - \frac{(Rating_{Max} - Rating_{Min})}{(Rating - Rating_{Max})}(Xvar - Var_{Max})$$

Then plug in the numbers:

$$Var_{Min} = \$500,000 - \frac{(10-0.5)}{(6-10)}(\$300,000 - \$500,000) = \$25,000$$

The minimum bank balance at Ameribux is $25,000

- -

Danali Trux has 20,000 social media followers. A recent survey regarding social media influence states that the minimum number of followers on average is 10 and the maximum, which makes on a celebrity, is 35,000. On a scale of 0.1 to 10, what is Danali's Power/Influence (PI) rating?

Answer (use the scalar transformation formula from above):

$$\frac{Power}{Influence} Rating(PI) = \frac{(10-0.1)}{(35,000-10)}(20,000 - 35,000) + 10$$

$$PI = 5.75$$

- -

Danali's subscriber base has now grown 20%, and a recent survey showed that the minimum average follower count is 20. If Danali's Power/Influence rating is a 6 on a scale of 0.1 to 9.99, what is the maximum number of subscribers to make one a celebrity?

Answer:

First, find Danali's new lever of subscribership (grows by 20%):

$$20,000 \times (1.20) = 24,000$$

Next, manipulate the scalar rating formula to solve for the maximum variable:

$$Var_{Max} = Xvar * \frac{(Rating_{Max} - Rating_{Min})}{(Rating - Rating_{Min})} + Var_{Min} * \frac{(Rating - Rating_{Max})}{(Rating - Rating_{Min})}$$

Then plug in the numbers:

$$Var_{Max} = 24,000 * \frac{(9.99 - 0.1)}{(6 - 0.1)} + 20 * \frac{(6 - 9.99)}{(6 - 0.1)}$$

$$Var_{Max} = 40,217$$

To reach celebrity status, one needs 40,217 according to the updated survey.

Suppose Sam Mule lives in Bumfukegypt where the maximum average annual income is $500,000 and the minimum is $30,000. Sam is considered a 7 on a scale of 0.5 to 10 with regards to his status by way of his annual income. What is Sam's current annual income?

Answer:

First, rearrange the rating formula in terms of the actual variable:

$$Xvar = Var_{Max} + \frac{(Income\ Rating - SMV_{Max})}{(SMV_{Max} - SMV_{Min})} * (Var_{Max} - Var_{Min})$$

Next, plug in the numbers:

$$Xvar = \$500,000 + \frac{(7 - 10)}{(10 - 0.5)} * (\$500,000 - \$30,000)$$

$$Xvar = \$351,578.95$$

Sam's current annual income is $351,578.95

How would LaDauna's rating change if she had 3 partners and a virgin is considered a 7 on the scale of 0.1 to 9.99? Answer:

Answer:

Since 3 partners is less than 4, we use the first equation:

If $Xvar \leq Var_{Mid}$:

$$Virtuousness = \frac{(SMV_{Max} - SMV_{Mid})}{(Var_{mid} - Var_{min})} (Xvar - Var_{mid}) + SMV_{Max}$$

$$Virtuousness = \frac{(SMV_{Max} - SMV_{Mid})}{(Var_{mid} - Var_{min})} (Xvar - Var_{mid}) + SMV_{Max}$$

$$Virtuousness = \frac{(9.99 - 7)}{(4 - 0)} (3 - 4) + 9.99 = 9.24$$

Ladauna would have a 9.24 based on the changed circumstances.

If the men became more liberal in their views and considered 50 partners sub optimal and 6 partners optimal, considering LaDauna had 12 partners and the scale rating stays the same, what would be her new rating?

Since 12 partners is more than 6, use the second equation:

If $Xvar > Var_{Mid}$:

Virtuousness (V) = $\frac{(SMV_{Min} - SMV_{Max})}{(Var_{max} - Var_{mid})} (Xvar - Var_{max}) + SMV_{Min}$

Virtuousness = $\frac{(0.1 - 9.99)}{(50 - 6)} (12 - 50) + 0.1 = 8.64$

LauDauna would be an 8.64 based on changing opinions.

Amanda Hugginkiss just successfully lost 10 lbs. in accordance with her New Year's resolution. Over the past 10 years, she has made the same resolution, but only successfully reached her goal six of those years. What is her current conscientiousness score?

Answer:

Since Amanda has made this resolution 10 times in the past, this new instance makes it a total of 11 times. Since she successfully completed it this time and adding to the six other times, she successfully completed her goal, making it a total of 7 successes. Therefore:

$$\frac{(7)}{(11)} * 10 = Conscientiousness\ Rating$$

$$6.36 = Conscientiousness\ Rating$$

Renee has looks rating of 6.92 and the distance from her eyes to mouth is 3 inches. What is the distance from her hairline to her chin?

Answer:

From the above table, an SMV (rating) of 6.92 is associated with a FLP of 0.44. Then we simply plug in the given information to get the answer:

$$FLP = Face\ Length\ Percent = \frac{Distance\ from\ eyes\ to\ mouth\ in\ inches}{Distance\ from\ hairline\ to\ chin\ in\ inches}$$

$$0.44 = \frac{3}{Distance\ from\ hairline\ to\ chin}$$

$$Distance\ from\ hairline\ to\ chin = 6.82\ inches$$

Patty is 25 years old. According to the Table 14, what can her Age rank be estimated as?

Answer:

Using the table, we get 5.34.

If Monica's BMI is 24, what is her BWR?

Answer:

Since Monica's BMI is less than 24.99, she is classified as "acceptable BMI" status. Therefore, the formula used is:

$$BWR = -0.7809\left(BMI_{F,acceptable}\right) + 24.515$$

And plugging in the numbers

$$BWR = -0.7809(24) + 24.515$$

$$BWR = -18.7416 + 24.515 = 5.77$$

Monica's ranking based on BMI is 5.77.

If Monica's WHR is 0.725, what is her BSR (round to one decimal place)?

Answer:

Use the following formula and plug in the numbers:

$$BSR = -31.633(WHR_F) + 32.14$$

$$BSR = -31.633(0.725) + 32.14 = 9.2$$

Monica's BSR based on her WHR is 9.2.

If Quintavious is a man who cares about how much a woman weighs 20% of the time and his main focus is her "coke bottle" shape, accounting for 80% of what he finds attractive; and sees Monica in the mall, what will his perception of her overall ranking for "W" be?

Answer:

Recalling that BMI is reflective of weight, which has to do with the BWR and the proportions ("coke bottle") have to do with BSR, we can start plugging in numbers:

$$Weight\ Ranking\ (W) = 20\%(BWR) + 80\%(BSR)$$

Then we go back to our previous two knowledge checks to find Monica's BWR and BSR, which are 5.77 and 9.2 respectively:

$$Weight\ Ranking\ (W) = 20\%(5.77) + 80\%(9.2) = 8.51$$

Quintavious would rank Monica as 8.51

Chapter 6 Knowledge Checks:

Biff works at the construction site in the wee hours of the morning. Depending on traffic, he gets to the site according to the following schedule:

Table 24 Answer:

TABLE A29.	Schedule Example (Transformed)	
X	**Y**	**Y' (transformed)**
Monday	4:59 AM	4.98
Tuesday	5:03 AM	5.05
Wednesday	**5:01 AM**	**5.02**
Thursday	5:19 AM	5.32
Friday	4:44 AM	4.73

Sum of the four known transformed values: 20.08

Simple average of the four known transformed values: 5.02

The time Biff gets in 5: (.02*60 = 1.2 minutes or approximately 1 minute) = 5:01 AM

Now, suppose that getting to work is easier on Monday and Friday, but harder on Tuesday and Thursday. Biff arrives on Monday and Friday with a 30% probability and on Tuesday and Thursday is 20% probability What is Biff's estimated arrival time Wednesday? Fill in the blanks.

Table 25 Answer:

TABLE A30.	Example Schedule with Probability			
			A	B	C = (A x B)
X	Y	Y'	Probability (weight)	Probability Shares
Monday	4:59 AM	4.98	30%	1.49
Tuesday	5:03 AM	5.05	20%	1.01
Wednesday	4:58 AM	4.97		
Thursday	5:19 AM	5.32	20%	1.06
Friday	4:44 AM	4.73	30%	1.41

Y' = sum of the probability shares = 4.97

Transformed back into time: 4: [(.97*60= 58 minutes)] = 4:58 AM

Johnny sees Katie and gives her a 7 on looks, a 6.7 on age, and a 5 on weight. Johnny says that looks are important to him 40% of the time and weight is important to him 30% of the time. What is the expected SMV of Katie?

Answer:

Plugging known variables into the equation:

$$E[SMV_F] = (w_L)L + (w_A)A + (w_W)W$$

$$E[SMV_F] = (40\%)7 + (w_A)6.7 + (30\%)5$$

Since we know that $\sum_i^n w_i = 1$ or 100%, we know that $w_A = 30\%$; so

$$E[SMV_F] = (40\%)7 + (30\%)6.7 + (30\%)5$$

$$E[SMV_F] = 2.8 + 2.01 + 1.5$$

$$E[SMV_{Katie}] = 2.8 + 2.01 + 1.5 = 6.31$$

Katie thinks Raymond's overall SMV is 7.45. If she gave him an 8 on looks, 6 on money and a 6.5 on status. Looks are important to her 70% of the time, and status is only half as important to her as money, what percent of the time is status important to her?

Answer:

First, substitute all knowns into the equation:

$$E[SMV_{Ray}] = (w_L)L + (w_M)M + (w_S)S$$

$$7.45 = (70\%)8 + (w_M)6 + (w_S)6.5$$

Performing operations, we get

$$7.45 - (70\%)8 = (w_M)6 + (w_S)6.5 =$$

$$1.85 = (w_M)6 + (w_S)6.5$$

Since we know that status is only half as important to Katie as money, we know that

$$w_S = 1/2w_M$$

We also know that

$$w_L = 70\% \text{ and } \sum_i^n w_i = 100\%$$

so

$$w_L + w_M + w_S = 100\%$$

$$70\% + w_M + w_S = 100\%$$

$$w_M + w_S = 30\%$$

And since we're trying to find w_S

$$w_S = 30\% - w_M$$

And since

$$w_S = 1/2w_M$$

$$2w_S = w_M$$

Substituting back in (to the definition of w_S)we have:

$$w_S = 30\% - 2w_S =$$

$$3w_S = 30\%$$

$$w_S = 10\%$$

Status is only important to Katie 10% of the time.

Chapter 7 Knowledge Checks:

Use the "Abridged SMV to Lambda Table" to answer the following questions:

Suzy the Sumerian has an SMV of 4.5. She is interested in Bobby the Babylonian, who has an SMV is 7.

1. What is the average male SMV equivalent based Suzy's SMV?
   a. **Answer:** 6.2
2. What is the average highest SMV of women who are attracted to Bobby?
   a. **Answer:** 5
3. Is Suzy less or more likely to be treated well? Explain.
   a. **Answer:** Suzy is less likely to be treated well because her SMV is lower than the highest SMV woman that Bobby can attract.

Chapter 7 Problem Set:

Connie Cro-Magnon, Holly Hunter-Gatherer, Hadley Homo-Erectus are at a party. Their lambdas are 0.76, 0.82, and 0.79, respectively. In walks Nathan the Neanderthal and they agree that he has a 7.7 in looks, 6.6 in money, and a 5.5 in status. They know that looks and money matter to them equally and that status matters to them 40% of the time.

What is Nathan's SMV?

Answer: first find out the weights for L and M. We also know that

$$w_S = 40\% \text{ and } \sum_i^n w_i = 100\%, \text{ so}$$

$$w_L + w_M + w_S = 100\%$$

$$w_L + w_M + 40\% = 100\%$$

$$w_L + w_M = 60\%$$

Since L and M matter to them equally:

$$w_L = w_M = w$$

And

$$2w = 60\%$$

So

$$w_L = w_M = 30\%$$

Next, enter back into equation to find SMV:

$$(w_L)L + (w_M)M + (w_S)S = SMV_{Nathan}$$

$$(30\%)7.7 + (30\%)6.6 + (40\%)5.5 = SMV_{Nathan} = 6.49$$

Nathan's SMV is 6.49

Chapter 7 "Woman most likely to date Nathan" Answer:

What are the SMVs of the women assuming their lambdas accurate? Which of the women is the *most* likely to date Nathan?

Use the above equation for ESMV and work backward using each of their personal lambdas:

TABLE A31.	SMV Example	
	A	B = (A x 6.49)
Woman	Lambdas	SMV based off Nathan's SMV
Connie	0.76	4.93
Holly	0.82	5.32
Hadley	0.89	5.78

Hadley is the most likely to date Nathan because her lambda is the least hypergamous.

Chapter 7 Knowledge Checks:

In the previous knowledge check, we dealt with Katie and Raymond. Based off of Raymond's value of 7.45, if $\lambda = 0.82$, what is Katie's expected sexual marketplace value?

Answer:

$$\lambda(E[SMV_M]) = E[SMV_F] =$$
$$\lambda(E[SMV_{Rayond}]) = E[SMV_{Katie}] =$$

$$0.82 * (7.45) = E[SMV_{Katie}]$$

$$E[SMV_{Katie}] = 6.11$$

Katie's expected sexual marketplace value is 6.11.

Nathan the Neanderthal, Cody Cro-Magnon, and Harry Homo Erectus, whose SMVs are 8, 7, and 6 respectively, are all interested in dating Foraging Franny. The market lambda is 0.77 ($\lambda = 0.77$). What is Franny's SMV?

Answer:

First find the weights by taking the ratio of each person's SMV to the total:

$$8 + 7\ 6 = 21;$$

$$\frac{8}{21} = 38\% \text{ or } 0.38 \text{ (Nathan's weight)}$$

$$\frac{7}{21} = 33\% \text{ or } 0.33 \text{ (Cody's weight)}$$

$$\frac{6}{21} = 29\% \text{ or } 0.29 \text{ (Harry's weight)}$$

$$SMV_{Franny} = 0.77 * [0.38 * (8) + 0.33 * (7) + (.29) * (6)] = 5.46$$

Which one of the guys would Franny most likely date?
5.46/0.77 = 7.10 is the SMV equivalent guy, so that or higher Franny is most likely to date Nathan.

Mesolithic Mary just got her PhD in Paleontology. She's so excited because the increase in her income has allowed her to accumulate a bank balance that puts her asset holdings in the 70th percentile of people in her region. When looking for a man, education is important to her 30% of the time and she would consider a guy with a PhD an 8 on the status scale. The amount of money a man has in the bank is only important to her 20% of the time. If you ask most guys, they will say she's average. What is Mary's ESMV and Expected Price? What market level of hypergamy would allow Mary to get away with her price? What does that mean in layman's terms?

Answer:

In Mary's assessment of herself, she has a 7 out of 10 on money (since she's in the 70th percentile). Since asset holdings are important to her 20% of the time, her relative importance weight on money is 0.20 or 20%. Her education is 8 out of 10, and her weight on education is 30% or 0.3. And most guys saying Mary is average means her ESMV is a 5 on the 10 scale.

$$E[SMV_{Mary}] = 5$$

$$E[P_{Mary}] = 5 + (w_M)M + (w_S)S =$$

$$E[P_{Mary}] = 5 + (0.20)7 + (0.30)8 = 8.8$$

To find the level of hypergamy, find the lambda that would equate her price to value:

$$\lambda(E[P_{Mary}]) = E[SMV_{Mary}]$$

$$\lambda(8.8) = 5$$

$$\lambda = 0.57$$

Calculating Valuation based on live public opinion

1. If the sum of the SMVs is 28, and the weights of Girl 1,2,3, and 4 are 14%,21%,29% and 36% respectively, find the SMV of each girl (y variable) rounding to the nearest whole number:

Table 29 Answer:

TABLE A32. Example SMV		
A	**B = C x Σ (C1:C4)**	**C**
Girl (x variable)	**SMV (y variable)**	**SMV Weight**
1	4	14%
2	6	21%
3	8	29%
4	10	36%

$$\sum SMV_s = 28$$

2. If Guy 1 has an SMV of 8 and Girl 2 wants to date him (he approaches her alone), what does her λ have to be?

Answer: $\lambda = 6/8 = 0.5$

3. If Guy 1 approaches Girl 2, who thinks Guy 1 is an 8. Girl 2 is in a group with Girls 1,3, and 4, and their opinions of Guy 1 are 10, 9, and 8.5 respectively, what is Guy 1's SMV based on these opinions?

Answer:

$\Sigma[(14\% \times 10) + (21\% \times 8) + (29\% \times 9) + (36\% \times 8.5)] = 8.75$

4. If the market λ = 0.7, which girls will date Guy 1?

Answer: Girls 1 and 2 (divide all SMVs by 0.7)

Calculating Valuation Based on Dating Site

- -

Samantha is excited; she just setup her OK Cupid profile and is ready to start dating. There are 4 guys that "slid" into her inbox DMs. She ascertains the following information about the guys based on their profile pic and other data:

Table 30 Answer:

TABLE A33.	Example SMV Calculation		
A	B	C = B/ Σ (B1:B4)	D = (C x B)
Guy (x variable)	SMV (y variable)	Weight	Shares
1	7.00	24%	1.66
2	7.25	25%	1.78
3	7.50	25%	1.91
4	7.75	26%	2.04

1. Finish the table, rounding to 2 decimal places
   Answer: in table above
2. What is Samantha's SMV based on the guys that are interested in her if the market lambda is 0.65?
   Answer: 7.39 (Sum of the SMV shares) * 0.65 = 4.80
3. If Samantha's lambda goes up to 0.8, what is her new SMV?
   Answer: 7.39 * 0.8 = 5.91
4. When Samantha's hypergamy factor (lambda) goes up, does she become more or less picky? She becomes less picky because her SMV is relatively higher given the same rating of guys

Long- or Short-Term Relationship

Stephanie tells her friends that she wants a long-term committed relationship. So far there are two guys who have expressed interest in being with Stephanie (and their attributive qualities are known to Stephanie)—Jake and Biff. Here is the data on the guys (fill in the "?" in the table to help you answer the questions):

Table 31 Answer:

TABLE A34. Long-Term Relationship Score Example

	A	B	C	D = (A x C)	E = (B x C)
Attributive	**Jake**	**Biff**	**Stephanie's relative importance weights**	**Jake's Shares**	**Biff's Shares**
Looks	8	5	.2	1.6	1
Athleticism	6	7	.2	1.2	1.4
Money	6	8	.2	1.2	1.6
Power	8	5	.2	1.6	1
Status	7	9	.2	1.4	1.8
Sum of Restricted weights (Looks and Power)	0.4		Sum of restricted shares	1.6 +1.6 = 3.2	1+1=2
Sum of Unrestricted weights (Athleticism, Money, Status)	0.6		Sum of unrestricted shares	1.2+1.2+1.4 = 3.8	1.4+1.6+1.8 = 4.8
Jake's SMV (Sum of all his Shares)	7				
Biff's SMV (Sum of all his Shares)	6.8				

If Stephanie places *equal importance* on each of the attributive values, fill in the table's blanks. Is Stephanie serious about having a long-term relationship? Do Jake and Biff fulfill the requirements for a long-term relationship? Who is better fit for a long-term relationship, Jake or Biff? Who is Stephanie likely to choose?

Answer:

Since Stephanie's unrestricted weights > restricted weights, she's serious about having a long-term relationship. Both Jake and Biff fulfill the requirement for a long-term relationship because the sum of their unrestricted shares > sum of their restricted shares. Biff is better suited than Jake for a long-term relationship because the sum of Biff's unrestricted shares > Jake's unrestricted shares. It is possible that Stephanie chooses Jake because his SMV is higher than Biff's.

If Stephanie's relative importance weights change to the following, fill in the table and answer the questions:

Answer:

Table 32 Answer:

TABLE A35. Long-Term Relationship Score Example

Attributive	Jake (A)	Biff (B)	Stephanie's relative importance weights (C)	D = (A x C) Jake's Shares	E = (B x C) Biff's Shares
Looks	8	5	0.2	1.6	1
Athleticism	6	7	0.1	0.6	0.7
Money	6	8	0.2	1.2	1.6
Power	8	5	0.35	2.8	1.75
Status	7	9	0.15	1.05	1.35
Sum of Restricted weights (Looks and Power)	0.2 + 0.35 = 0.55		Sum of restricted shares	1.6 + 2.8 = 4.4	1 + 1.75 = 2.75
Sum of Unrestricted weights (Athleticism, Money, Status)	0.1 + 0.2 + 0.15 = 0.45		Sum of unrestricted shares	0.6 + 1.2 + 1.05 = 2.85	0.7 + 1.6 + 1.35 = 3.65
Jake's SMV (Sum of all his Shares)	2.85 + 4.4 = 7.25				
Biff's SMV (Sum of all his Shares)	2.75 + 3.65 = 6.4				

Based on the information in the table, is Stephanie looking for a long-term relationship?

No, because her Restricted Weight totals > Unrestricted Weight totals.

Which man is better suited to enter into a long-term relationship with Stephanie? Why?

Biff is, because his Sum of Unrestricted Shares > Jake's Sum of Unrestricted shares.

If Stephanie says she wants a long-term relationship, but dates Jake, what is likely to happen?

A "pump n' dump"; Jake won't stay around long

If Stephanie's relative importance weights change to the following (fill in the table to answer the questions):

Table 33 Answer:

TABLE A36.	Long-Term Relationship Score Example				
	A	B	C	D = (A x C)	E = (B x C)
Attributive	Jake	Biff	Stephanie's relative importance weights	Jake's Shares	Biff's Shares
Looks	8	5	0.15	1.2	0.75
Athleticism	6	7	0.2	1.2	1.4
Money	6	8	0.2	1.2	1.6
Power	8	5	0.25	2	1.25
Status	7	9	0.2	1.4	1.8
Sum of Restricted weights (Looks and Power)	0.15 + 0.25 = 0.40		Sum of restricted shares	1.2 + 2 = 3.2	0.75 +1.25 = 2
Sum of Unrestricted weights (Athleticism, Money, Status)	0.2 + 0.2 + 0.2 = 0.60		Sum of unrestricted shares	1.2 + 1.2 +1.4 = 3.8	1.4 + 1.6 + 1.8 = 4.8
Jake's SMV (Sum of all his Shares)	7				
Biff's SMV (Sum of all his Shares)	6.8				

What can we say about Stephanie's preferences now?

Stephanie prefers a long-term relationship because her unrestricted weights > restricted weights

Which guy must she choose to realize this (look at the sum of unrestricted shares)?

She'd be wise to choose Biff

Chapter 8 Knowledge Checks:

Jerry and Jan are a match made in heaven. Jerry is the breadwinner and Jan is a stay-at-home wife. Jan is a 2.5 on the 10 scale, has a lambda of 0.8, and spends 10 hours per day fulfilling "wifely duties" of cooking, laundry, and taking care of their son, Tyler. Jan spends 30% of her time taking care of Tyler and the rest of her time is spent equally between cooking and laundry.

Based on the above table, answer the following questions:

What is Jan's occupational value?

Answer:

$$V(Occ(Jan) = (30\%)(11.08) + (35\%)(18.84) + (35\%)(10.60) = \$13.63$$

What is Jerry's SMV?

Answer:

$$\lambda SMV_{Jerry} = SMV_{Jan}$$

$$SMV_{Jerry} = \frac{SMV_{Jan}}{\lambda}$$

$$SMV_{Jerry} = \frac{2.5}{0.8} = 3.13$$

If Jerry and Jan are a couple for 20 years, and Jan works every day, what is the total gross endowment value of Jan's role as a wife?

Answer:

$$Endowment\ Value = (10hrs/day)(365days/year)(20years) * \left(VOcc(Jan)\right) =$$

$$Endowment\ Value = (10)(365)(20) * (13.63) = \$994{,}844$$

If Jan was a 4.5 on a 10 scale, how would the above answers change? It involves Excel Regression work

Answer:

Based on the above table the regression equations for the occupations are

$$V(Cooking) = 0.93 * (SMV) + 15.86$$

$$V(Laundry) = 0.68 * (SMV) + 9.20$$

$$V(Child\ Care) = 0.85 * (SMV) + 9.18$$

Based on a 4.5:

$$V(Cooking) = 0.93(4.5) + 15.86 = 20.01$$

$$V(Laundry) = 0.68(4.5) + 9.20 = 12.26$$

$$V(Child\ Care) = 0.85(4.5) + 9.18 = 13.01$$

Based on 30% time spent on childcare and 35% spent on cooking and laundry, Jan's occupational value is

Answer:

$$V(Occ(Jan)) = (30\%)(13.01) + (35\%)(12.26) + (35\%)(20.01) = 15.20$$

Based on Jan being a 4.5, and a lambda of 0.8, Jerry's SMV is

Answer:

$$\lambda SMV_{Jerry} = SMV_{Jan}$$

$$SMV_{Jerry} = \frac{SMV_{Jan}}{\lambda}$$

$$SMV_{Jerry} = \frac{4.5}{0.8} = 5.63$$

If Jerry and Jan are a couple for 20 years, what is the total value of Jan's role as a wife?

Answer:

$$Endowment\ Value = (10)(365)(20) * \left(VOcc(Jan)\right) = \$1,109,600.00$$

Based on the above equation, answer the following question:

If Molly spends her time equally between each of the occupations above, and her SMV is a 6.25, how much should Hal pay if he's taking her out to dinner for 2 hours?

Answer:

$$Hourly\ Social\ Benefits(SB) = (9.95) * (6.25) + 4.97 = \$67.16$$

$$Hourly\ (SB) * hours = total\ benefit\ endowed = \$67.16 * 2 = \$134.32$$

Hal should pay no more than $134.32 on Molly's dinner.

If Lustin' Larry would spend 175.00 to go out on a date with a woman whose SMV he considers to be 0.5, fill in the following table, then answer the questions:

Table 42 Answer:

TABLE A37.		Social Benefits Points			
t	A	$B = \sqrt{A}$	$C =$ $(B_{t+1} + B_t)/B_t$	$D =$ $D_{t+1}*(1 + C_t)$	$E =$ $(D_t + D_{t+1})$
Index	SMV	Social Benefits Points	SB % Chg.	Social Benefits Dollars	Marginal Dollars Spent
1	0.0	0	n/a	n/a	n/a
2	0.5	0.71	n/a	175	n/a
3	1.0	1	41%	246.48	71.48
4	1.5	1.22	22%	300.71	54.23
5	2.0	1.41	16%	347.54	46.83
6	2.5	1.58	12%	389.44	41.90
7	3.0	1.73	9%	426.41	36.97
8	3.5	1.87	8%	460.92	34.51

9	4.0	2	7%	492.96	32.04
10	4.5	2.12	6%	522.54	29.58
11	5.0	2.24	6%	522.12	29.58
12	5.5	2.35	5%	579.23	27.11
13	6.0	2.45	4%	603.88	24.65
14	6.5	2.55	4%	628.53	24.65
15	7.0	2.65	4%	653.18	24.65
16	7.5	2.74	3%	675.36	22.18
17	8.0	2.83	3%	697.54	22.18
18	8.5	2.92	3%	719.72	22.18
19	9.0	3.00	3%	739.44	19.72
20	9.5	3.08	3%	759.16	19.72
21	10.0	3.16	3%	778.88	19.72

How much would Lustin' Larry spend on a date with women he considered to be a 4.5, 6.5 and 8?

Answer: $522.54, $628.53 and $697.54

How much would Lustin' Larry spend on a date with women he considered to be a 5, 7 and 8.5?

Answer: $552.12, $653.18 and $719.72

If Larry's current girlfried is a 6, and he had the opportunity to go out with at woman who is a 7, how much extra would a date cost him?

Answer: add up the marginal dollars, so $24.65 (to go from 6 to 6.5) + $24.65 (to go from 6.5 to 7) = $49.30

If Larry's current girlfriend is a 7 and he has an opportunity to go out with at woman he considers an 8, how much extra would it cost him?

Answer: add up the marginal dollars $24.65 + $22.18 = $46.83

Based on the previous answers (Larry trading up from a 6 to a 7 or a 7 to an 8), in which situation is it riskier to trade up ("cheaper to keep her")?

Answer: it is riskier to leave the 6 to go for a 7 marginally. Therefore it's cheaper to stay with the 6.

Chapter 10 Knowledge Checks:

Mary likes Marlboro Reds and Jack Daniels on summer nights. She is 35 years old. The health ministry says that life expectancies are decreased by 11% and 13% for smoking and drinking, respectively. Also, the female life expectancy is 82 years.

What is Mary's depreciation rate if she had no vices (her NDR)? Round to three decimal places and express as a percent.

Answer:

$$NDR = \frac{1}{Age_t} = \frac{1}{82} = 0.012 \text{ or } 1.2\% \text{ per year}$$

What is Mary's Effective Age?

Answer:

Remember she only smokes and drinks during the <u>summer</u>, which is 3 months out of a 12-month year, therefore the estimate is scaled by 3/12 = 1/4.

$$EAge_t = Age_t(1 + v_1) * (1 + v_2) = (EAge_t) =$$

$$= 35\left(1 + 0.11\left(\frac{1}{4}\right)\right) * \left(1 + 0.13\left(\frac{1}{4}\right)\right) = 37 \text{ years old}$$

Based on the above calculations, what is her gamma? Round to three decimal places and express as a percent.

$$\delta_t = \frac{EAge_t}{Age_t} * \frac{1}{LE} = \frac{37}{35} * \frac{1}{82} = 0.013 \text{ or } 1.3\% \text{ per year}$$

Chapter 11 Knowledge Checks:

- -

Henry meets two girls in a coffee shop, and on just looks alone, he estimates that they both have an SMV of 7.5. What he does not know is that girl one has a δ of 5%, and girl two has a gamma of 8%. If Henry is willing to pay the "average" price for the two girls, which girl will he attract?

Answer:

δ of Girl 1 = 0.05

δ of Girl 2 = 0.08

The average price Henry is willing to pay is:

$$SMV_{avg} = 7.5 \left(1 - \frac{0.08 + 00.5}{2}\right) = 7.0$$

And since:

$$SMV_{f1} = 7.5(1 - 0.05) = 7.1$$

$$SMV_{f2} = 7.5(1 - 0.08) = 6.9$$

Henry will attract girl two. Girl one will not be attracted as Henry is not willing to pay for her higher SMV.

Ingram Content Group UK Ltd.
Milton Keynes UK
UKHW020820090323
418164UK00011B/123